INTRODUCTION TO SHIPPING

ip

The Distance Learning Programme
of
The Institute of Chartered Shipbrokers

Shipbroker A person having one of several occupations, chartering agent or owner's broker, negotiating the terms of the charter of a ship on behalf of a charterer or shipowner respectively; sale and purchase broker negotiating on behalf of buyer or seller of a ship; ship's agent, attending to the requirement of a ship, her master and crew while in port on behalf of the shipowner; loading broker, whose business is to attract cargoes to the ships of his principal.

Published and Printed in England by
Witherby & Co. Ltd., 32-36 Aylesbury Street, London EC1R 0ET

Published for the Institute of Chartered Shipbrokers
First Published 2005

ISBN 1 85609 274 7

© Institute of Chartered Shipbrokers

WITHERBYS
P U B L I S H I N G

British Library Cataloguing in Publication Data

Introduction to Shipping
  1. Shipping. 2. Introduction
  I. Institute of Chartered Shipbrokers
  657.8'39

ISBN 1856092747

Notice of Terms of Use

While the advice given in this document ("document") has been developed using the best information currently available, it is intended purely as guidance to be used at the user's own risk. No responsibility is accepted by the Institute of Chartered Shipbrokers (ICS), the membership of ICS or by any person, firm, corporation or organisation [who or which has been in any way concerned with the furnishing of information or data, the compilation or any translation, publishing, supply or sale of the document] for the accuracy of any information or advice given in the document or any omission from the document or for any consequence whatsoever resulting directly or indirectly from compliance with or adoption of guidance contained in the document even if caused by a failure to exercise reasonable care.

Published and Printed by
WITHERBY & COMPANY LIMITED
32–36 Aylesbury Street,
London EC1R 0ET, England
Tel No. 020 7251 5341   Fax No. 020 7251 1296
International Tel No. +44 20 7251 5341   Fax No. +44 20 7251 1296
E-mail: books@witherbys.co.uk   Website: www.witherbys.com

[5844]

THE INSTITUTE OF CHARTERED SHIPBROKERS

The Institute of Chartered Shipbrokers is the only internationally recognised professional body representing shipbrokers, ship managers and agents throughout the world.

With 24 branches in key shipping areas, 3,500 individual and 120 company members, joining ICS represents a commitment to maintaining the highest professional standards across the shipping industry worldwide.

In today's world it is essential for reasons of

- competitiveness
- efficiency and
- safety

that all key players understand the contractual relationships between themselves.

Staff with ICS qualifications subscribe to a common worldwide standard of professional competence and conduct. They have a thorough understanding of all aspects of shipping including law, insurance and economics and by doing so can communicate effectively with specialist professionals.

"ICS is the only source of professional and vocational qualifications in shipping. Take it from us, all other things being equal, the ICS qualified candidate will get the job."
Phil Parry, Managing Director, Spinnaker Consulting

Companies employing ICS qualified staff can be confident that they have played their part in ensuring that professionalism, industry knowledge and risk awareness are of paramount importance to their Board and management.

To find out more about ICS and membership either as an individual or company, please contact us at:

85 Gracechurch Street
London EC3V 0AA
UK
T: +44 (0)20 7623 1111
F: +44 (0)20 7623 8118
E: info@ics.org.uk

www.ics.org.uk

PREFACE

Professional education through TutorShip distance learning courses

The Institute of Chartered Shipbrokers (ICS) is the professional body for all concerned in the business of commercial shipping. Passing its examinations and being elected to membership (MICS) provides a successful candidate with the only internationally recognised qualification for shipbrokers.

The complete syllabus covers the following subjects:

Introduction to Shipping
Legal Principles in Shipping Business
Economics of Sea Transport and International Trade
Shipping Business

Dry Cargo Chartering
Ship Operations and Management
Tanker Chartering
Ship Sale and Purchase
Liner Trades
Port Agency

Shipping Law
Financial and Management Accounting
Logistics and Multi-modal Transport
Marine Insurance

The Institute believes it is essential that a qualified shipbroker has a thorough knowledge of certain profession-specific subjects plus a sufficient knowledge of the law, insurance, economics etc so that they can communicate with a specialist professional. This results in less confusion, misunderstanding and hopefully less contractual risk. Professionally qualified personnel are consequently ideally placed to undertake the key executive roles in the shipping service sector.

The true value of these course books is only gained if the student enrols on the TutorShip distance learning programme and all TutorShip Courses are accredited by the O.D.L.Q.C. (the Open and Distance Learning Quality Council). We would suggest that there is nowhere better to turn to than ICS TutorShip courses for preparing yourselves for a highly successful career in the shipping profession.

We further recommend these books for practitioners and those already working in the Shipping Industry and allied trades. They will ensure you are kept abreast of developments as well as acting as useful everyday knowledge based texts for every aspect of this 'shipping business'.

Further details can be found at www.ics.org.uk

CONTENTS

5 THE TANKER CHARTERING MARKET (continued)

6 LINERS 53

7 THE PRACTITIONERS IN SHIPPING BUSINESS 63

9 ACCOUNTS (continued)

10 LAW OF CARRIAGE 93

Appendices 105

Mock Exam 187

The Purpose and Scope of this Book 191

Chapter 1

THE REASONS FOR SEA TRANSPORT

1.1   INTRODUCTION

Shipbroker is a time-honoured title of a profession which can certainly trace its roots back to the 17th Century but to a few people the name conjures up a somewhat narrow concept of its meaning instead of the many and varied specialised tasks which today's shipbroker may undertake. So whilst the members of the Institute are proud to call themselves Shipbrokers you will often find reference to shipping business as your reading proceeds. There is more about the different specialities that are encompassed by the term shipbroking in Chapter 7 of this book and it will be seen that they all concern themselves with the business of shipping.

Designed as an introduction to the fascinating world of shipping business, the Chapters in this publication will not explore the great depths and intricacies of the different aspects but will endeavour to touch upon many of the topics that provide the background knowledge necessary for anyone seeking to embark upon a career in this profession.

As well as dealing with ships themselves, and the markets in which their business is arranged, it will explore the geography of the maritime and commercial world, consider some of the legal aspects of working in the business of shipping and, as all commerce must eventually concern itself with money, look at basic accounting matters and corporate structures.

1.2   WHY SHIPS?

More than two thirds of the world's surface is covered in water but, with the exception of passengers who go on cruises, nobody wants merchant shipping for its own sake. Some passengers certainly need ships to take them from one place to another but the matter that this book is mostly about, is the need for ships to carry **cargo**.

The demand for ships is derived from the demand for the goods that they carry; that is why economists refer to merchant shipping as a **derived demand**. The customer, who is usually but not always, in a different country from the producer of the goods, wants those goods to be delivered to him safely and at minimum cost. Note that the word 'quickly' was not included with the other two requirements. Speed is certainly important for some commodities and for these there are other forms of transport such as air freight which is ideal for small but highly valuable items of cargo. But air freight is very costly so that it would be ridiculously expensive to transport, say, coal or iron ore by air even if it were possible.

Sea transport may be considered a relatively slow but inexpensive form of transport and because modern ships are capable of carrying hundreds of thousands of tonnes, the cost per tonne/kilometre adds only a small amount to the cost of the commodity being carried. As will be explained later in this text, this enables bulk materials to be moved half way around the world and still arrive at an economic price. That is why by far the greatest volume of goods involved in international trade is carried by sea.

Earlier, the statement was made that the customer for the goods being carried is usually but not always, in another country from the seller of those goods. One must not overlook the fact that, as shipping is the way to move large quantities of goods cheaply, it is equally suitable for transporting commodities from one place to another in the same country. This is, of course, especially important if the country concerned is made up of a series of islands. Coastal shipping, as it is often called, is vital to several countries and you may encounter it under its more technical name of **cabotage,** although this term tends to be used in reference to countries seeking to restrict such trade solely to ships owned in that country.

Inland shipping between countries across lakes and on rivers is a common form of transport in many parts of the world but, although related to ocean transport, unless the vessels involved venture out to sea there is very little common ground between the two industries.

It was also suggested that speed of transport was not important when considering shipping. If one is comparing the equivalent of 20 kilometres per hour with 800 kilometres per hour, achieving the higher speed will be far too expensive for relatively low valued goods. However, you will see that when comparing the equivalent of 20 kph with 40 kph, many factors may favour the higher speed so at these levels of comparison speed can be important, you will also learn that speeds at sea are referred to in **knots** which is the word for nautical miles per hour. A nautical mile is 1852 metres (approx 6080 feet) and how it is derived will be explained in the Chapter on geography.

1.3   AN INTRODUCTION TO THE THEORY OF TRADE

The movement of cargo by sea comes about as a result of one party – the **exporter** – selling a commodity to another party – the **importer** – this sale from one to another is, of course, referred to as **trade.** You will often hear the exporter referred to as the **consignor** or **shipper** and any subtle differences between these terms will be explained later in the course. Similarly you may see the importer referred to as the **consignee** or as the **receiver**.

The first obvious question is why should "A" buy goods from "B"? The immediate and equally obvious answer is that "A" needs or wants what "B" produces. This comes about due to the uneven distribution of resources throughout the world. Note that the reference was to distribution of **resources** not simply the distribution of commodities. For example, Great Britain, once a major exporter of coal still has substantial reserves but only a very small annual production because extraction is uneconomic. Australia also has coal and although the two countries are more than 10,000 nautical miles apart, Australia is able to sell coal to Britain.

Before dealing with this apparent paradox, let us concentrate first upon the implications of 'resources', there are two more expressions commonly used by economists that need to be mastered when considering the theory of trade. The first is **absolute advantage,** which refers to a commodity that one country has in exportable quantities but which another country has none. Examples could be bananas or coffee, these cannot be produced in Northern Europe whilst they are in abundance in the West Indies and Brazil. Such an absolute advantage is the result of **climate.** Absolute advantage may also come about through **geology** and a good example is copper that is mined in several parts of Southern Africa whereas many countries that need it to produce goods have no such mineral deposits of their own..

Thus, in the case of absolute advantage, the resource is simply the physical availability of the commodity. Other factors are, however, involved which lead to **comparative advantage**. In simplistic terms this means where one country produces a commodity more cheaply or in a more desirable form than another.

In addition to climate and geology there are other **factors of production** that create a comparative advantage. These factors tend to fall into four categories namely Land, Labour, Capital and Enterprise. No two countries have exactly the same resources and few, if any, countries can be considered as being self-sufficient. For example, even with the wide-ranging natural resources that are present in a country like South Africa, the lack of appreciable quantities of oil prevents the country being self-sufficient.

Land incorporates climate and geology in terms of absolute advantage but it can have a profound effect also in the case of comparative advantage. Reference was made to the fact that Australia can sell coal to Britain, which actually still has vast reserves of coal. Where geology plays its part is in the way that coal in Australia is much easier and therefore cheaper, to extract from the earth.

Labour takes cognisance of the fact that the cost of living in some countries is considerably lower than in others and so they can produce certain items at a much lower cost. This has been particularly demonstrated in the case of shipbuilding which was at one time almost exclusively carried out in northern Europe and the USA but is now much reduced in those places but has developed enormously in countries like Japan, South Korea and, more recently, China.

Capital does not simply mean money, but just as much the things which money has provided, such as manufacturing equipment, roads, ports and all the other items which permit goods to be produced and brought to a place from which they can conveniently be exported.

Both Labour and Capital may be involved in **enterprise.** Countries with high labour costs have used their skill and knowledge to develop a high degree of automation in production enabling the same amount of work to be carried out by far fewer people (labour) but automation demands a huge amount of money (capital) to be invested.

Land (geology and climate) may be considered static as most mineral deposits have been located, even if not yet being worked, and despite the effects of global-warming the changes in weather patterns are not hugely affecting global production. Short term changes though can be brought about by natural phenomena such as drought or flooding.

Labour and Enterprise, however, can change radically in a relatively short time. Mention was made earlier how shipbuilding moved from Europe to South Korea but before South Korea attained its present capacity, Japan was the leader in this activity. Japanese workers, however, began to seek higher wages so that, despite more and more automation, their country's competitive edge was eroded. Today a similar situation has occurred in South Korea with the result that China, where workers are paid much less, is experiencing a boom in shipbuilding for export. The world leader position is still a struggle between Japan and South Korea although both countries have admitted that within 10 years China may have surpassed them both.

Enterprise tends to change by evolutionary processes through populations becoming more technologically advanced but more drastic changes may be brought about by **politics**. A narrow comparative advantage favouring imports can easily be reversed by the imposition of **customs duty** which would make the imported goods more expensive thus favouring a boost to domestic production in order to reduce unemployment. The converse may be where a government gives money to manufacturers in its own country in the form known as a **subsidy**. The object here being to enable the goods so produced to be competitive in the export market. This device was practised for several years in UK and other European countries in a vain attempt to retain their position as major shipbuilders. The theory of subsidies is that it is better to use tax-payers money to maintain competitiveness in manufacture and earn foreign currency rather than use possibly more money paying benefits to large numbers of unhappy unemployed workers.

Another example of politics bringing about rapid changes is in the former Soviet Union. Throughout the 1980s and 1990s vast amounts of grain were imported to supplement the inefficient collective farming system, but at the end of 2002 Russia and the Ukraine are both net exporters of grain having altered farming practices after the collapse of the state run economy.

Patterns of Trade influence imports and exports where politics as well as enterprise can have their effect. Until the middle of the twentieth century, several European countries, especially Great Britain, had direct interests in territories overseas; countries which were at one time parts of their empires. Traditional trading patterns were, therefore, between the mother countries and these overseas nations many of which deliberately developed items which were required in

Europe. Typical of these were the farming and dairy products (meat, butter sugar etc.) that are so important to such areas as Australia and New Zealand.

Latterly the economic and political links forged in **Europe** have brought about a reduction in the amount of trade with former colonies. This in turn has had the effect of countries like Australia creating new trading patterns with the Far East and in so doing finding it logical to boost its extraction of coal, iron ore and other minerals.

Politics can also have a direct influence on trading patterns in other ways. Warlike operations in the Middle-East have caused the Suez Canal to be closed for long periods on more than one occasion. This produced the incentive to design and build the 'Capesize' tankers needed to transport crude oil round Africa instead of via the Suez Canal and still deliver it in Europe at the same price.

The dominance of Arab countries in oil production and complicated Middle Eastern politics surrounding attitudes of the Western world to Israel and its neighbours have led on several occasions to oil prices rising so steeply that world-wide trade recession have resulted.

An important influence upon trade and trading patterns that has little or nothing to do with the actual factors of production has been the technological advances in ship design and production. Until the 1950s, 10,000 tonnes was large for a dry-cargo ship and a so-called "super-tanker" carried 42,000 tonnes.

Today ships more than ten times these sizes are commonplace. Such increases in size brought about what economists call **economies of scale.** Very simply this means that one does not need a crew ten times the size for such bigger ships. Indeed, other technological advances have had the reverse effect and crew numbers on a modern 100,000 tonner are often less than a third of those of a 1950s 10,000 tonner. Similarly one does not need an engine burning ten times the amount of fuel to propel the larger ships.

The effect of these economies of scale has been to enable quite inexpensive raw materials to move half way round the world and still arrive at a competitive price. Mention was made earlier of the way Australian coal can be marketed in Europe. Not only raw materials move long distances cheaply, one can move goods in freight containers vast distances and only add a few dollars to their unit price; a small amount in the overall price of, for example, washing machines or television sets.

All these practical and political influences on trade and trading patterns are not the end of the story. Simple preference, encouraged by clever advertising, can take advantage of the cheapness of modern sea carriage. The USA has the biggest car producing companies in the world and yet one can encounter German, British and many types of Japanese cars in American streets. Walk along the aisles of a supermarket in any European country and food items from all over the world can be found on the shelves. These countries are able to produce almost all the food that is essential for life but here again, personal fancy is now an important part of comparative advantage. This has led to the term '**globalisation**' being applied to the worldwide distribution of, especially, consumer goods.

1.4   THE DIFFERENT SHIPPING MARKETS

It is important, from the outset, to grasp that shipping is divided clearly into two types, one of which divides into two again. The two divisions are the **liner trades** and the **tramp trades.** The tramp trades then divide again into **dry cargo** and bulk liquids known as the **tanker trade.**

1.4.1   Liners

Liners are so-called because they trade according to a schedule of ports of loading and discharge, usually adhering to a published time table on set conditions of carriage and often charged at a published rate of freight. Their cargoes are made up of a large number of different

consignments from a number of different shippers. Each consignment has to be separately documented and could be as small as one carton or as large as several tonnes. Documentation is a subject that will be dealt with in a later Chapter.

Liner cargo is *almost always* made up of manufactured or partly-manufactured goods; the italics are used because there are occasional exceptions. The vast majority – perhaps as much as 90% – of liner cargo is now carried in **containers**. The standard cargo **container** was introduced in the early 1960s and since the 1970s each new generation of liner ships have been specially designed to accommodate them. Full details of containerisation will be dealt with in later lessons but the containers themselves are so familiar, being seen on roads and railways throughout the world. In the ports, ships are rapidly loaded with hundreds or thousands of these containers that are emptied of their cargo at their destination after the ship has discharged them and has sailed away.

Prior to the introduction of containers liner cargo, usually referred to as **general cargo,** was loaded piece by piece needing expert knowledge to decide how and where it should be stowed in order to ensure its undamaged arrival; it was a very slow, labour-intensive process. Not every exporter has enough cargo to fill a container so that the expression 'generals' is still used to these small LCL (less than container load) consignments that have to be **consolidated** into containers in order to be loaded.

There are still a very few routes which are not containerised and one still sometimes hears their cargo referred to as **conventional** cargo which is a throw-back to the days when containerisation was still an innovation. More usually non-containerised cargo is now referred to as **break-bulk** cargo and comprises those items that are genuinely impossible to containerise.

1.4.2   Bulk Dry-cargo

Bulk dry-cargo is carried in ships that, even today, are referred to as **tramps**. Not because they are dirty and disreputable like a tramp (hobo or vagrant) but because like a tramp, they go from place to place depending upon where they can find cargoes. They do not follow a schedule but go where the market draws them so that they may load a cargo at place A discharge it at B and if they cannot actually load another cargo at B they will sail empty (in ballast) to C and load for D and so on.

The expression "even today are referred to as tramps" was used at the beginning of this section because in recent years, some dry bulk cargo ships have become highly specialised and whilst they do not follow an advertised schedule like liners they do tend to stay in one trade which often involves returning from the discharging port back to the loading port empty. Details of the different types of bulk dry cargo ships will be dealt with in a later lesson; it is sufficient here to visualise a market in which many of the ships are extremely large, built with certain bulk cargoes in mind together with a many more general-purpose ships that continue to fulfil the role of typical tramps.

Unlike liners, tramps are *almost always* carrying raw materials or semi-raw material, *almost always* carrying only one commodity at a time and *almost always* carrying a cargo from only one shipper on behalf of a **charterer**.

Typical cargoes in the tramp market are coal, iron ore and other minerals, grains, fertilizers, steel and timber. Again, unlike liners tramp cargoes are carried at rates and upon conditions individually negotiated in each case.

1.4.3   Bulk Liquids

Bulk liquids are carried in ships called **tankers** that may be looked upon as highly specialised tramps. The main cargo carried in tankers is, of course, **oil** and some of the world's largest ships have been built for this trade. The oil these monsters carry is **crude oil**, that is in the state that it comes out of the ground. This material is then transported to **oil refineries** which tend to be situated close to the main area of the consumption of the finished product. Some of these products may be transported overland by pipeline, railway or road vehicle but much of it is carried by smaller ships. These ships will be just as specialised, some designed to carry the simpler products, referred to as **refined petroleum products** which include such things as petrol (gasoline), kerosene (paraffin), diesel oil, fuel oil, lubricants etc.

Some by-products of oil refining are chemicals for various purposes that require smaller tankers many of which have to be very carefully constructed so that they are not harmed by the chemicals they carry or do not contaminate the chemicals they are carrying. Included under the tanker heading are some of the world's most sophisticated ships, the gas carriers. Designed to carry liquefied petroleum gasses such as butane and propane or Liquefied natural gas (Methane) the ships are referred to as LPGs and LNGs respectively. Whilst most of the world's tankers are employed in carrying oil or gas, there are other liquid trades including chemicals, acids, vegetable oils, wine, molasses and even orange juice.

Freight rates for the carriage of liquid cargoes are also freely negotiated and fluctuate according to the market's demands but as will be learnt in a later Chapter the tanker chartering market is separate from and rather different from the dry cargo market.

1.5   WHO TRADES?

Mention has already been made of the principal characters in the trading world – exporters and importers, shippers and receivers, consignors and consignees but as this text proceeds, more detail will be given about the many other parties involved in international trade. Meantime, set out below are some preliminary definitions within the scope of this Chapter.

This being seaborne trade, the **shipowner** plays a very important part. Most, but by no means all, ships are owned by companies. Some may own just a few ships whilst others may have very large fleets. Some shipowners, especially those with small fleets or institutions who have bought ships as a speculative investment, employ **ship managers** to manage their ships for them.

Where bulk cargoes are concerned, the entity employing the ship, if not the owner carrying his own cargoes, is referred to as the **charterer**. A charterer may be the actual exporter or importer but might also be a **trader** who acts between them. With bulk cargoes it is most usual for the entire ship to be chartered although part-charters occasionally occur. The charterer may take the ship for a **single voyage** when it is customary for the owner to charge a rate per tonne or a lumpsum to carry the goods from A to B. The charterer may, however, need to have more flexibility than a voyage charter permits and will then take the ship on **time charter** in which case it is customary to pay a rate per day for the time agreed. Sometimes a charterer may have large volumes of cargo to move and rather than negotiating many individual voyage charters he will enter into a **Contract of Affreightment (COA)** with a single ship owner. The owner must then provide ships as they are needed according to the pre-arranged agreement.

The shipowners and charterers involved in arranging the fixture are referred to as the **principals** but is quite usual for the actual chartering deal – called a **fixture** – to be negotiated on behalf of the charterer and the shipowner by **shipbrokers**.

For greater clarity it is common for the shipbroker representing the owner to be referred to as the **owner's broker** and the one acting for the charterer to be called the **charterer's agent** or **charterer's broker**. The term charterer's agent is also (loosely) used in another context when referring to port representation, this is discussed in a later Chapter. Such shipbrokers may be, and often are, independent firms or companies but among the larger shipowners and charterers it is quite common for the shipbrokers involved to be members of departments within the principal's own company. Some individuals also make a living in this field.

Mention has already been made of the way in which liners carry goods for many different exporters in which case the person, firm or company contracting with the owner will be the **shipper** who may be the actual manufacturer or may be a trader.

Again, the contract for the carriage of those goods may be arranged by the shipping department of the actual exporter, or alternatively an independent firm or company known as a **freight forwarder** (sometimes referred to as a **forwarding agent** or even a **shipping and forwarding agent)** may make the arrangements for them. Such a forwarder or agent will perform whatever duties the exporter requires in order to arrange for the goods to move from the premises to where the shipowner takes over responsibility.

With the majority of general cargo now moving in containers there has been a development of the function of freight forwarders in which a firm or company takes on the role of carrier instead of acting as an intermediary. These are known as **NVOCs (Non Vessel-Operating Carrier)**. As the name implies, they do not own ships, they may or may not even own road transport. They do, however, take on the full responsibility for moving the goods from the exporter's factory right the way through to the importer's premises which they achieve by contracting with hauliers and shipowners in their own name. For once the lawyer's definition is a simple rather than complex way to understand what an NVOC does as they are described as "deemed to be the carrier but not actually the carrier". You will often see the initials as **NVOCC**, the additional "C" refers to the word "common" because in some countries such as the USA, the law insists that such people refer to themselves in this way. Very briefly a common carrier is one who offers its services to the public at large. The alternative (a private carrier) would be a ship under contract to a charterer.

One further definition is **ship operator**. It is quite common for companies, even major companies, to operate ships as if they own them either on a line or in the tramp trades without actually owning them. This is done by taking the ships they require on time charter or another form of long term lease known as a bareboat charter, in which event they may be referred to as the **disponent owner.** The definition of a disponent owner is "deemed to be the owner but not actually the owner". The reason for acting in this way is that the operator has much greater flexibility to react to market changes and of course, does not have to find the large amounts of money that would be necessary in they were to buy all the ships they need. The term ship operator is also used in a more general sense to cover ship owners, ship managers and ship operators collectively.

1.6   CONCLUSION

Earlier in this Chapter the point was made that the demand for shipping is **derived** from the demand for the commodities they carry. It was also stressed that, especially in the 'tramp' trades, the cost of carrying those commodities – rates of freight – are freely negotiated and you may hear economist stating that the international chartering market is the nearest one can get to **perfect competition**.

Some of the competition and the rate fluctuations that flow from it, directly spring from the supply of ships. In its simplest terms, two ships and only one cargo makes a weak market, two cargoes and only one available ship makes a firm market.

The major fluctuations in demand for ships follow the fluctuation in the demand for commodities. These can be long or short term and can arise from a wide variety of reasons. For example, a poor grain harvest in one part of the world may increase the demand for imports whilst, conversely, a bumper crop could have the opposite effect. Even something as short-term as a serious strike could create a sudden demand for a particular type of ship that might have repercussions in other markets.

Trade recessions, which could originate from a variety of reasons, can have a profound effect of the demand for ships. Political decisions such as the OPEC countries raising the price of crude oil can cause world-wide changes in the demand for all types of ships. Conversely, the outbreak of war can create a sudden and enormous increase in demand for shipping space with a commensurate soaring of freight rates.

1.7   SELF-ASSESSMENT AND TEST QUESTIONS

Attempt the following and check your answers from the text.

1.   Why is shipping referred to as a "derived demand"?

2.   How is the speed of a ship referred to?

3.   What does "cabotage" mean?

4.   What is the definition of a disponent owner?

5.   What is the definition of an NVOCC?

6.   What is the term used to describe the agreement between a charterer and an owner?

7.   Why were "Capesize" tankers designed and built?

Having completed Chapter One, attempt the following and submit your essay to your Tutor:

1.   Give details of two trades of your choice (not oil) which are driven by:
   a)   Comparative advantage
   b)   Absolute advantage

   One of the chosen trades should be most suited to carriage in a tramp ship, the other most suited for liner transport.

   In your essay indicate factors that might cause the demand of the commodity to fluctuate also what might cause the demand for sea transport to change while the demand for the commodity remains constant.

2.   Identify and discuss a major change in an international trading pattern **different from** those mentioned in this Chapters text.

Chapter 2

THE SUPPLY OF SHIPS

To understand the shipping industry one must appreciate the environment in which it operates. The aim of this Chapter is to give an insight into some important aspects and constraints that have created – and are continuing to shape – the shipping world of today.

2.1   A BRIEF HISTORY

Ships have been used for **trade** for thousands of years but shipping business today is really the result of technology and practices established over the last 150 years.

Today's ships owe much to the inventors of the 19th Century and two developments in particular that caused the eventual demise of wooden sailing ships.

Firstly came the use of **iron** for ship construction. It took quite a long while for people to have confidence in iron instead of wood with many claiming that it would be impossible for a heavy material like iron to float. However, common sense prevailed and it was discovered that larger ships than had been possible with wood could now be built. It was at this time that the magnificent 'tea clippers' reached the height of their splendour. However, even the stoutest sailing ships were still at the mercy of the weather and knowing when (or even if) a ship would complete its voyage was not possible with any accuracy. Note the reference to 'iron' as the material because the general use of steel came much later; the first **steel** ship was launched in 1877.

Then came the development of the **steam** engine first as a supplement to sails and finally to replace wind power altogether. Steam engines had been around for many years and had been doing useful work on land from the end of the 17th century. It was not until 1830, however, that steam engines were considered reliable enough to propel ships. Although early attempts would probably not be considered a roaring success, the first – s.s. *"Hindostan"* only carried 200 tons of cargo but needed 500 tons of coal for fuel.

Steamship development was relatively slow at first because the high cost of operating machinery had to compete with the continued development of sailing ships which were still being built for the carriage of low value cargoes until well into the 20th century. The main advantage of steam-propelled ships was, however, their ability to adhere to a timetable in all but really extreme weather, something sailing ships still could not do. In addition, steam ships could take more direct routes as they were not obliged to follow the prevailing winds.

In the early days of steam it was, of course, the requirements of passenger traffic rather than cargoes that encouraged owners and builders to develop ocean shipping. By the turn of the century the White Star Line had built the first of the 'luxury' liners the s.s. *"Oceanic"* 17,274 tons and capable of 21 knots.

There was a third 'milestone' in the development of merchant shipping which was **wireless telegraphy**. In these days of electronic and satellite communications it may be difficult to imagine the enormous step forward which was achieved when it became possible not only to communicate instantly with customers overseas but also to make contact with the ships themselves. In the late 1990s all seagoing ships were obliged to update their radio and communications equipment when the Global Maritime Distress and Safety System (GMDSS) convention came into full effect. A consequence of this is that all ships must now carry Inmarsat C equipment which, providing the appropriate contracts with airtime suppliers is in force, also allows ships to send and receive e-mails.

The spur to international trade provided by these technological advances was matched by advances in port development and the constructing of canals for ocean going ships – The Suez Canal in 1869, Kiel Canal in 1895, and the Panama Canal in 1915.

The Suez Canal was so effective in shortening the voyage time to the Indian sub-continent that the world suddenly experienced an effective over-supply of ships that was responsible for the formation of the first Liner Conference in 1875.

Development of passenger ships continued, including the class that included the ill-fated *"Titanic"* (1912) and the magnificent *"Queen Mary"* (1936), advances in machinery included oil-burning steam turbines for the best of the luxury liners. **Oil** also started to became the fuel of choice for reciprocating steam engines and the first **diesel** engines began to appear in the 1930s although coal-fired tramp ships were still very much in service well into the 1950s.

The second World-War had a profound effect on merchant shipping. First, of course, because a major element in the initial years of the war was submarine warfare that resulted in thousands of merchant ships being sunk. To counteract these losses a type of ship was designed which could be mass-produced by semi-skilled labour. The vast majority of these ships were built in North America, they were all of a similar pattern being about 10,000 tons deadweight, oil-burning reciprocating engines and capable of about 10 knots on 24 tons of fuel oil per day.

The most famous of these was the *"Liberty"* class and although they were looked upon as being 'expendable' they continued in service for many years after the war was over. Furthermore, towards the later months of the war the counter-measures against submarines had become so effective that merchant ship losses were minimal but the production lines were going full pelt. The result was that despite a massive upsurge in world trade in the late 1940s early 1950s, there was an ample supply of ships to fulfil requirements. For this reason there was no strong incentive to develop merchant shipping for several years after the war and even passenger liners were feeling the effect of improved air transport.

Eventually the end of the "Libertys" was predictable and so far as bulk cargoes were concerned, the demand for economies of scale became pressing. Provided the loading and discharging terminals could be developed in step with ship sizes there was no apparent limit to the increase. This meant that, as oil companies had little difficulty in extending refinery jetties, progressively larger tankers could be accommodated. Sizes quickly rose from the wartime 15,000 tons to 50,000 tons (which were called "super tankers" at that time). It was then only a matter of evolution for ships in the 100,000 to 200,000 ton sizes to be developed under the name of Very Large Crude Carriers (VLCCs) and then eventually even larger which earned the name of Ultra Large Crude Carriers (ULCCs), the largest of which is around half a million tons cargo carrying capacity.

Cargoes such a iron ore, coal, grain etc although experiencing rather more modest growth also sought to achieve economies of scale as new loading and discharging terminals were built with new ore and coal deposits being developed.

There is, however, no economy with size if the **time in port** is prolonged and the improvement in port time for ships handling **manufactured goods** showed little if any improvement. Time is more clearly money to a ship than to many other business activities. While a ship is at sea, on passage, money is being earned. Remaining still in port for anything other than the minimum of time is not earning money. Quick port turn-round allows more voyages per year to be undertaken. It was not, therefore, until the advent of **containerisation** that commenced in the 1960s, that significant developments took place with ships intended for the **liner** trades. Once the switch to freight containers was firmly established and, aided by a massive investment in new port infrastructure and equipment, it took less than three decades for container ship sizes to increase from barely 2000 container capacity to more than 6000, with ships able to carry over 8000 containers now being delivered on a regular basis from the shipyards in Asia.

2.2   THE SUPPLY OF SHIPPING

The effective supply of shipping world-wide is influenced by four main factors:

1.   The number of ships.

2.   The size of ships.

3.   Ship speed.

4.   Time spent in port.

It will be seen that these four factors are interdependent. If there are two ships of 10,000 tons, they provide the same carrying capacity as one ship of 20,000 tons. Similarly if a ship steams at 20 nautical miles per hour (20 knots) it will spend only half the time and therefore provide twice the carrying capacity as a ship capable of steaming at only 10 knots. And the effective increase in tonnage capacity as a result of rapid port turn-round of ships is just as easy to envisage.

Numbers of ships this century have increased three-fold and when it is remembered that ship sizes have, in many cases, increased more than ten-fold, the increase in world trade can be seen to be of very substantial proportions.

The chronology of ship **size** increases is most easily seen in tankers and is shown in the following table:

By 1914 a large tanker was	8,000dwt	
" 1945 " " " "	15,000dwt	
" 1952 " " " "	50,000dwt	
" 1959 " " " "	100,000dwt	
" 1967 " " " "	200,000dwt (VLCC)	
" 1972 " " " "	300,000dwt (ULCC)	
" 1974 " " " "	555,000dwt	

(world's largest tanker)

It is worth noting that tanker sizes have not increased since 1974 and you may pause to consider that as well as economies there can be **_diseconomies_** of scale. Whilst it is true that a ship of twice the size of another will not need twice as big a crew or need twice the fuel consumption to drive it, there comes a time when big is no longer beautiful. Larger ships need larger ports but a stage is eventually reached when a port cannot be deepened further or can only be deepened at prohibitive expense. Refineries or other industrial processes only need to be big enough to meet the demands of the markets they supply so that facilities to take in far more raw material than they can handle is counter-productive. Thus the oil companies appear to have decided that VLCCs providing a steady supply, make more economic sense than over-large sporadic consignments even though, in theory, the cost per ton-mile of oil in a bigger ship is lower. Nevertheless ULCCs are still being produced, the latest being Stena's innovative and sophisticated VMax class which, unusually for large tankers, have twin engines and propellers making them more manoeuvrable and safer than many smaller ships.

Perhaps the best example of economies of scale in the shipping business has been in container ships. Ships of 2000 and 3000 twenty-foot equivalent units (TEUs) were once considered "large" (containership-capacity is generally measured in TEUs because containers are standard size 'boxes' of 8 feet wide, 8'6" high and either 20 feet or 40 feet long thus one 20 foot container is one TEU and a forty foot is two TEU's). Throughout the 1970s world trade increased so rapidly that naval architects were pressed to design the largest container ship that could transit the Panama Canal, the so-called "Panamax" size. This took container capacities up to nearly 4000 TEUs and by stretching design skills to the limit the "Panamax" dimensions can be made to carry 5000 TEUs. The tremendous economies that ever-larger container ships provide has had the effect of world trade virtually 'feeding on itself'. The cost of carrying manufactured goods in containers from one side of the world to the other now adds so little to the final cost that goods can compete one with another with very little concern as to distance travelled.

This **"global economy"** has encouraged even bigger container ships. Liner companies calculated that with substantially larger ships they could trade economically *other* than via the Panama Canal and sizes quickly rose from the 4000 TEU level to 6000 TEUs which many thought was the limit. In fact it was being said towards the middle of the 1990s the "the idea of an 8000 TEU container ship was just as idiotic as the one million ton tanker". Whilst no tankers larger than the *"Seawise Giant"* 555,000 dwt (now renamed "Jahre Viking" and with a 564,763 dwt after re-building) were ever seriously contemplated, 8000 TEU container ships are now reality.

Container traffic has an advantage over some other transport methods due to its **intermodalism** which is the word used to describe the way, because of their standard design, containers can easily be transferred from one transport medium to another. This allows for trucks or trains to be involved in pre- or post-shipment movement and also allows for ports too small to be called at by giant container carriers to be served by **"feeder"** ships. Thus the port with greatest capacity becomes the "hub" port in a container service. In fact a number of ships with a declared capacity of 9,200 TEU are now under construction in South Korea. None of these vessels will be as large as the *"Axel Maersk"* class owned by A P Moller which, although having a declared capacity of just 6,600 TEU, many experts believe could actually be the first 10,000 TEU ships ever built. Quite why the owner has decided to under-declare their capacity remains a mystery. Unfortunately for ship designers, intermodalism is also a double edged sword. Because of inland trade, more containers travel by road and rail than by sea and in recent years larger lorries have been introduced in Europe and the US. This means that even when carrying a 40 foot box, there is unused space on the lorry trailer. As a result boxes of 45 feet length are growing in popularity. Many of the latest container ships being built have holds designed to take a mix of 40 feet and 45 feet boxes. Each new design seems to have more space allocated to the larger containers indicating that at some point 45 feet containers will be the most popular.

The **speed** of merchant ships has improved considerably since the 10 knots or less of the WW2 period. There is always a balancing act with the speed of merchant ships in that whilst the faster a ship travels the more voyages (and so more income) it can achieve in a year, more speed has always meant more fuel being burnt. After a certain rate of speed, any increase will require a disproportionately greater increase in fuel consumption and there is usually an ideal speed range for every size of ship and above *or below* this speed is uneconomical running.

Engine designers have made considerable advances in machinery since **diesel** engines became the standard power plant for ships. Marine diesel engines use more or less the same grades of oil as used to be burnt in the boilers of reciprocating steam engines and not the lighter fuels used by road vehicles. Two targets have been aimed at by designers, the first is obviously that of high speed with maximum fuel economy and the second is the widest possible range of economical speeds so that a ship is able to maintain a **lower speed** to save money when markets are poor. In more prosperous times a wide margin of economical speeds enables a ship to increase or decrease its speed in order to comply with a schedule; a most important factor for container ships. Currently the large container ships have the capability of cruising at 24 – 27 knots although bulk carriers and tankers tend to be content with speeds around 15 knots.

It is engine designers who now predict that container ship sizes will pause for some time at the maximum 8000 TEU level and then, if sizes do increase, expect a jump to 11000 TEUs. The reason they give is that ships have now probably reached the maximum size that can be driven by a single propeller. This will mean that until the earning capacity of the ship can justify the extra capital cost of twin engines/propellers there will be no incentive to produce larger ships.

The likelihood of seeing these Ultra Large Container Ships (ULCS) in the very near future depends on the commercial risk owners are prepared to take. Following the terrorist attacks in New York in September 2001, some owners of brand new 7-8,000 TEU ships delayed using them because trade levels did not warrant paying the increased port charges such ships would incur. Even some of the most successful lines were obliged to introduce a programme of rolling lay-ups for their ships to avoid forcing down freight levels.

Events like this highlight one of the biggest problems that ship operators face when trying to gauge future demand. Ships can be as long as two years in the design and build stages before they are ready to carry cargo and in that time the perceived demand that decided the owner to opt for a new ship may have evaporated. Fortunately for those owners, world trade proved more resilient than many had thought and by the middle of 2003 freight rates had not only regained their previous levels but had moved to highs never before experienced. This was mostly due to China gaining membership of the World Trade Organisation and the opening up of its massive markets – both import and export.

While most engine manufacturers and naval architects are looking at ways to increase the size of container ships there are others preparing to take advantage of promising new technologies in ship propulsion. The ship of the future could well be electric powered using multiple podded propulsion units such as are now being installed on large passenger ships, and water jets that are already used for fast ferries that can achieve speeds of close to 40 knots. The ships would generate their own electricity using a combination of diesel generators, gas turbines burning "clean" LNG and Hydrogen fuel cells. The ships envisaged for a trans Atlantic service would be around 1,500 TEU but would travel at 40 – 50 knots.

Bulk carriers are another type that appears already to have found its optimum sizes which are a complex combination of maximum economies of scale coupled with the demands of the consumers plus certain limitations imposed by the physical problems of exceeding certain dimensions. The sea is capable of being savage and there have been too many casualties to bulk carriers that experts say have been due to structural failure caused by a combination of design faults and poor maintenance. The matter has become so urgent that in 2002 the leading classification societies introduced much stricter building standard requirements for new bulk carriers and compulsory structural changes to existing vessels at certain stages of their working lives.

Improvements in ship design would have been of little use without a corresponding improvement in port facilities so **Port authorities** have tended to keep pace with advances in the ships themselves. In the case of bulk cargoes, the terminals are often owned or operated by the organisations that are extracting or utilising the minerals concerned. In other cases the pressure imposed by commercial competition has been sufficient to ensure that the size of the port or terminal is appropriate to the ships that wish to use it.

The effect of competition between ports is particularly noticeable in the container industry. The key is, of course, intermodalism which is such an important aspect of container traffic. A container moves smoothly from the ship to a road or rail vehicle and then remains on wheels until it reaches its final destination. For this reason it is no longer vital for the ship to call at a port as near as possible to where the importer or exporter is based. Shipowners can, instead, choose their ports on the basis of what provides the most beneficial result to the voyage.

The first consideration would be the port's geographical position because it is in the owner's interest to ensure that the voyage is kept as short as possible. After location would come accommodation so that even the largest of the owner's ships can approach the berth with little or no delay. The port authority can often influence this by employing dredgers to deepen the approaches to – and areas alongside – the berths. The port of **Rotterdam** for example increased its depth of water by 15 metres (50 feet) over the course of the 20th Century.

The next selling point that the port would have to offer is its **equipment** and **infrastructure**. Loading and discharging ships today – especially container ships – is considered in terms of minutes and hours, not days and weeks as was the case thirty or forty years ago. The accommodation and equipment available will determine the time a ship takes in port and time is money. Money also is directly involved in the decision-making because of course, what the port charges per ton of cargo or per container moved will influence a shipowner.

2.3 WHY OPERATE SHIPS?

The most obvious reason for owning and operating ships is to make a profit. There are, however, other reasons that might apply particularly to governments and these can result in a state-owned merchant fleet or a government policy which encourages the owning of ships under the national flag. The main reasons for a government encouraging the development of a shipping industry are:

2.3.1 Conserving Foreign Exchange

Nations with a limited ability to earn foreign currency through exports may seek to ensure that all, or most, of the goods they export or import are carried in their own ships. This means that the freight charges are paid to themselves rather than to foreign vessels. As the major costs of operating their own ships are paid for in their own currency there is no drain on foreign reserves. This limiting of use of foreign ships has been implemented in some cases by directing cargo to state-owned ships and in others by arranging preference to be given to ships flying the national flag.

2.3.2 Control of Trade and 'Prestige'

There was a tendency, when many of the former colonies of European countries were first becoming independent, for the governments of these new countries to seek to break away from the influence of the maritime 'establishment'. Thus, in some cases, the desire to have a national line and to control all the country's trade went beyond merely wishing to conserve foreign exchange. It seemed essential first for an airline to be established and then a shipping line. Those countries have become more sophisticated and more financially viable so that whilst national airlines still seem indispensable the desire for national shipping fleets is far less apparent. Often this is because their original plans were based around fleets of second hand 'tween deckers' that were once widely used in liner trades. Containerships are more costly to build and require additional expenditure on the containers themselves so, as lines switched to containers, the older ships became obsolete and too expensive to replace.

2.3.3 Earning Foreign Exchange

Some countries have seen that operating ships, especially passenger cruise ships, can be profitable in foreign currency terms and often in real terms as well. The former Soviet Union, with its major construction and operating costs all being in roubles, was able to provide reasonable quality, low-cost cruising with a substantial profit left over for the state operators. Attempting to achieve similar profits with merchant ships is more difficult because of the high cost of competing in the open market against the major maritime nations unless the country concerned has sufficient natural resources that are in demand. Then of course the state can restrict shipment to its own flag ships ensuring a good basic income for local shipping companies.

2.3.4 Strategic Needs

During the time that the 'cold war' was a major world problem, many countries felt that they had to have a minimum level of merchant tonnage under their own national flag to be used for moving strategic supplies should actual fighting break out. With less of a threat of a major war this attitude is less apparent but has not disappeared entirely.

2.4 PROTECTIONISM

The foregoing are typical methods of protecting a nation's shipping industry either state or privately owned; few of them have proved entirely successful. The main problem has been that many of the cargo preference schemes or state-owned lines were established initially when the countries concerned were far from prosperous so that the ships had to be acquired as cheaply as possible and thus had a very limited life. When the time came to replace them the problem of raising enough finance meant seeking funds from the world markets. Having to expend vast sums of interest and loan repayments in foreign currency tended to undermine the whole purpose of cargo preference. This became steadily more apparent as both bulk carriers and tankers (and more especially container ships) became larger, more sophisticated and therefore much more costly. Thus, only countries with a substantial shipbuilding industry of its own (such as South Korea) have been really able to maintain a viable cargo preference scheme.

There are, however, other forms of protection that a state may afford to its shipping industry. It must be remembered that shipping is a truly international market, which means that the same rates of freight are payable – the same income is achieved – regardless of the ship's nationality. But different countries have different economies and different costs of living so that the wage levels in, say, the USA or Germany are vastly different from the wage levels in, say, the Philippines or Sri Lanka. Crewing costs are a major cost item for ship owners, consequently if one is able to employ a crew from the Philippines, at wages appropriate to their local level, such ships will be far cheaper to operate than a similar ship employing a European crew.

The most obvious way for a government to assist its shipping industry is by granting a direct cash subsidy for the purchase of ships which is, for example, how the USA has maintained a sufficient fleet of ships to satisfy what it perceives as its strategic merchant fleet requirement. Direct subsidies to the ship builders are almost as effective and have been practised by many countries as a means of maintaining a viable shipbuilding industry against otherwise unbeatable competition.

Several countries prefer to operate a form of indirect subsidy which may be in the form of special income tax concessions. Others operate a scheme of providing capital finance at rates of interest far below the market level.

2.5   SHIP REGISTRATION

All seagoing ships have to have a nationality. Just as a person needs a passport when travelling to other countries, so a ship must have a register showing which country is its 'home'; in fact a ship's register gives the actual **port of registry**. That same port is printed beneath the ship's name across the stern and the vessel flies the national flag of its country of registry on the short mast at the stern; you will often hear the expression that a ship is **flagged** in a certain country which is the same as saying she is registered there.

Incidentally you will see another national flag flying from the ship's mainmast whenever she is in port, this has nothing to do with its place of registry but is the flag of the country the ship is visiting at the time and is called the **courtesy flag.**

Originally flagging was simple. A ship was registered where the owner had his office and although this is always called the 'port' of registry it is sometimes not actually a port. Countries like Switzerland and Zambia own ships from time to time but theirs are never able to reach their home 'port'.

However, as mentioned earlier in this lesson, ship owners began to find that registering ships in their own country was no longer financially comfortable. Taxation might be far too severe, or local wage levels far too high to be competitive. Over-enthusiastic governments or over-zealous trades unions might impose minimum numbers of crew members – manning levels – higher than those of other countries.

Shipowners were faced with giving up ship-owning or seeking a remedy and this caused them to seek countries with no taxation, little or no imposition of control upon ships under their flag and a simple scheme to enable shipowners to establish a 'shell' company – often a brass plate

10cm x 5cm outside a lawyer's office – for a nominal fee and to register ships for a similarly modest charge. Countries such as Panama and Liberia were in the forefront of this movement, in fact the Liberian flag was actively encouraged by American shipowners who found they had no chance of surviving under their own flag unless they were among those fortunate enough to get government assistance.

Many other countries have followed the pattern of Panama and Liberia; they are now known collectively at **flags of convenience.** In latter years the traditional maritime nations have made attempts to meet the problem half way by creating **'open registries'** which retain the national flag and the national compliance with international safety conventions but relax many of the financial and crewing strictures.

The major problem with some Flags of Convenience (**FOCs**) is that their lack of imposed control carries with it a lack of care about the observance of safety measures. The sea can be a very dangerous place and there are several international safety conventions that have been agreed within the **International Maritime Organization (IMO),** a part of the United Nations based in London. The most famous are the **SOLAS (Safety of Life at Sea)** and the **MARPOL (Marine Pollution)** conventions, all traditional maritime nations *as well as many flag of convenience countries* have ratified these agreements. Several, sadly, have not done so and such flags tend to attract some shipowners who have scant regard for the safety of their personnel or for the cargoes they carry. This is a great pity because "there are no bad flags – only bad shipowners" but the fact remains that even the good owners and the more responsible FOCs tend to find themselves undeservedly sharing the same reputation as the owners of the "rustbuckets".

It is worth noting that most IMO conventions require ratification by a certain number of states controlling a certain percentage of the world fleet before they are effective. Without the support of FOC countries like Panama and Liberia none of the conventions would have attained the levels required to make them effective. In some instances FOC countries are much more supportive of the conventions than traditional maritime states. Liberia for example was the first nation to ratify the section of MARPOL that controls polluting emissions from ships' engines. Despite being home to a major share of the world's shipowners and managers, Western European countries are particularly slow at ratifying IMO conventions. So much so that the EU Commission often found itself promoting regulations more severe than those formulated by the IMO in an attempt to persuade member states that some action is necessary.

Criticism about their lack of control of ships flying their flags has lead to many FOC countries taking a greater interest in control and enforcement of standards on board, some have begun the process of removing the worst ships, while others have closed the doors to newcomers. It should be understood that many of the FOC registers, particularly those with the worst standards, are not run by the governments of the countries concerned but are commercial enterprises who pay part of their income to the government. The countries are usually very small with very low GDPs and so allowing a FOC to operate is seen as a way of generating income for the government. There are also many states around the world with national-flag ships that compare unfavourably with the average FOC ship and yet they do not seem to attract the same attention that the FOC states do.

Attempts are made to counteract the problem of **sub-standard** ships. An international affiliation of transport trades unions known as the **International Transport Workers Federation (ITF)** from time to time arranges a 'swoop' on a ship employing what the ITF considers an underpaid and/or badly accommodated crew and tries to ensure that all the unions in the port where the ship is lying 'black-list' the ship until the owners agree to sign a contract with its crew on terms laid down by the ITF. Unfortunately, as with many militant organisations, there are occasions when principles become confused and the blacklisting is more aimed at trying to force the shipowner to employ European crews rather than seeking to improve the lot of Asian crews.

The ITF campaign against FOC vessels is not new having begun more than 50 years ago, shortly after the end of WW2. It was then that a great many shipowners were exploring the use of FOCs, not just for financial reasons but more to avoid the situation that had occurred just a few years earlier with ships being requisitioned by governments whose countries were at war.

The ITF was at that time still mostly a European organisation and was concerned with ensuring employment for merchant seaman being released from military service. Since then it has expanded globally and does seek to look after all its members. Perhaps the most justified criticism of the way the ITF works is that a uniform wage for seamen pitched near the salary levels of developed countries, will actually encourage more workers from poorer states to seek employment as seafarers.

The differences in wage levels is well illustrated by a survey carried out by the International Shipping Federation who found that, for example, the cost of employing a UK seaman is almost two and a half times that of one from the Phillipines. The cost of employing a Norwegian Chief Officer is nearly four times that of one from the Phillipines.

There is, however, another side to the equation. Countries like the Philippines are unlikely ever to be significant ship-operating nations and yet one of the major sources of foreign exchange, that they depend upon, comes from the wages earned by their seafarers serving on ships flying free flags.

2.6   PORT STATE CONTROL

Throughout most of history governments of nations with ports and access to the sea have taken little interest in the condition and operating standards of ships belonging to other states. Providing they paid their dues, such ships were free to trade without any controls or sanctions from the states of the ports they visited.

In the last two decades of the 20th century a growing emphasis on safety and environmental issues was clearly in evidence. Public pressure was forcing authorities to take measures that would be seen as protecting the environment around their coasts, and it was in this atmosphere that the idea of port state control was developed.

At first, individual states gave themselves the power to intervene and impose restrictions on any ships that were in such a condition as to pose a threat to the interests of the state, irrespective of which flag they were flying. But acting alone, this was not effective as it might be since incidents such as pollution may have originated in the waters of a nearby state.

In 1982 several European states reached agreement to form a regional group of nations co-operating in implementing PSC. The agreement was reached in Paris and as a result the group is known as the **Paris Memorandum of Understanding (MOU)**. Later Canada joined the group to extend PSC across the North Atlantic.

Ten years later a second regional group was formed by Latin American countries. Rapidly followed by Pacific (Tokyo MOU) and Caribbean Groups. Meantime the USA was also operating a PSC regime but outside of any regional group. Other groups have since been formed namely, the Indian Ocean, Mediterranean, West and Central Africa, The Black Sea and The Gulf MOUs

Ships are targeted using a number of criteria such as past record, flag, class, ship type and owner. Vessel selected are boarded by Inspectors who initially only check ships documents. If problems are uncovered by the document check or if the inspector judges the ship to require an expanded inspection he will begin a more thorough examination of all aspects of the ship including construction, navigation, safety and pollution prevention.

There is supposed to be a standardised procedure for inspections although understandably standards may vary. At the end of the inspection the PSC Officer will record details of any deficiencies found. If the deficiencies are sufficiently serious the vessel may be detained until they are rectified, otherwise the vessel will be allowed to sail but a time limit will be set for rectifying each identified deficiency.

Results of all reports are stored on a central computer by each MOU and in the USA. Ships that have been detained are recorded on the central computer and details are also publicised in newspapers and on Internet websites in an attempt to shame the owner/operators into improving conditions on the ships. The ultimate sanction is a complete ban of the vessel entering any port within the regional MOU.

2.7   SHIP CLASSIFICATION

It is important to have clear in your mind the difference between *registration*, and *classification*, which is the subject of this section. Registration, it will be recalled, is the establishing of a ship' nationality – its flag.

Classification is a way of a ship obtaining a certificate of quality without which no one will want to insure it or the cargo it carries and no wise person would want to entrust its cargo to such a ship. Classification is by no means mandatory in all countries but some states do insist upon it. Usually that is because the roles of flag inspection and classification society are combined within a single organisation. Russia and South Korea are both examples of this, India too has a similar system but most Indian shipowners choose also to class their ships with one of the European classification societies for commercial reasons.

Classification is provided by **Classification Societies,** some of which are extensions of governments and some commercial organisations. At one time all Classification societies were considered reputable but alongside the growth in FOC registration there has been a huge increase in the number of bodies calling themselves classification societies but operating to very dubious standards. It is difficult to say exactly how many classification societies there are because some of the poorest standard ones have short lives. The best estimates would be in the 30 – 50 range.

Class societies are so obviously linked to the condition of the vessels that they class, that Port State Control authorities actually target ships for inspection based on their classification. Those that have the worst record sometimes close and re-open under a new name to avoid this targeting strategy.

The largest and most reputable societies are all members of the **International Association of Classification Societies (IACS),** an organisation established to ensure consistent standards and to jointly develop regulations and undertake research into all aspects of ship design and construction. Probably the best known of the 15 members of IACS are:

Society	Symbol	Founded	Nationality
Lloyds Register	LR	1834	British
American Bureau	AB	1862	American
Bureau Veritas	BV	1828	French
Germanischer Lloyd	GL	1867	German
Det Norske Veritas	NV	1864	Norwegian
Nippon Kaiji Kyokai	NK	1899	Japanese
Registro Italiano Navale	RL	1861	Italian

Of these Lloyds Register is the foremost and its Register Book is particularly valuable to shipping business practitioners because it includes *every* ship in the world over 100 tonnes deadweight regardless of whether it is classified by Lloyds or not. For this reason, all those concerned with shipping should become familiar with the format and content of the Lloyds Register volumes.

Appendix 1 provides a sample of the manner in which Lloyds Register is laid out.

The accepted classification with Lloyds is **100A1** which indicates that the ship has been surveyed by Lloyds personnel and found to be complying with their standards of seaworthiness. Where a ship is shown to have a Maltese Cross symbol after the 100A1 (spoken of as Hundred A1 Star) it signifies that the ship was actually constructed under the supervision of Lloyds surveyors.

To maintain its class a vessel must undergo periodical surveys which include inspections afloat and in dry dock. The 'special survey' has to take place every four years (or 5 years if the ship is on a Continuous Survey cycle). Each special survey tends to become more rigorous as the vessel ages. All parts of the ship are subject to survey, the hull of course, the machinery, boilers and tailshaft (the shaft linking the engine to the propellor) all have their own survey programme.

It was stressed at the beginning of this section how important it is to keep Classification separate in one's mind from Registration. This emphasis is made because most countries entrust some parts of their registration procedure to a classification society, particularly safety certification. Some flags leave the entire process of registration in the hands of a classification society which is why there is a risk of confusing the two processes.

2.8   SELF-ASSESSMENT AND TEST QUESTIONS

Attempt the following and check your answer from the text:

1. What three technological developments have had the greatest effect on world-wide merchant shipping?

2. What is the size of the largest tanker ever built?

3. How large do the experts consider container ships will become in the foreseeable future?

4. What speeds can modern container ships maintain?

5. What does 'intermodalism' mean?

Having completed Chapter Two, attempt the following and submit your essays to your Tutor.

1. Explain why ships have got larger and why some ships are larger than others?

2. Discuss the different tactics shipowners can and have adopted to protect themselves against periods of low freight rates. What could be some of the problems which may arise when some Governments help their merchant fleets excessively.

3. Refer to the page from Lloyd's Register (**Appendix 1**) and answer the following:

    (a)   What type of ship is the "*Amphion*"?
    (b)   Where would you expect the "*Amro 2*" to operate, doing what?
    (c)   Where was the "*A
    mrado*" built and by whom?

Chapter 3

THE SHIP

The ship is obviously the fundamental tool of all commercially related shipping activities and although the finer points are beyond the scope of this book, there are certain basic aspects that need to be grasped by ALL working in the industry.

3.1   TONNAGE AND LOADLINES

When describing a ship it is quite common to hear people state that she is "so many tons" and leave it at that. In fact in shipping the word "ton" (or the metric equivalent "tonne") has many different meanings and ways of being calculated.

For instance, when referring to a ship's carrying capacity in volume terms the word "ton" does not refer to a weight ton at all. It was originally derived from the word "tun" and referred to the 252-gallon barrel used in the wine trade in the days of sail. Then a convenient way of estimating a ship's size was to calculate how many of these barrels she could carry and that figure was used as the ship's **register tonnage.**

From that tradition, and after engines were added to ships, there evolved **Gross Register Tonnage (GRT)** and **Nett Register Tonnage (NRT).** These were a measure of the enclosed space in the ship calculated on the basis of a ton being 100 cubic feet. **Gross** being the total space, while **Nett** was the total space less that used for machinery and accommodation.

There tended to be variations from country to country in the method of measuring ships for their GRT and NRT so that a new system of measurement was internationally agreed and came into full force in 1994. The size of the 'ton' now varies between 95 and 105 cubic feet depending upon the size and the type of vessel. To differentiate between the old and the new system the word 'registered' was dropped so that we now have **Gross Tonnage (GT)** and **Net Tonnage (NT)**. Because the change is still relatively recent a lot of people, even seasoned professionals, still mistakenly refer to GRT or NRT when they mean GT or NT. But the old terms are not completely obsolete because some countries still calculate minimum manning levels based on the old figures.

These somewhat curious uses of the word "ton" are retained because entities such as port authorities, who seek to make their charges on some sort of size basis, see these measurement tonnages as a fairly reasonable way of charging according to an approximation of the revenue earning capacity of the ship. Gross tonnage is also the most popular way of referring to the sizes of **passenger** ships.

Despite world-wide discussion and agreement, the **Suez Canal** and the **Panama Canal** authorities decided to retain their respective unique methods of measuring ships for the purpose of calculating canal charges.

Ships do have other measurements that use weight as the basis of measurement. At one time the type of ton used depended upon the ship's nationality, today the metric tonne is used almost universally. Incidentally it should be noted that while the British use "tonne" to distinguish metric tonnes of 1,000 kg from imperial tons, other European countries simply use ton since they had no need to distinguish between the measurements.

3.1.1 Displacement Tonnage

This is the actual weight of the ship and the word displacement is used in reference to Archimedes Law, which states that the weight of a body is equal to the weight of water it displaces. Loaded displacement which is the total weight of the ship and all that it is carrying has no interest in merchant shipping but is commonly used as a way of referring to the size of warships.

3.1.2 Light Displacement

Is the actual weight of the empty ship, which is of interest to technical people and also to **ship sale and purchase brokers** when negotiating the sale of a ship to the scrap trade since it is a measure of the quantity of steel (and a few other metals) that is being sold.

3.1.3 Deadweight (dwt)

Coincidentally this is the difference in tons between the light and loaded displacement but its commercial importance is that it represents the total weight a ship can carry which includes cargo, fuel, stores, fresh water etc. To clarify one may encounter the initials **DWAT** standing for **deadweight all told.**

More importantly to those concerned with the ship commercially are the initials **DWCC** standing for **deadweight cargo capacity.** This indicates the potential earning capacity of a ship but it is not a figure that is cast in stone. When quoted in a ship's description it assumes that the maximum quantity of stores and bunkers are on board. In practice the operator may increase the DWCC by carrying less bunkers

3.1.4 Loadlines

The amount of a ship's deadweight is determined by its loadline and this varies slightly because a ship has a maximum depth (draft) to which it is permitted to be loaded. This differs according to the part of the world in which the ship is loading and what season of the year. When reference is being made to a ship's deadweight without any qualification it invariably refers to the amount that can be loaded on 'summer marks'.

The ship's maximum draft and its variations are determined according to an internationally established formula. This international convention was the first one dealing with ship safety and started life in **1876**. It was then that **Samuel Plimsoll** a campaigning British politician succeeded in persuading the government of the day to pass a Merchant Shipping Act. This gave the authorities several powers to detain unsafe ships and by an amendment drawn up in 1894 it particularly introduced a **loadline.** This was the deepest draft to which a ship could be loaded and was shown on the starboard side of the ship by a painted circular disc 12 inches in diameter with a line 18 inches long drawn horizontally through its centre to show the loadline. Because of Plimsoll's involvement, the loadline is sometimes referred to as a Plimsoll Mark

The decision as to where the load line shall be situated is made at the time the ship is constructed and the decision process is overseen by the ship's Classification Society which issues the Load Line Certificate and supervises the placing of the loadline. This mark is situated approximately amidships on both sides of the vessel. The Classification Society's initials (e.g. LR, GL etc) are included in the loadline (see diagram page 23). The maximum draft allowed is calculated according to a formula laid down in the loadline convention but an owner can opt for a lesser draft and if he does so a lower NT can be assigned to the ship. An owner who intends to use his ship for carrying lightweight cargoes might choose this option because it means that port charges calculated on the ship's GT or NT will be lower.

Although, commercially, one associates the load line with the **draft** of the ship, the depth of the ship **in** the water, the safety aspect of the load line is concerned with the ship's **freeboard,** the amount of the ship's hull between the water level and the loadline deck. The level of the deck is indicated by a horizontal line painted on the ship's side above the loadline itself.

Different parts of the world and different seasons are considered to vary in their degree of danger and so vary in the amount of freeboard necessary for safety. International convention has divided the world into zones the least dangerous of which is titled 'Tropical' zone and the most dangerous is 'Winter, North Atlantic'. Furthermore, salt water provides more buoyancy to a ship than fresh water so that if the ship loads in fresh water she may be loaded to a deeper draft as she will rise up to the correct draft when reaching the ocean.

For these reasons a ship's loadline can have as many as six marks, each of which has an initial against it which represents:

TF   =   Tropical Zone, Fresh Water

F   =   Fresh Water

T   =   Tropical Zone (Salt water)

S   =   Summer (in other zones)

W   =   Winter (in other zones)

WNA =   Winter North Atlantic

The actual mark (the disc with a line through it) is the Summer Mark. On the line are placed the initials of the Classification Society that surveyed the ship to determine the positioning of the mark. In the illustration is LR (Lloyds Register) but there are several more such as AB (American Bureau) or RI (Registro Italiana) and so on.

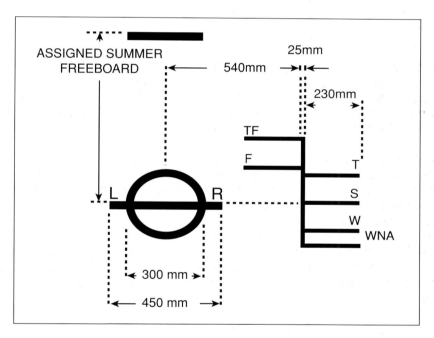

Ships used for carrying lumber (timber) can be granted an additional privilege because of the inherent buoyancy of the cargo and allowed to load deeper than ships carrying other cargoes. Additional loadline marks (corresponding to those mentioned above) are painted on the ship and prefixed with the letter L. If the ship happens not to be carrying timber on a particular voyage then the maximum draft will be in accordance with the standard marks.

3.1.5   Draft

This word, which can also be spelt 'draught', so far as this Chapter is concerned refers to the distance between the bottom of the ship (the **keel**) to the level of water on the ships side (the **waterline**).

The more cargo (weight) the ship loads the deeper the ship will lay in the water – the greater her draft.

Every ship has a characteristic progression of increase in draft with weight so that it is possible to produce a **deadweight scale** like the example shown in **Appendix 2**. From this will be seen that for every state of the ship's draft there is a corresponding total deadweight. The scale is such that if the ship knows that it can increase its draft by a certain amount it is possible to give a close approximation of the amount of cargo required. The formula used is the **TPC** (Tonnes per Centimetre) or **TPI** (Tons per Inch) in case of older British and most US ships.

For some bulk cargoes, the taking of a draft reading before commencement of loading and then again when loading is finished gives a good check on the weight of cargo that has been loaded. This is called a **draft survey** and when it is of critical importance it is usually carried out either jointly by personnel from the ship and from the terminal or by an independent surveyor.

The word draft (draught) is also used in reference to the **depth of water** available at a certain place in a sentence such as "the draft available at low tide is 6 metres".

3.1.6 Ship measurement based on volume

There is another important reason for knowing the measurement of the interior of the ship apart from Gross and Net Tonnage. Some cargoes are far bulkier than they are heavy. Visualise the difference in the space that would be occupied by a ton of feathers compared to a ton of steel. It would be pointless arranging for a quantity of cargo equivalent to the ship's DWCC if there was simply insufficient room in which to stow it.

For this reason it is vital to know the **stowage factor** of the cargo, that is the number of cubic metres or cubic feet to the tonne, **(see Appendix 3)** and to know the cubic capacity of the ship. A ship always has two cubic capacities one is referred to as the **grain cubic** which is the measurement of the total cargo space on the basis that materials like loose grain flow into all the spaces in the holds. The other figure, the smaller of the two, is the **bale cubic** that measures around rather than in and out of all the beams and girders in the hold. This, as the name implies, imagines the way bales of materials could not occupy the awkward corners. The difference between the two will vary according to the construction of the ship but in older vessels the bale cubic is very roughly ten percent lower than the grain cubic. More modern ships have an inner skin over the side beams so that the bale and grain cubic are much closer. The designed cubic capacity of a ship will depend upon the trade for which it is intended. If its life is to be exclusively in the iron ore trade it will not need to have so much space as if it were intended for grain, for example.

3.1.7 Stowage

All cargoes have their own characteristic density which for the purpose of shipping is referred to as the **stowage factor**. This was at one time always referred to as so many cubic feet to the ton (cuft/ton) and general purpose ships until well into the middle of the 20th century tended to have a cubic capacity with a ratio of about 40 cubic feet to the ton deadweight. For this reason, cargoes with a stowage factor of around 40 cuft/ton were referred to as **'deadweight cargo'**. Light cargoes, conversely are referred to as **'measurement cargo'**.

In more recent times two things have changed. First, most countries have now adopted the metric system and secondly, general-purpose ships now tend to have a rather more generous cubic capacity, nearer 50 than 40 cuft/ton. This means there is a rather wider range of cargoes with which a ship can be 'full and down', which is the expression seafarers use to refer to a ship which has its holds full to the top and the water line level with its loadline.

Although cubic capacities are now measured in cubic metres many shipbrokers all around the world still use cubic feet when quoting stowage factors. Partly this is because it is easier to work with and remember stowage factors when quoted in cubic feet. Wheat for example has a stowage factor between 40 and 44 cubic feet/tonne, the equivalent in metric would be 1.133 to 1.246 m^3/tonne. Of course the ship's cubic has to be converted into cubic feet but this involves just a single multiplication of the quoted figures although in most cases the owner will simply give the cubic in cubic feet when describing the ship.

Appendix 3 is a list giving examples of the stowage factors of a variety of cargoes and although you are not expected to memorise them, it is vital that you get an appreciation of the manner in which different cargoes can have widely differing stowage factors. When actively engaged in shipping business, knowing stowage factors becomes vitally important. An example of why this should be so concerns the time that Great Britain became more concerned with importing coal than exporting the material. British coal is mainly deep-mined and thus very dense so that shipowners were safe in assuming coal to be a 'deadweight' cargo. When coal from places like North America were being chartered, the market came to realise that shallow mined coal can stow considerably lighter than deadweight and some unhappy disputes arose before charterers and owners came to terms with realising that enquiring as to the stowage factor was important after all.

Note also in the appendix that there are comments alongside some commodities. Students should certainly acquire the habit of memorising any crucial characteristics about cargoes such as a tendency to spontaneous combustion, a tendency to contaminate the holds, or the need to take special care to keep the cargo dry, cool, well ventilated etc.

3.2 TYPES OF SHIPS

So far mention has been made of many different types of ships and how they have evolved. This section will take a closer look at some of them and their principle features.

3.2.1 The Bulk Carrier

These are, without doubt, the simplest of ships in terms of construction. As the name implies their purpose is to carry homogenous cargoes in bulk. What they will have in common is a single deck with clear holds and large hatches. Almost all existing bulk carriers are of single skin construction. However new regulations currently being discussed by the IMO will require new vessels to build with double hulls in the very near future. In anticipation of this many new ships are already being built with double hulls.

Bulk carriers vary in size from small coastal ships of a few thousand DWT up to ships capable of carrying well over 200,000 tonnes of cargo, there are at least five accepted terms that can be applied depending on size.

3.2.2 Capesize

Refers to any vessel too large to pass through the Suez or the Panama canals. The latter effectively puts a lower limit on the DWAT of around 76,000 tonnes. Anything above this size would be considered a Capesize vessel.

Typically a ship of this type would have nine cargo holds of approximately equal size. Capesize vessels are rarely if ever equipped with gear and are used mainly in the grain, coal and ore trades. A noticeable feature of most recently built vessels is the absence of a forecastle – a factor that many believe contributes to their vulnerability in heavy weather. The same dicsussions at the IMO that will lead to double hulls may also see a requirement to include a forecastle in new vessels.

3.2.3 Panamax

These ships are as the name suggests the largest size of ships able to pass through the Panama Canal. Effectively this puts a ceiling of around 75,500 DWT on ships, although vessels at the higher end may not be limited by length or beam, their draft when fully laden may make them to deep. Such ships will therefore need to be part loaded or full with high stowage factor cargo if they are to make use of the shorter routes made possible by the Panama canal. Panamax vessels typically have seven holds and are often also equipped with gear. In the main Panamax vessels participate in much the same markets as the Capesize ship but are more flexible being able to call at a wider range of ports.

3.2.4 Handy and Handymax

Such ships follow essentially the same designs with Handy size ships running from 20-35,000 DWT and above that being referred to as Handymax. Both classes will have five or six cargo holds and are much more likely to be geared than the Panamax and Capesize ships. Probably the most marked difference will be in the shape of the cargo holds, as both of the smaller types are usually square sectioned rather than hopper shaped. This factor reveals that aside from grain and ore cargoes, these ships are also highly active in the steel and forest product trades. As a consequence the hatches need to open to give access to as much of the hold as possible, and often extend virtually the full width of the ship – leading to them being referred to as "open hatch vessels" (not to be confused with open hold container ships which have no hatch covers whatsoever).

Ships below the sizes mentioned above are commonly referred to as **small bulkers** or in the case of the coastal ships **mini-bulkers**.

If you look at the cross-section of such a ship you will see the way in which they are 'self-trimmers' in that they are hopper-shaped at the top and bottom. The effect of this is that, as discharging proceeds, the cargo falls towards the centre and thus will be under the square of the hatch so that all the cargo is accessible to grabs without any manual labour being needed to 'trim' it from the sides. When loaded the shape reduces the free surface so that the extent to which the cargo is able to shift in bad weather is kept well within safe limits.

There is a further safety feature in this design because the sloping sections are water ballast tanks. More often than not, bulk-carriers have to travel long distances without any cargo in the holds. This would mean the ship would be so high out of the water that she would be almost unmanageable in even moderately rough weather with the propeller probably half out of the water. By filling those tanks with water the ship can be brought down to a safer draft with sufficient ballast above the water line as well as below to make for a comfortable passage.

Such a design, with cubic capacity adequate for most bulk commodities, is by no means ideal for one of the most common bulk cargoes – iron ore. Such material is extremely dense and so would only provide a relatively small heap in the bottom of each hold. Without going into the technicalities of stability diagrams, if all the weight is concentrated at the bottom, the ship will behave like a pendulum in any sort of rough sea. Such a movement, apart from being most uncomfortable for those on board, imposes undue stresses on the fabric of the ship.

The solution lies, of course, in purpose-built ore carriers which have a smaller cubic capacity than a general purpose bulk carrier. Such ships are also specially strengthened along the fore and aft line to cope with the strain that is imposed during loading and discharge, when parts of the ship are full while other parts are empty.

3.2.5 Tweendeckers

Typical General Cargo Ship

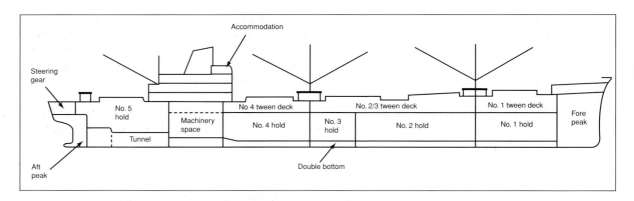

The above sketch shows a typical general purpose tramp of the 1970's and with so much emphasis today on specialised carriers one is inclined to overlook the fact that there is a substantial proportion of the world's trade still being carried in such ships.

Today the tweendecker is more likely to be referred to as a multi-purpose ship a term that is quite vague and has different meanings to different people. While some do apply it to traditional tweendeckers others believe that for the term to be valid some additional feature must also be present. There are for instance vessels that have folding or moveable tween decks and some also which have a RORO ramp included into the design.

Virtually all multi-purpose ships are able to carry containers both in the holds and on deck. Almost certainly a multi-purpose ship will be equipped with cargo handling gear. Today most vessels are equipped with cranes although derricks are by no means obsolete. Crane capacity will vary, but around 30 tonnes is probably the most common choice unless the vessel is intended for trades where heavy lift cargo is frequently carried. As well as being employed in general cargo liner services, multi-purpose ships are often chartered for tramp voyages to carry cargo that is not easily containerised. They are used in the bulk trades for cargoes such as steel and forest products and, for vessels equipped with folding tween decks, grain, fertilisers and coal are also popular cargoes. To allow for the variation in stowage factors many multi-purpose ships also have moveable bulkheads that can be adjusted to prevent cargo shift or to allow separation.

The number of holds will vary between two and five and folding MacGregor hatches are the norm. Ships with a low number of holds often include a very long hold that can accommodate cargoes of exceptional length that needs under deck stowage.

Tween decks add to a ship's versatility because apart from the obvious need to have a simple way of separating consignments, there is a limit to how many bags, drums, crates etc one can place one on top of another before the bottom tiers collapse under the weight of those above.

3.2.6   Container Ships

Containership Typical Layout

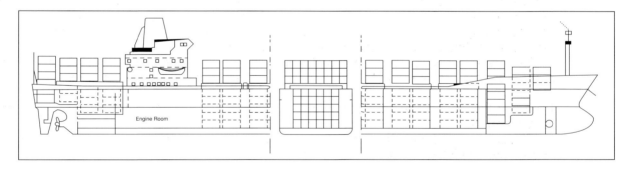

Are used mostly in the regular liner trades and carry most of the worlds trade in manufactured goods. This type of ship has already been well described in earlier chapters.

The large purpose-built container ships are 'fully cellular' which means that the holds have vertical metal guides into which containers can slide. Such a configuration obviates the need for any further securing of the containers in the ship as well as allowing loading to take place much more quickly. Such ships will load several tiers of containers on deck that will, of course, have to be secured by substantial methods of lashing.

Many of the largest liner shipping operators have been adding latest generation 6,000-8,000 TEU vessels to their fleets during the past two years, and there are many more ships of this size being built.

3.2.7   Roll-on/Roll-off (Ro-Ro)

These ships as the name suggests are designed for any type of wheeled cargo. They range from small ferries for short-sea crossings, to trans-Atlantic ships well up into the 20,000 DWAT class. Common to all Ro-Ro ships is some form of ramp so that the cargo may be driven or towed on board. As well as Cars, Trucks, Trailers and the like, Ro-Ro ships often operate on a conventional cargo route. The usual procedure for such an operation is for the cargo to be pre-loaded on to special trailers that are towed on by a specially designed tractor. Alternatively the cargo can be conveyed on to the vessel and stowed by forklifts.

RO-RO ships designed specifically for the carriage of new cars are easily distinguished from other types of ship by their slab sided construction and minimal superstructure. Frequently the bridge on these vessels is located in a forward position although the engine room remains aft. RO-RO ships for carrying cars are often referred to as Pure Car Carriers (PCCs) or Pure Car and Truck Carriers (PCTCs), ships that are used on freight ferry services are often called RO-PAX vessels today.

For the most part RO-RO ships are built with single hulls but there is an increasing tendency for ferries to be built with a catamaran hull. Some of these are what are termed "Fast Ferries" and are capable of speeds up to 40 knots, to help achieve this extensive use of aluminium is made in the superstructure and instead of propellers the ships are equipped with waterjet propulsion systems.

RORO vessels have been designed with their ramps in almost every conceivable position. Some have straight ramps that project directly forward or aft of the bow or stern respectively. Others have quarter ramps which project at an angle from on or other of the stern quarters whilst some have side access doors. Vessels with quarter or side access can usually berth alongside any normal quay whereas those with straight stern or bow ramps will require an 'L' shaped berth to work effectively. One advantage of the straight ramp is that extremely long loads can drive directly into the ship, something which is not possible with quarter or side access.

ROROs commonly have their capacity measured in lane metres. This measure gives an indication as to the total length of space available for vehicles of given widths.

The sketch below shows one of the larger types of Ro-Ro ships that would probably carry a mixed cargo of containers on deck and wheeled cargo under deck.

Typical Ro/Ro ship

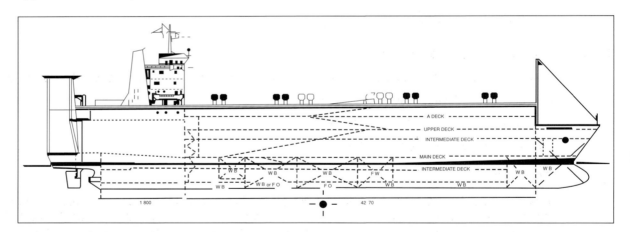

3.3 CARGO HANDLING GEAR

A means whereby cargo may be loaded in and discharged from a ship has to be available. With highly specialised ships like the larger bulk carriers and container ships, this process is carried out by appliances on the shore as the greater space and lack of need to worry about weight enables shore gear to be faster and have a great capacity. Tankers, of course depend upon pumps, shore pumps to put the cargo in, shipboard pumps to discharge it. (its has to be this way because pumps can push very efficiently but only 'suck' rather poorly)

It is with the smaller bulk carriers, container feeder ships and general purpose ships that one finds shipboard cargo handling equipment and if the trade needs a ship with cargo gear there are various features which have to be considered.

What type? At one time there was little choice, ships used winches and derricks. A **winch** is an electric or steam driven winding engine, and a **derrick** is a pole hinged to the mast near the deck over which runs hoisting wires which are linked to the winch. Crude though this system sounds it served the shipping industry extremely well for many generations, is very simple to maintain and operate which is why it is by no means obsolete yet.

More recently the trend has been towards **deck cranes** that are more expensive, need more sophisticated maintenance but operate at a far faster rate and as time is money to a ship the higher cost is offset by time saved. The other major question is its capability.

The principle factor here is the weight that it can safely lift – its **Safe Working Load (SWL)**. Winches and derricks tend to be around five or ten ton SWL although **heavy lift derricks** can be constructed to lift enormous loads and it is not unusual to hear these describe as 'jumbo' derricks.

The SWL of cranes varies considerably depending upon the trade the owners had in mind. Usually they are in the range of 10-40 tonnes but there is a trend towards slightly higher capacity cranes of 60 tonnes. Heavy lift ships, such as those being introduced by the German operator, Rickmers on its specialised liner service are equipped with a variety of cranes including two 320-tonne cranes that can work in tandem to lift upto 640-tonne loads.

3.4 TANKERS

These are vessels which carry liquids in bulk and for the purposes of this Chapter we shall split them into two main categories:

a) Crude Oil and Product Tankers

   and

b) Chemical and Specialist Tankers

3.4.1 Crude Oil and Product Tankers

The following terms are used to describe the various types of tankers which fall into this category.

i) ULCC's (Ultra Large Crude Carriers)

ii) VLCC's (Very Large Crude Carriers)

iii) MCC's (Medium Crude Carriers)

iv) Product Carriers.

The term ULCC describes tankers which range from 300/500,000 DWAT. They are mainly used for long haul operations between The Gulf and the Far East, Europe and North America discharging their cargo at terminals especially constructed to handle such large vessels.

VLCC's are vessels ranging from between 150/299,000 DWAT and are employed on similar routes to ULCC's but their relatively smaller size allows for greater flexibility. They can discharge at many terminals within the Mediterranean, North West Europe, West Africa, etc; they also have the advantage of being able to transit the Suez Canal in ballast condition.

MCC's range between 70/150,000 DWAT and are, in the main, used for short haul trips world wide. They have the advantage of being able to load at most terminals within the North Sea, North Africa and the Mediterranean, West Africa and the Far East. Their reduced size also gives flexibility within the ports they serve allowing many more options to Charterers and Shipowners.

This type of vessel can use the Suez Canal in either fully laden or part laden condition depending on its size.

Product carriers can also be sub-divided into two main tonnage groups; the larger carrying products in quantities between 26,000 and 50,000 tonnes whilst the smaller, so-called 'Handy Size' loads between 12,000 and 25,000 tonnes; this latter type of vessel is often called a GP or General Purpose type.

Tankers are constructed to a simple but well tested system. The vessel is divided by longitudinal and lateral bulkheads that normally give vessels a series of centre tanks flanked by two wing tanks. In modern times some of the wing tanks are used only for water ballast and being segregated, do not become contaminated with oil. The ballast can then be discharged overboard into the sea thus enabling the vessel to call at terminals that do not have the facility to handle dirty or contaminated ballast water. Tanks designated purely for water ballast are referred to as 'segregated ballast tanks' or SBTs for short.

Tankers have traditionally been built with a single skinned hull, but there have been so many pollution incidents caused by ruptures to a tanker's hull that public opinion has forced authorities into taking some preventative action. As a result all new tankers now have to be built with a double hull and there is a programme in place to phase out all older single skin tankers within a relatively short period of time.

Tankers are invariably self-discharging and most are equipped with at least four pumps that operate at high speed enabling a fast turn round in port. The rate of discharge is of course affected by local conditions such as climate, small shore lines, distance of receiving tanks from the berth, etc.

When carrying certain types of oils, tankers require heating coils within the tanks to keep the cargo fluid. Those coils, usually fitted in the bottom of the cargo tanks, can maintain a constant heat of up to approx. 50°C. Heating coils are not usually found in ULCC's or VLCC's as they are usually too large to load at terminals that supply the heavy and sticky crude oils.

3.4.2   Chemical and Parcel Tankers

In the last thirty years the expansion of the petro-chemical industry has seen the need for specialist vessels to carry the sophisticated products now produced. The smallest speck of rust or drop of water can in some cases ruin the specification of many petro-chemical cargoes. To counter this, modern Chemical Tankers are built with cargo tanks internally coated with types of epoxy, silicates or polyurethanes, and the different coatings are compatible (respectively incompatible) with different chemicals. The most sophisticated chemical carriers are those whose tanks, pipes and pumping systems are made of stainless steel.

Chemical/Parcel tankers are usually small in size ranging though up to a maximum of 50,000 DWAT. It has to be emphasised that the main requirement in this type of vessel is not only the ability to carry the maximum number of different products. It must be able to keep them so completely separate during loading, on passage and during discharging that there is no risk of one product contaminating another and, of course, no risk to human life or the environment.

3.4.3   Gas Carriers

The movement of gas, both Natural and Petroleum is now a major trade within the shipping industry.

As their names imply, Natural Gas is the gas which comes out of the ground in that form and can be used with little or no treatment. The North Sea gas which fuels most homes and many factories in the UK is a typical example. Petroleum Gas, on the other hand is a by-product of the refining process of crude oil. It has many uses, the ones with which we are probably most familiar are the small cylinders of Butane which are used in portable stoves for camp cooking or, smaller still, for cigarette lighters.

Both types of gas are carried in liquified form and, of course, both need purpose-built ships. They do, however, need quite different types of ship.

3.4.4   Liquid Petroleum Gas (LPG)

Diagram of LPG Carrier

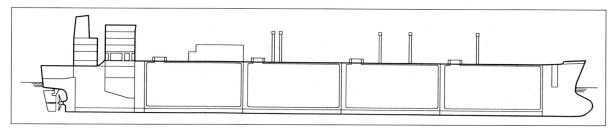

By kind permission of Syd Harris from *Fully Refrigerated LPG Carriers*

The two main types of LPG, Butane and Propane, have the advantage from the transportation point of view, that they can be kept in a liquid state so long as a high pressure is maintained. As with all gases in a liquid state, however, they are able to be kept that way more easily at a low temperature.

Gases can, therefore, be carried under any one of the following conditions either:

a)   at ambient temperature under pressure, or

b)   in insulated tanks at liquefaction temperature but at atmospheric pressure, or

c)   in a combination of liquefaction temperature under pressure.

For loading purposes the gases are liquefied by reducing their temperature by an amount dependent on the actual product involved; this operation is normally carried out by the shore installation. Most modern LPG carriers are, however, fitted with refrigeration equipment which allows them to reduce and maintain the cargo temperature as required usually to minus 50°C, thus any vapourising during the voyage or discharging can be liquefied by the internal system onboard the vessel. The size of the LPG carrier has increased over the past twenty years from vessels that carried 700 cubic metres to vessels in excess nowadays of 70,000 cubic metres.

Cargo tanks in LPG carriers are normally cylindrical in shape constructed from aluminium alloy and are self supporting and free standing. Further they are insulated to keep the heat out by a coating of a suitable material such as polyurethane foam.

3.4.5   Liquid Natural Gas (LNG)

Natural gas cannot be liquefied by pressure alone and so has to be carried at very low temperatures. The main types of natural gas are Ethane and Methane. Ethane requires to be carried at minus 104°C and Methane at minus 163°C, both being carried at atmospheric pressure.

There are two very different systems used in the design on LNG ships although both of them rely on insulated tanks to store the cargo.

Firstly there is the Moss system named after its designer which is instantly recognisable by the spherical tanks protruding high above the ship's deck. The tanks themselves are made from an aluminium alloy surrounded by insulation and protected by a steel outer shell. The tanks are connected to the ship's hull but do not form part of it.

Diagram of LNG Carrier

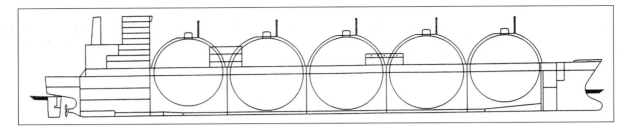

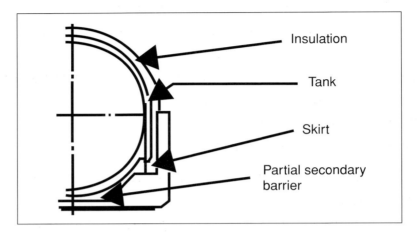

The second types of ship are referred to as membrane types. Unlike the spherical tanks of a Moss type LNG tanker, the prismatic tanks of a membrane LNG carrier are fully integrated into the hull. The cargo containment system is fitted inside the tanks, between the inner hull and the liquid cargo.

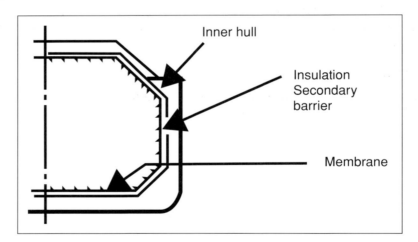

Neither type of storage system is fully effective and, the gas cargo boils off at the rate of around 0.15 per cent per day. Ordinarily this would be considered a negative factor but for the fact that most LNG ships are designed to make use of this tendency and are equipped with gas turbine engines that are mostly fuelled by the Boil Off Gas (BOG). For this reason LNG carriers only need to take on bunkers for auxiliary engines and for running the boilers for the turbines in port.

Most LNG carriers are built to service the needs of specific contracts as there is no spot trade in LNG. This is a situation that is likely to change very soon as the properties of LNG as an alternative fuel to petrol and diesel are being more and more appreciated. LNG consists of almost 96% Methane which when burnt produces very few so-called greenhouse gases. Although most LNG is extracted from underground reserves in the same way as oil (and in the same geographical locations), it can be produced ashore from waste materials. It is a fuel that is growing in importance and as such the demand for LNG carriers is also growing.

The most usual size for an LNG ship is 135,00 – 145,000 M^3 (equal to about 60-70,000 DWAT) and although larger ships are planned most of the shore facilities have been built to accept the present sizes of ships.

3.5 SELF-ASSESSMENT AND TEST QUESTIONS

Attempt the following and check your answers from the text:

1. What expression is used to denote how much cargo a ship can carry?
2. What is the purpose of a Loadline?
3. What is the approximate difference between grain and bale cubic capacities?
4. How is oil pumped into and out of a tanker?
5. What are ballast tanks used for?
6. What do the initials SWL mean?

Having completed Chapter Three, attempt the following and submit your answers to your tutor:

1. **Deadweight**

   Refer to the deadweight scale in the **Appendix 2** and answer the following:

   If the draft before loading was 3 metres and on completion of loading was 11 metres, approximately how much cargo had the ship loaded?

2. **Stowages**

   A 20ft container has a cubic capacity of approximately 30m^3, referring to **Appendix 3**, estimate what weight of oranges in cases would fill it? Would this be a measurement or deadweight cargo?

3. **Ships**

   Discuss the factors which have influenced the development of ships during the second half of the twentieth century.

Chapter 4

THE DRY-CARGO CHARTERING MARKET

4.1   INTRODUCTION

The different sectors within shipping business are usually referred to as 'markets' because at some stage there is the sort of negotiation between two parties that is characteristic of a market. The bulk trades, especially, are essentially driven by the laws of supply and demand on an international basis. So free are these markets that economists refer to the chartering markets as "perfect competition".

Like the kind of market one might find in a country town, with its several different stalls, the dry-cargo chartering markets are comprised of their own different specialities such as grain, coal, iron ore etc. Where it differs from the town market, is the way that one finds the same trades being worked in different centres throughout the world. Not only the same trades but– such is the influence of international communication – at the same 'prices' or, to use a more appropriate shipping term, the same **rates**.

At one time the only significant market-place for dry cargo chartering was **London** because at that time, the world's largest merchant marine was under British flag. The actual place where this all took place was the **Baltic Exchange**, in a street called St Mary Axe which is in the heart of the City of London.

It might be argued that the origins of the 'Baltic' go back almost to the early part of the fifteenth century when there was an active import export trade between Britain and the countries surrounding the Baltic sea. A more tangible link is seen with the seventeenth century when in 1666 there was a catastrophic fire which destroyed much of the City of London including the then Royal Exchange which was a meeting place for all types of commercial activities. It was some years before a new (the present) Royal Exchange was built and during the interim, tracers tended to meet in taverns. However they were not happy with this because they found they spent far too much on alcoholic beverages during a working day. As this was the time when coffee was becoming a very fashionable drink, coffee-houses became popular as merchants' meeting places and the first genuine foundation of the Baltic Exchange was when two coffee houses – the Virginia & Maryland and the Baltic Coffee houses – amalgamated with the specific intention of providing a meeting place for shipowners and merchants to come together to negotiate business. There is, of course, a wealth of history between that beginning and the establishment of an actual exchange in the middle of the nineteenth century from which today's exchange emerged. Paradoxically, there is now very little trade between Britain and the Baltic Sea conducted on the Baltic Exchange.

For many years, indeed until well past the middle of the twentieth century, the chartering of dry-cargo ships took place on the 'floor' of the Baltic, the business being conducted by word-of-mouth which is why the motto of the Baltic, which it shares with the Institute of Chartered Shipbrokers, is "Our Word Our Bond".

Of course the tremendous advances in electronic communication from the 1950s onwards has overtaken the face-to-face negotiation system and has encouraged the establishment of chartering markets in several other cities such as New York, Hong Kong, Hamburg, Oslo, Tokyo etc. Even so London is still by far the most active of all the market-places. The Baltic Exchange still exists although the wheel seems to have turned a full circle and now the trading floor has been rented out as offices while the 50-60 brokers who still come to the Exchange on a Monday morning have for some time held their meetings in the bar.

4.2 CHARTERING

The formal contract between a shipowner and the merchant seeking the use of his ship who is known as the **charterer** is called a **charter party**. The name is derived from the Latin *Charta Partita* (divided document). This dates from the time when an agreement was drawn up on a single sheet of parchment and then torn in two, one portion for each of the two parties. If they had a disagreement they had to bring the two halves together to test that they were the original agreement.

There is nothing new about chartering ships, the earliest written voyage charter is in the British Museum and is dated AD 236. It contains all the basic elements of a modern charter party.

There are two basic ways a ship can be chartered

4.2.1 Voyage Charter

By this means the merchant charters the ship to carry an agreed quantity of cargo from A to B. Payment is by means of **freight** which is usually expressed in terms of dollars per tonne but may sometimes be agreed as a 'lumpsum', a total amount rather than an amount per tonne.

In any case the actual level of rate of freight will be reached by negotiation, the dominant factor being the strength or weakness of the market at the time.

Voyage charters may be for a single voyage or can be several voyages of the same ship on a **consecutive voyage** basis. A variation of this is to ship an agreed quantity of cargo over a period of time. This is called a **contract of affreightment.** Such an agreement is a benefit both to the charterer, whose requirements will be covered for the period in question, and for the shipowner who can employ whichever of his ships is most conveniently placed rather than having to bring the one ship back in ballast on each occasion. Contracts of Affreightment can be of special benefit to 'pools' of shipowners

4.2.2 Time Charter

In this instance the charterer hires the vessel for a period of time and instead of paying a rate of freight per ton the charterer pays **hire rate per day**. During this time the shipowner still operates the ship and still provides the crew. (There is an exceptional special sort of time charter, mentioned later in this section where this does not apply). The difference is that the charterer tells the ship where to go and what to do and pays for all the fuel (bunkers) consumed as well as the expenses incurred in entering and leaving ports and in loading and discharging cargo. Thus the charterer acts in many ways as if he were the owner and is known as the **disponent owner** which is the legal expression used for the entity that is "deemed to be the owner but not actually the owner"

All the terms of a time charter have to be negotiated in just the same way as for a voyage charter. The principal items to be agreed are, of course, the rate of hire and the period of the charter, which may be for a few months or for several years or even, on some occasions, for a **trip.** In this latter case the job the ship carries out is very similar to a voyage charter being from place A to place B but being paid at a rate of hire per day rather than a rate of freight per ton. The reason for a charterer preferring this way of chartering is that, although the charterer bears any risks of delays, it does give far more flexibility than could be easily built into a voyage charter.

The type of time charter where the shipowner does not take any part in operating the ship and does not supply the crew is called a **bareboat** charter or in more legal terminology a **demise** charter. In these cases the charterer really does act just as if he owns the ship and this method of chartering is only resorted to when a significant period is required. In fact bareboat chartering is perhaps more easily visualised if it is looked upon more as a way of financing the ownership of vessels without having to raise the capital to buy them.

It may help to perceive these different methods of chartering ships if one thinks of voyage charter being like hiring a taxi for a single journey, a time charter like hiring a car with a driver by the day and bareboat chartering like renting a self-drive car for a period of time. Naturally the extent to which these analogies may be stretched is rather limited.

Chartering, as has been stressed already, is achieved by negotiation of a commercial contract between charterer and owner, usually through the medium of shipbrokers, in a completely free international market governed only by the laws of supply and demand. Because in most countries, the law permits consenting adults to agree to anything that is not in itself illegal, there is considerable freedom of choice as to what is included in a charter party.

To avoid the chaos that such a scenario might suggest there is, first of all, a fair degree of self-regulation especially among practitioners who bind themselves to the motto "Our Word Our Bond".

Secondly there are many **standard forms** of charter party (abbreviated as C/P) many of them specific to individual trades and a representative list will be found in **Appendix 4.** Do not attempt to learn this list parrot fashion but study it sufficiently to grasp the following points:

1. There are very many forms and this list is far from complete as there are scores of private forms used exclusively by individual charterers or groups of charterers. Even the standard forms are rarely used exactly as they are printed because changes are made to reflect special conditions applying to some particular voyages and shippers and charterers both have favourite amendments which they like to incorporate into the standard forms.

2. Many of the forms are very old. Even those shown as fairly recently established are in many cases revisions of standard forms originally compiled in the nineteenth century. A typical example is the "Americanised Welsh" coal charterparty, which as the name implies, was derived from a Welsh Coal form. It was, in fact, based upon a form adopted by the Chamber of Shipping of the United Kingdom in 1896.

    Conservatism on the part of owners and charterers tends to favour well-established forms even though they may need many amendments to comply with modern conditions. The value of such tried and trusted documents is that almost every part of them has at some time been tested in Law courts.

3. Some forms for very specific trades were devised by the charterers and will tend to be biased in favour of the merchant. Conversely those that have been approved, adopted or actually compiled by The Baltic and International Maritime Council (BIMCO) an owners' organisation tend to favour the shipowner. Bias can, of course always be corrected by negotiation and amendment of the wording; to what extent this can be achieved in favour of one party or the other depends upon the strength of the market at the time.

Appendix 5 is a copy of one of the most famous time charter forms, the **"Baltime"** and shows an example of the 'box' layout.

Appendix 6 displays a copy of an extremely well-used voyage charter form, the **"Gencon"** which is the form used for any trade for which there is not a suitable (or acceptable) standard form.

Compare these two forms with the help of the summary in **Appendix 7** which highlights the major differences between voyage charters and time charters.

Note that **time charters** require more details of the ship including the speed and consumption of bunker fuel (for which the charterer pays). Owners will demand the inclusion of trading limits, and the exclusion of certain types of cargo. The place and time of delivery and re-delivery are important to both parties and of course the period and rate of hire are crucial

In **voyage charters**, in addition to the obviously important items such as where from and where to, the cargo and the rate of freight, much attention is paid to **time.** First there is the time when the ship has to present to load.

Secondly the amount of time allowed for loading and discharging. "Time is money" is as true if not more so to a shipowner as it is in many trades. Too much time spent in port means less time for sailing and so less cargoes carried in a year. Thus many words are devoted in voyage charters to **Laytime,** which is the word used to cover loading and discharging time. If a charterer takes longer than the agreed amount of time to load or discharge, the charter will provide for a penalty called **demurrage** to be paid to the owner. In several dry cargo charters there is also provision for the charterer to be rewarded by a sort of bonus for taking *less* than the agreed amount of time, this is called **despatch money** and is usually based on half the amount per day as is agreed for demurrage.

One of the most important clauses gives details of how and when the **Notice of Readiness (NOR)** is to be given. An NOR is a statement given by the ship, or an agent acting on its behalf, to the charterer advising that the ship is ready to start loading or discharging. On the face of it this seems like quite a simple procedure, but it is complicated by events such as berth congestion, obtaining clearance for the ship by port authorities, confirmation from the charterer that the condition of the ship is acceptable and a whole host of other possible obstructions to starting work. Usually as well some time is allowed to the charterer after receipt of the notice to arrange labour and equipment to work the vessel.

Despite all the attempts to make things clear as to when time commences to count and what periods are excepted, there are more legal disputes over laytime than any other element in chartering.

Appendix 8 gives a representative list of the abbreviations and acronyms used in chartering negotiations and it will be seen how many of these relate to laytime. Even these can be further complicated such as with SHEX which means that Sundays and Holidays do not count against the number of days allowed for loading/discharging. But what if the charterer decides to continue working during these excepted periods? To cover this eventuality one may find the letter "uu" added after SHEX which means "unless used". If the market is in charterers favour the added letters may be "eiu" meaning "even if used" which would allow the charterer to work over the weekend without any of that time counting. The overtime cost to the charterer might be more than compensated by the despatch money earned.

Somewhere in all voyage charter parties is a clause that details what form the **Bill of Lading** should take and how many are issued. A Bill of Lading is one of the most important documents that you will come across in the shipping business. A Bill of Lading is a document which carries information about the cargo, the terms on which it is being carried and who is entitled to take possession of the goods after discharge.

In legal terms it is a receipt for the goods, evidence of a contract and a document of title. The last makes it just as valuable as the goods themselves since the holder can sell the goods while they are at sea merely by transferring the Bill of Lading to the buyer. More detail of the functions of a bill of lading are explained in the section on liner trades.

Important as these are, all the foregoing probably only accounts for half of the total wording of the charter party. The rest comprises clauses that cover a number of other aspects that are either essential procedures or provision for unexpected eventualities.

Essential procedures includes things such as which party is to arrange and pay for the cargo handling or who has the choice of agents at the ports. The unexpected eventualities cover matters such as war, strikes, ice affecting navigation and also a clause that covers the cancelling procedure if the vessel is unable to arrive in time to commence the voyage.

There are also clauses that provide protection for either party in case the other side does something which causes additional expense or damage. Damage to the cargo is a common problem and the parties can agree beforehand what causes of damage are excluded or included. Most charter party forms also have a **clause paramount** that incorporates internationally agreed rules on cargo carriage, these rules are either the Hague rules or the Hague/Visby rules. Although they can apply to charter parties if specifically included they almost

There are even speculators who think that they can trade ships more profitably than the owners themselves and will take ships on time charter and then re-let them on a voyage basis hoping to make a substantial profit between the cost of the time charter and the income from the voyage charter.

4.3.2 Chartering and the Internet.

There is a lot of history attached to the way the chartering market works and sometimes it may seem that the process is unnecessarily complicated, particularly the use of brokers as intermediaries to bring together shipowner and charterer. There have been several attempts to break with tradition and use the Internet as a platform for chartering whereby charterers and owners both subscribe to a site where details of cargoes or available ships can be matched and contracts concluded on-line. So far all attempts have failed and yet fresh attempts are made with monotonous regularity. Some sites are happy just to show details of cargoes and ships along with the contact details of the parties concerned, leaving it to brokers or the parties themselves to make the traditional negotiations. These sites seem to have a much longer life than the former type

It is not hard to understand why this should be. Buying and selling goods and services on standard terms over the Internet is a well established method, but each combination of ship/cargo/port/charterer and shipowner brings its own unique final charter party outcome and so is not best suited to the Internet business format.

Another reason why brokers are unlikely to be made redundant by the Internet is the very internationalism of the shipping business. With owners and charterers likely to be several thousand miles apart and perhaps unable to speak the same language, brokers who can negotiate for them and conclude an agreement which might well be in a third language are an essential element. There is too the high degree of personal trust which exists in shipping markets and which cannot be replaced by computer screens.

While Internet broking may not be so attractive as IT enthusiasts anticipated, the use of electronic communications and e-mail has made chartering much easier. Not only are communications faster, but charter parties can be stored on computers and edited as required rather than having to be retyped each time.

4.4 SELF-ASSESSMENT AND TEST QUESTIONS

Attempt the following and check your answers from the text:

1. How do economists describe the chartering market?
2. In which city does most chartering take place?
3. What is the motto of the Baltic Exchange?
4. What basis is used for charging for the use of a ship under a time charter?
5. What does the abbreviation SHEXuu mean?
6. What is the penalty a charterer pays if too much time is used for loading/discharging?
7. What is the title of the charter party form that is used for chartering ships for American coal?

Having completed Chapter Four attempt the following and submit your answers to your Tutor.

1. What major differences in conditions would you expect between a Time Charter and a Bareboat Charter and which would pay the higher rate?

2. What is the difference in laytime calculation between SHEXuu and SHEXeiu?

3. Explain what is meant by a firm offer and a counter-offer.

4. In a time charter, what would you negotiate concerning the hire money apart from how much? See **Appendix 5**.

5. Explain the cancelling clause shown in the "Gencon" charter. See **Appendix 6**.

6. What would be suitable charter forms for (a) coal; (b) sugar; (c) iron ore; (d) wood?

7. What type of charter party is known as the New York Produce Exchange C/P?

Chapter 5

THE TANKER CHARTERING MARKET

5.1 INTRODUCTION

Although oil has been found and used for many thousands of years its real commercial significance only began to emerge during the second half of the nineteenth century. This was in the USA where the first well specifically drilled for oil was in Pennsylvania in 1859. The chief interest at that time was in kerosene (paraffin oil) for lighting. Other products after extracting kerosene from the crude oil were simply burnt in furnaces and the lighter constituents like gasoline (petrol) were something of a problem. The automobile did not come upon the scene until almost the end of that century but when internal combustion engines became more widely used, gasoline ceased to be a surplus commodity.

Prospecting for oil in the USA proceeded at a rapid pace and for many decades, America dominated the oil production market, which is why, even to this day, the multi-national oil companies are predominately American. The British and Dutch joined the race and oil fields were being developed in Latin America and South East Asia; Russia also discovered major oil reserves.

Although America, Britain and the Netherlands retained their dominance in *refining and distributing* petroleum products, by the 1930s the development of the vast oil deposits in the Middle East ensured that the Arab nations would, eventually, firmly dominate the oil *supply* market.

5.2 THE DEVELOPMENT OF TANKERS AND THE TANKER MARKET

For many years the demand for oil was small enough that it could be met by transporting it in metal receptacles usually packed in wooden crates and referred to as "case oil". The first steamship designed to carry oil in bulk was built in 1886 and had a deadweight capacity of 2300 tons.

Initially oil refining took place close to where the oil wells were located but political as well as economic considerations made it wiser to site oil refineries near to the place of consumption rather than at its place of origin. Although this meant, in effect, that the oil would be "carried twice" it made a great deal of sense both at the time and subsequently.

Political sense, because a tendency was developing for some countries, having granted concessions to western nations for the exploration, extraction and refining of oil, later to nationalise these assets with minimal compensation.

Economic sense, because refining oil as near as possible to the area of most consumption simplifies the distribution of the many products of refining either by small specialist tankers, trucks or overland pipelines. An added advantage, probably not thought of at the time, is that having the refineries near consumption rather than near production means that there is no great problem if other areas of production become important. Consequently, when oil was discovered in the North Sea, turning countries like Norway, The Netherlands and Great Britain into oil producers as well as oil consumers, the existing oil refineries had no difficulty in adapting. The major advantage of carrying oil in its crude state is that it permits maximum **economies of scale** in terms of the ships used to transport it.

In the 1940's, when refined oil was the main cargo, 15,000 tonnes capacity was 'large' for a tanker, in the 1950s a so-called 'super-tanker' carried about 50,000 tonnes. By the mid-60s almost all oil refining was taking place near the areas of consumption and tankers carrying 200,000 tonnes emerged, these were given the name of **Very Large Crude Carriers (VLCCs)**.

Then when the Suez Canal was closed as a result of the Arab-Israeli wars, not having to comply with canal dimensions there was no restriction on ship size but every incentive to maximise carrying capacity which resulted in ships around 350,000 tonnes becoming common. They gained the title of **Ultra-Large Crude Carriers (ULCCs)**. The ship was originally built in 1976 and named "*Seawise Giant*", she was severely damaged by an Exocet missile during the Iran-Iraq war and needed to be rebuilt. As a single hull ship its sailing days are nearly over and it is expected that it will be converted into a Floating Storage Offshore (FSO) unit in common with many tankers of its generation. The biggest ever built is the "*Jahre Viking*" which has a capacity of over 555,000 tonnes. Million tonne tankers were designed but never built.

For many years the major oil companies owned vast fleets of tankers so that they could move oil around with complete flexibility. Some independent tanker owning was encouraged because the oil companies enjoyed being able to supplement their own fleets from time to time. Nevertheless, to maintain the flexibility that was essential, they usually took these ships on time charter unless they had a specific port-to-port requirement when voyage chartering could be utilised.

The oil companies, however, later became anxious to reduce the sizes of their owned fleets as these tied up vast millions of dollars of company capital. For them the ideal situation would be to use some method of voyage chartering which was so devised as to continue to provide the flexibility for them to direct or re-direct the ships to the refinery with the most pressing demand.

The device was the creation of "scales" which first took place at the time of World War II. At that time the USA, through the United States Maritime Commission, developed their scale and the British, through the Ministry of Transport, developed theirs. This somewhat cumbersome system of two dissimilar scales continued until the 1960s when the American and British got together and created a single scale the first of these combined scales was called **INTASCALE** and then, in 1966, it was further developed and given the name it bears today - **WORLDSCALE** – or, to give it its full title, **The New Worldwide Tanker Nominal Freight Scale**.

The system of Worldscale is to produce a freight rate in dollars for almost every conceivable oil tanker voyage (about 60,000 altogether). Each rate takes into consideration the distance, port costs, canal dues etc so that as far as is possible the same income per day would accrue regardless of the voyage performed. This enables charterers to take ships on charter with wide loading and discharging options with both sides being content with whatever load and discharge ports are finally declared.

The rates are listed in the Worldscale under the port of discharge showing the rate and the distance of the voyage in nautical miles for example:

PHILADELPHIA	USD/MT	Miles
Banias	8.38	10728
Bonny	8.28	10364
Cinta	17.63(C)	23998
Cinta	15.94(S)	20838

Note the different rates via the Cape of Good Hope (C) and via Suez Canal (S).

Of course the tanker market fluctuates just the same as any other chartering market and this is catered for by chartering at Worldscale followed by a number. Thus Worldscale 100 would be the flat rate as in the scale, Worldscale 175 would mean 175% of the flat rate and Worldscale 75 would be 75% of the flat rate. Market strength or weakness is not the only factor to influence the rate at which a ship may be fixed. The scale is calculated using an arbitrary ship size, speed and consumption as its basis so that if one's ship is widely different from that basis, a different rate will be sought.

The use of Worldscale is not only convenient for chartering single voyages but lends itself very conveniently to the use of **Contracts of Affreightment** which allows for a long term commitment and gives the charterer almost all the flexibility of time charter with none of the responsibilities for delays and no sudden gaps in supply in case of breakdown.

The ratio of tanker ownership has now reversed with the oil companies no longer having vast fleets of their own and the independents bearing the greater part of the benefits (and risks) of tanker ownership. Not surprisingly, they have their own dedicated international association – **INTERTANKO** – (The Independent Tanker Owners Association) which gives them a unified voice even to the extent of devising their own standard charterparty the **INTERTANKVOY.**

Independence is by no means confined to tanker owning. Reference has already been made to multi-national oil companies – the **oil majors** – of which there are several, probably the best known include EXXON (American), BP (British) and Shell (Anglo-Dutch). There are, however many smaller oil companies, some privately owned and some state-owned. These companies and countries are obviously reluctant to be dependent upon the majors for their supplies of crude oil or refined products. Their needs have encouraged the emergence of independent **oil traders** who buy the oil and charter the ships in their own names and then sell the cargo on to whichever oil company will pay the best price. Inevitably there is now a thriving oil market, the dominant centre being in Rotterdam. The stage has now been reached where the oil traders form a very significant segment of the tanker chartering market.

5.3   TYPES OF TANKERS

5.3.1   Crude Carriers

Most reference so far in this lesson has been to those tankers designed to carry crude oil. Crude, as its name implies, is the oil just as it comes out of the ground. In that state it is a complex mixture ranging from heavy, dark coloured substances which are virtually solid at normal temperatures at one end to very volatile gases at the other. In between these two extremes is the fluid which, when processed through a series of refining processes, produces all the liquids which one tends to associate with petroleum such as gasoline (petrol), kerosene (paraffin oil), diesel oil, fueloil and several more besides. In addition the refining process produces a large number of liquid chemicals with a host of uses from specialised solvents to the raw material from which plastics are made. Crude oils vary considerably depending upon their origins some, like that from the parts of the Middle East, are so thick and heavy that if allowed to cool becomes almost a solid. One the other hand crude oil from the offshore wells in the North Sea is lighter in colour and freely pourable at normal temperatures.

The crude oil is transported in the largest ships in the tanker group. And the sketch overleaf shows a typical crude carrier).

A typical crude carrier

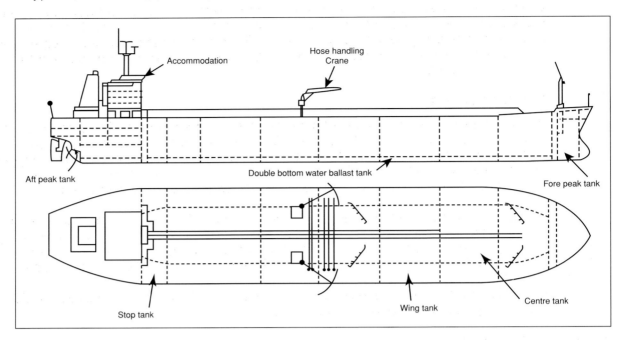

Reference was made earlier in this Chapter to VLCCs and ULCCs, these ships are relatively straightforward in their construction because there is no requirement to take elaborate precautions against contamination. Thus their division into a series of tanks is more for structural strength than for cargo segregation. The fact that these separations do exist naturally makes it possible for more than one discharging port to be served if necessary.

For many years, tankers were constructed with single plating, that is to say just one skin of metal between the cargo and the sea. However, some catastrophic instances of pollution of the sea and the sea shore through tanker accidents has led to increasing anti-pollution controls. The most stringent of these was the USA Oil Pollution Act of 1990 (OPA90) which required all tankers operating in United States waters to have 'double hulls'. That requirement has also been internationally adopted under the MARPOL convention so all new tankers are built with double hulls and an enforced scrapping programme means that by 2015 no single hull oil and chemical tankers will be trading.

The words "relatively straightforward" were used to describe the construction of crude carriers but they still include a fair amount of complex machinery and instrumentation. First there are cargo pumps which have to be capable of emptying the entire ship in no more than two days. Each tank must have its own set of pipelines with accompanying systems of valves and instruments to allow the right combination of tanks to be selected. Then there has to be a method of getting the heavy residues away from the sides of the tanks when discharging. This now usually achieved by a system known as **'Crude Oil Washing' (COW)** which comprises devices somewhat like huge, inverted lawn sprinklers which spray oil from the ship's own cargo around the insides of the tanks to wash the residues down.

Many types of crude oil are extremely viscous and would even become almost solid if cooled down, therefore crude carriers are equipped with 'heating coils' which, as the name implies, is a system of pipework in the tanks through which steam may be pumped to keep the oil at a pourable temperature.

Yet another set of pipelines is involved in providing the 'inert gas system'. Reference was made earlier to the fact that one component of crude oil is a volatile gas at normal temperatures. This gas when blended with air will produce a highly explosive mixture. To prevent air reaching it, the empty area above the level of the oil in the tanks is covered with a blanket of inert gas. The exhaust gases from the main engine supply some of this gas but most ships have an inert gas generator for the purpose.

As crude oil carriers invariably have to ballast to their loading ports, an efficient system of ballast tanks is also essential to enable this leg of the voyage to be carried out safely. In the early days of tankers, ballast water was simply run into the cargo tanks but this caused pollution of the sea when pumped out ready for loading. Tankers now, therefore, have 'segregated ballast tanks', that is tanks separated from the cargo tanks to avoid contamination of ballast water by cargo residues.

5.3.2 Product Carriers

Petroleum products, so far as the tanker market is concerned are divide into two categories, Clean products and Dirty products. Clean includes the lighter spirits and oils such as gasoline, kerosene, gas oil and diesel oil. Dirty covers the heavier oils such as the different types of fuel oil especially the so-called residual oils which are now the main type of bunker fuel for ships. (NB In chartering fixture reports the expression "Dirty" also covers crude oil.)

Tankers carrying clean products have to be meticulous in their cleanliness and cargo segregation because their cargoes are for use – often in delicate engines – without any further refining so that contamination would cause serious problems. Heavy fuel oils are not so sensitive but even so have to arrive in a satisfactory condition for immediate use.

Product carriers for clean cargoes are usually in the 40,000 range whereas dirty product carriers can be any size even up to 150,000 tonnes.

5.3.3 Chemical Carriers

Cleanliness and freedom from contamination in the chemical trade has to be almost obsessive. Furthermore some of the chemicals are so corrosive that the tanks have to be coated in order that the cargo cannot make any contact at all with the metal. The coatings vary widely depending upon the intended cargoes. Load a cargo into a ship with the incorrect coating and the liquid could dissolve the coating and then start on the metal. There are even chemical carriers with tanks constructed of stainless steel.

5.3.4 Parcel Tankers

These are a very specialised type of chemical carrier which have an extremely high degree of segregation with each tank having not only its own pipeline system but its own pumps. These tankers are almost the 'liners' of the tanker trade as they are able to load several different parcels for different shippers. In this way quantities of chemicals can be shipped that in themselves would be insufficient to comprise a full cargo for even the smallest tanker. The specialist knowledge of the operators of parcel tankers and that of their seafarers has to be of the very highest order.

5.3.5 Gas Markets

There are two distinct types of gas regularly carried in ships as liquids. The first is **Liquid Natural Gas (LNG)** which is **methane** and as the name suggests, is gas as it comes out of the ground. This has to be carried in insulated tanks with a very powerful refrigerating system to keep it in liquid form. LNG is the gas that is piped to factories and homes replacing the town gas that used to be made from coal.

The other type is **Liquid Petroleum Gas (LPG)** – **propane** and **butane** – which are gases produced as a by-product of oil refining. They only requires a modest amount of cooling but have to be kept under very high pressure to maintain a liquid state. These gasses are used where fixed connections are not usually available such as remote facilities and housing, camping and caravanning fuels and lighter fuels.

The gas markets are very closely connected to the crude oil trades since natural gas is found in the same sort of locations as crude oil and LPG is, as already stated, a by product of refining. Most of the gas supplies are controlled by the same major energy companies that produce crude oil and, since the ships required to carry it are highly specialised and hugely expensive to build, they are not built speculatively.

LNG particularly is seen as a very clean fuel because when burnt it only produces water vapour and carbon dioxide and not the more harmful acidic pollutants that oil does. For this reason there is a growing demand for it; as the fuel for power stations to produce electricity, for direct burning to supply heat and hot water and more recently as a fuel for vehicles and ships themselves.

As a consequence there will be an increase in the number of ships that can carry it and, most probably a growing spot market for them which may encourage speculative building.

The major reserves of natural gas are located near the crude oil reserves but there are also many places where, although extracting the crude oil would be uneconomic, taking out the gas is easier and this opens up the possibility to revisit some of the "worked out" crude deposits. Natural gas also occurs in places where crude oil has not yet been located.

There are gas fields in the North Sea, Mediterranean North Africa, The Middle East, Caribbean, US Gulf, Canada, Alaska, Indonesia, Australia and West Africa. Consumption tends to be in the nearest densely populated area with Europe and the US being the largest importers.

Since most of the ships now in existence are carrying cargo for their owners, there is not a huge charter market for them and when they are chartered it is usually on time charter or bareboat terms. However there is one voyage charter party form "Gasvoy" published by BIMCO that is used regularly for shipping LPG and is readily adaptable to LNG cargoes.

5.3.6 Other liquid cargoes

Oil and the chemicals derived from oil are not the only liquids to be carried in tankers. Non-oil cargoes include chemicals such as phosphoric acid, sulphuric acid, liquid ammonia etc. There is also a separate market in edible liquids including vegetable oils, molasses even orange juice and wine.

With such cargoes areas of production are much more difficult to define that with oil and gas. The ships too may not follow the same design basics that apply to oil tankers. Juice carriers for example are much closer to dry-cargo ships and indeed some of them actually have provision to carry containers on deck as well as cargo in the removable tanks installed in the holds.

5.4 TANKER CHARTER PARTIES

There are, of course, many elements in tanker charters which follow the same lines as dry cargo forms but there are several significant differences. The tanker market has its own standard forms but with perhaps only two exceptions, these forms have been devised by the oil companies themselves.

Appendix 9 is an example of a "Shellvoy 5" voyage charter party (A new version of this charter party – Shellvoy 6 – will be published during 2005 and may incorporate some changes.) and after the **preamble** giving the names of the parties, which is similar to any other standard form, The next clause "Description of Vessel" introduces some of the important differences. Lines 19/20 refer to a **heating system** which is a system of heating coils through which steam can be passed. The reason for their presence is because many crude oils would become solid and un-pumpable if allowed to cool to the sort of low ambient temperatures in, say, a north European winter.

The Shellvoy form is designed for use for any type of liquid cargo so that Line 21 refers to **tank-coating** which would not be of interest if the cargo was crude oil but vital if chemicals are involved.

Note that even tankers need winches or cranes (lines 22/23) but these are only needed to handle the hoses required for cargo handling.

Lines 24/27 are important as they deal with the capacity of the ship's **pumps**. Remember that the shore installation pumps the cargo **in** and the ship pumps it **out**. This is because pumps are very good at 'pushing' but not very efficient when 'sucking'. Refer also to lines 122/126.

If the ship is intended for loading clean products, her previous cargoes could leave a small amount of residue and some products could be contaminated by the merest trace of foreign matter. Thus lines 28/31 deal with the ship's **last cargoes**.

Mention was made earlier about **crude oil washing** and **inert gas systems**; these are covered by lines 32/34. The temperature of the cargo on loading is covered in line 50 which cross refers to clause 27 (lines 327-332) which covers the ship's responsibility to heat the cargo.

The wording then follows more or less customary terms until line 56 where reference is made to the laytime. Note that this does not deal in so many tonnes per day loading and so many tonnes per day discharging but simply says **running hours** (i.e. SHINC) because almost always the agreed total length of time for loading and discharging is **72 hours** regardless of the size of the ship. The ship's pumps are invariably designed to match the size of the ship and shore pumps always have plenty of spare capacity. Running hours, as the words imply, mean no breaks for Sundays and Holidays because oil installations by their very nature work 24 hours a day and almost every day of the year.

Lines 57/60 deal with **demurrage** and it should be noted that tanker charters have **no provision** for despatch money.

Read through all the form in order to gain a general impression. Most of the clauses are not dissimilar from a dry cargo form but you will see reference to oil pollution, which, despite some very damaging and highly publicised incidents, is in fact quite rare.

Older versions of the c/p contain reference to TOVALOP (the Tanker Owners Voluntary Agreement concerning Liability for Oil Pollution) which was a fund to which most tanker owners subscribed to ensure that there was always a huge sum of money available should it be needed to deal with a major oil spill. This voluntary agreement is now defunct having been made obsolete by stricter regulatory regimes.

Shellvoy 5 now contains the **Shell ITOPF Clause** which replaces lines 561-565 and reads:

> Owners warrant that throughout the duration of this charter the vessel will be:
>
> 1. owned or demise chartered by a member of the International Tanker Owners' Pollution Federation Limited and
>
> 2. entered in the Protection and Indemnity Club stated in part 1(A) 1 (xii) of SHELLVOY 5 as amended December 1996

5.4.1   **The Civil Liability and Fund Conventions**

The international compensation regime for damage caused by spills of persistent oil from laden tankers was based initially on two IMO conventions – the 1969 International Convention on Civil Liability for Oil Pollution Damage (1969 CLC) and the 1971 International Convention on the Establishment of an International Fund for Compensation for Oil Pollution Damage (1971 Fund Convention). This 'old' regime was amended in 1992 by two Protocols, which increased the compensation limits and broadened the scope of the original Conventions.

The 1969 CLC entered into force in 1975 and lays down the principle of strict liability (i.e. liability even in the absence of fault) for tanker owners and creates a system of compulsory liability insurance. Claims for compensation for oil pollution damage (including clean-up costs) may be brought against the owner of the tanker which caused the damage or directly against the owner's P&I insurer. The tanker owner is normally entitled to limit his liability to an amount that is linked to the tonnage of the tanker causing the pollution.

The 1971 Fund Convention provided for the payment of supplementary compensation to those who could not obtain full compensation for oil pollution damage under the 1969 CLC. The International Oil Pollution Compensation Fund (1971 IOPC Fund) was set up for the purpose of administering the regime of compensation created by the Fund Convention when it entered into force in 1978. By becoming Party to the 1971 Fund Convention, a country became a Member of the 1971 IOPC Fund. Payments of compensation and administrative expenses of the 1971 IOPC Fund were financed by contributions levied on companies in Fund Convention countries that received crude oil and heavy fuel oil after sea transport.

In 1992, a Diplomatic Conference adopted two Protocols amending the 1969 CLC and 1971 Fund Convention, which became the 1992 CLC and 1992 Fund Conventions. These 1992 Conventions, which provide higher limits of compensation and a wider scope of application than the original Conventions, entered into force on 30th May, 1996. As in the case of the original Conventions, the tanker owner and P&I insurer are liable for the payment of compensation under the 1992 CLC, and oil receivers in countries that are party to the 1992 Fund Convention are liable for the payment of supplementary compensation through the 1992 IOPC Fund. 1992 Fund Convention countries were required to denounce the 1969 CLC and 1971 Fund Convention, at midnight on 15th May 1998. As more States ratify or acede to the 1992 Conventions, the original Conventions have rapidly lost significance and the 1971 Fund Convention was terminated altogether on 24 May 2002.

In October 2000 the Contracting States to the 1992 CLC and 1992 Fund Convention approved a proposal to increase by about 50% (to about $260 million) the amount of compensation available under the terms of the Conventions. This came into effect on 1 November 2003.

Some countries that have not ratified the international compensation Conventions will have their own domestic legislation for compensating those affected by oil spills from tankers. Some of these may be highly specific, such as the Oil Pollution Act of 1990 in the USA, whereas other countries may rely on broader laws originally developed for other purposes.

5.5 NEGOTIATING THE CHARTER

Negotiation by means of offer and counteroffer are similar to those for dry cargo with a few significant differences. Reference has already been made to the way the majority of tanker fixtures, especially those for crude oil, are conducted according to **Worldscale** with the number being in line with the strength of the market at the time.

In almost all cases there tends to be only one broker between the charterer and the owner, unlike the dry cargo market where there is usually a charterer's agent and an owner's broker.

Negotiations in the tanker market tend to be far brisker than in dry cargo because both the charterers and the owners specialise in the oil business so that there are far fewer terms and conditions about which to haggle. Also, as the single broker is probably dealing directly with decision-makers on both sides, the time limits on offers and counter offers can be very short.

Unlike dry-cargo chartering which was, until recently, a face-to-face type of trading, tanker chartering always was (like all chartering now is) essentially desk-based. Tanker brokers have always been specialists and they usually tend to confine that specialisation to one segment of the market so that those working in crude oil are quite apart from those concentrating on refined petroleum products and chemical brokers are separate again.

5.6 SELF-ASSESSMENT AND TEST QUESTIONS

Attempt the following and check your answers from the text:

1. In which country are most multi-national oil companies based?
2. What is meant by saying oil is "carried twice"?
3. Where is the principle oil market used by oil traders?
4. What is the name of the independent tanker owners association?
5. What is COW?
6. Why do tankers have an inert gas system?
7. What are the two liquid gases called?
8. Why are some tanks coated?
9. How long are tankers normally allowed in which to load and discharge?
10. How many previous cargoes does the Shellvoy form wish to know about?
11. Who pays the cost of loading and discharging?
12. Who nominates the agents at ports of loading and discharge?

Having completed Chapter Five, attempt the following and submit your answers to your tutor.

1. Explain the reasons for oil companies deciding to base oil refining remote from the areas of production.

2. From your study of the "Shellvoy" charter party and the text, analyse what owners undertake to do to ensure the minimum damage to the environment from oil pollution.

3. Explain the origins of Worldscale and the advantages arising from its use.

Chapter 6

LINERS

6.1   INTRODUCTION

A liner is a ship which is employed in a **service** between one port (or range of ports) and another port (or range of ports). It does this with a regularity and frequency which will conform to an **advertised schedule** which, in the main liner trades, is on a fixed day of the week basis. This in contrast to a tramp which follows no schedule and may trade among a wide variety of ports according to the market at the time.

A liner is a **common carrier**. If one recalls the analogy of the taxi in Lesson 4 one could then think in terms of a liner being the equivalent of a bus service. Common carrier means that any shipper may have his cargo carried so long as he is prepared to pay the rate quoted and abide by the liner operator's terms and conditions. This in contrast to a tramp which is a **private carrier** as the cargo carried under a charter is individually negotiated and an agreement signed. In some countries (e.g. the USA) the expression "common carrier" has strict legal connotations.

Whereas a tramp *almost always* carries raw materials, very often in bulk, a liner *almost always* carries manufactured goods, very often in small consignments. A tramp *almost always* carries the goods for one shipper whereas a liner always carries the goods of several, often very many, shippers; it is for this reason that goods carried by liners is referred to a **general cargo**. (Where italics have been used in this paragraph it is because there are rare exceptions)

Because a line carries many consignments the contract of carriage is not the subject of individual negotiation, the shipper accepts the line's standard conditions of carriage. These are set out in what is the most important document in liner business is the **Bill of Lading** which among other functions is the **evidence of a contract**.

If the lack of a formal contract signed by both parties is difficult to grasp, refer back to a bus service. The issue of a ticket in exchange for the fare and the passenger's acceptance of that ticket is evidence of a contract between the bus company and the passenger, subject to the bus company's terms and conditions. In the same way a Bill of Lading is evidence of a contract between the carrying line and the shipper and it is rare indeed to alter by negotiation any of the other terms and conditions of carriage laid down by the liner operator; unlike in chartering where almost anything can be negotiated.

The freight paid by the shipper for liner transportation (liner terms) includes the full cost of loading the cargo from the quay and discharging it to the quay at destination. This does not include the charges (usually called **terminal handling charges**) for handling the container into and out of the container terminal. With liner contracts there are no complex time counting provisions and no demurrage or despatch **except** demurrage will become payable if a container is delayed beyond the stipulated time by the shipper or consignee.

6.2   A BRIEF HISTORY OF LINERS

Regular lines did not really exist until steam propulsion enabled shipowners to predict voyage times with some accuracy as their ships were no longer totally dependent upon the wind (and somewhat less likely to become victims of adverse weather). Thus lines, as such, began in the second half of the nineteenth century.

The principal area to benefit from the improvement arising from steam propulsion was the carriage of passengers for whom the line operators competed with each other in the provision of comfort and (for the wealthy) luxury. This was the time that European nations were expanding their interests in their colonial empires so that links with these overseas territories were a prime objective for those governments who encouraged the development of liner companies for passengers, mail and cargo. As trades evolved, the lines developed separate services for cargo so that the passenger liners could concentrate on offering maximum luxury and fast passage times for mail services.

The importance of passenger carrying continued into the middle of the twentieth century when air transport took over this traffic. Passenger carrying today is largely confined to ferry services and to cruise liners, which continue the tradition of providing comfort and luxury.

6.3   CONTAINERISATION

It is debatable whether the advent of steam propulsion replacing sailing ships was a revolution in sea transport or merely evolution. However, the next development in the carriage of goods by sea was certainly revolutionary.

Cargo liners had steadily improved in their speed and efficiency with the regularity and frequency of services matching the demands of steadily increasing international trade. Further improvements were, however, hampered by the fact that general cargo came in all shapes and sizes. From massive crates of machinery to drums, bales, bags and cartons. Over a thousand separate consignments per sailing was not unusual and all these had to be stowed by hand. (This piece-by-piece cargo is now referred to as **break-bulk** or **conventional** cargo). Extraordinary skill was needed to ensure that the different consignments did not damage each other and were carried safely even in heavy weather. The time taken in port was such that there was no scope for any economies of scale because larger ships meant even longer in port. The cost of building faster ships would be lost as the time in port could not be improved.

An attempt was made to improve matters by **"unitising"** cargo, which was putting all cargo on to **pallets** or placing **"skids"** under heavy crates and cases. This process took place before the ship arrived – a rebate was offered to shippers who delivered their cargo already on pallets or skids. This meant all cargo could be handled by fork-lift trucks and even loaded into the ship through side ports accessed via ramps on the shore. Unitisation raised productivity in the docks from 1.7 tonnes per man-hour to 4.5 tonnes per man-hour.

Then, in the latter half of the 1960s, **containers** were introduced and this was, and still is, referred to and the "container revolution"; productivity in the docks shot up to 30 tonnes per man-hour and subsequently much more. This now meant that shipowners could think in terms of port stays being measured in hours and minutes rather than days and weeks.

Containerisation began in the United States where the first experiments took place in 1956. A year later a container service began operating across the North Atlantic and international discussions on standardising the dimensions of containers took place.

6.3.1   The Container

The first international standards were for a "box" measuring 8 feet wide, eight feet high (later increased to 8'6") and lengths of 10 feet, 20 feet, 30 feet and 40 feet. The 10' and 30' were never very much in demand and the 20' size was most popular in the early days which is why the TEU (Twenty feet Equivalent Unit) became the unit of reference; thus a 40' unit is measured as 2 TEU. Other standard sizes were later agreed but are generally in only limited use.

Other items were included in the standardisation including the security of doors etc. Probably the most important standard, however, is the **corner casting** which, by means of three oval holes on each corner of the container, standardised lifting, lashing and securing (e.g. to the bed of a road vehicle). This allows containers to be handled speedily anywhere in the world. (See **Appendix 10**)

Quite early in the container's history it went beyond simply being a box. Anything which could be fitted within those eight corner castings set at the standard dimensions was capable of carriage as a container (see **Appendix 11**) In addition to a general purpose container which is a sealed air and water-tight box there is also a **ventilated** container which is ideal for cargoes such a coffee beans which are still 'alive' and so must be ventilated. The ventilation ducts can be closed when used for cargo that does not need them. Still with sensitive cargoes in mind there is an **insulated** 'port hole' container which, as the name implies, is a container with insulating material top, bottom and sides and is used for cargo which has to be kept at a constant temperature. It has ports (round openings) in one end which can connect it to the ship's (and eventually shore-based) refrigeration plant. Similar to the insulated container is the **refrigerated** container (usually referred to as a **reefer** container) this one has its own refrigeration unit and can be set to sub-zero temperatures in necessary.

For pieces of cargo which are too heavy to be loaded horizontally by fork-lift and can only be handled by crane there is the **open top** container, which may have a removable tarpaulin providing a **soft top** (or tilt cover) or a steel roof giving a **hard top**. For more awkward shapes and sizes there is the **flat rack** and even a simple **platform**, several of which can be used side-by-side for really large items.

Bulk cargoes are not ignored as there is the **dry bulk** container, which has man-holes in the top for cargo to be poured in; these are ideal for cargoes like malt. Then for liquids there are **tank** containers which may be used for anything from sensitive liquid chemicals to liquid foodstuffs; they are, of course, dedicated to one type or the other.

The principal reason for containerisation was, of course, to reduce port time to a minimum and so allow liner operators to reap the same benefits from economies of scale as bulk-carrier and tanker owners were enjoying. There was, however a considerable by-product which was **intermodalism**. The standard sizes and lifting/securing systems of containers allowed them to be carried with ease on rail wagons and road vehicles so that extolling the benefits of **door-to-door** transport was the main advertising ploy by the pioneers of containerisation.

6.3.2   Container Progress

It may be argued that the real "revolution" began in the late 1960s when a consortium of the lines operating between Europe and Australia formed Overseas Container Lines (OCL) and took delivery of six 29,000 tonners each initially capable of carrying 1250 twenty foot equivalent units (TEUs). Each of these ships could carry the equivalent of four or five conventional general cargo ships. It was many years before the proponents of containerisation admitted that they were so fearful that the conservatism of shippers might defeat the container concept that those first ships were designed so that they could become grain carriers if the idea failed – today it is difficult to believe such pessimism existed.

The Australian service was soon followed by the Europe/Far East services by which time shippers were beginning to prefer containers instead of having to be persuaded to accept them and all the major routes eventually became containerised. The word "revolution" is hardly an extravagant expression when it is realised that in no more than three decades the world's general cargo trade has changed from the old 'conventional' method to the situation where it is reckoned that 90% is now containerised and container ships of 8000 TEU are trading with even larger ships in the design stages.

Shippers fondness for containers is such that more than 70%, on some services nearer 90%, of cargo is presented to the line as **Full Container Loads (FCLs)** but there is no problem for shippers with smaller consignments. These can be presented to the line a **Less than Container Loads (LCLs)** and the line consolidates such shipments into containers for the line's convenience. In the early years of containerisation, enterprising freight forwarders offered their services to shippers of LCL consignments, charging them rather more attractive rates than the line's minimum freight. These forwarders consolidated the shipments into containers which they then presented to the line a FCLs. Their profit came from the difference between what they paid the line for the FCL and the aggregate of what they charged the various shippers.

It was from these tentative beginnings that a whole new branch of shipping entrepreneurs evolved, these are the **Non-Vessel Operating Carriers (NVOCs)** who take the role of the actual carrier but do not operate their own ships. In some places (e.g. USA) these are referred to as **NVOCCs,** the extra "C" covers the word "common" because local regulations insist that these operators are Common Carriers in the eyes of the law.

Today, NVOCs specialise in house-to-house services on a world wide basis, providing a value-added service to merchants, all as part of today's 'global market'. Some now handle more FCL units than quite important shipping lines. They buy space (often referred to as 'slots') in bulk and retail them on supply chain management basis. Although most still offer a service to FCL shippers at rates less than the lines themselves, some NVOCs no longer handle LCL business at all.

Containers and the intermodalism that they have allowed are such a feature of modern trading in manufactured goods that it is almost inconceivable to think that anything could restrict their use or hinder the productivity increases they have allowed in port working.

However because so many illegal immigrants are entering countries by stowing away in containers and the fact that it is so easy to smuggle goods and weapons inside sealed boxes have lead to moves by the US to insist on much more rigorous security checks. To this end some ports in other countries allow US Customs officials a presence in their ports to screen and inspect cargo in containers.

If these moves do not produce results there is every chance that a security conscious US may insist on all boxes being emptied in the ports rather than allowed to proceed inland unchecked. Scanning equipment and other security devices are being developed and installed by container terminals in an attempt to avoid the massive disruption that would result from official action.

6.4   CONFERENCES AND FREIGHT TARIFFS

Shortly after its opening, the Suez Canal 1869 proved so successful in reducing the passage time between Europe and South Asia that there was suddenly far too many ships. Shipowners started slashing rates to increase their cargo share but realised that this was benefitting no one. Thus, in 1875, the lines came together and formed the UK/Calcutta Conference which eventually became the India Pakistan Bangladesh Conference and as such it thrived for well over a century.

Eventually, virtually all liner routes had their conferences whose principal objectives were to regulate the number of lines in the trade and the frequency of their sailings. Also to produce a tariff of freight rates with which all the member lines undertook to charge. These tariffs became complex volumes because the aim always was to attract low-value cargo by charging inexpensive rates but compensating for any loss by charging high value goods much higher rates. This concept of charging "what the traffic would bear" seemed to suit everyone and helped to achieve what all owners wanted, a full ship providing an overall income that was profitable. Conferences also standardised bill of lading terms and conditions which all their member lines used.

Conferences only admitted members who could provide a service at the same standard as the other members and the cargo share and frequency for each member line was also agreed. This meant that a shipper using a conference service knew that regardless of which actual line it was, the rate and terms would be the same and the line concerned would be of reasonable quality. As no single line could offer the frequency and regularity that shippers needed, the conference system suited merchants as much as the shipowners.

The fact remains that liner conferences were price-fixing cartels. In the long-distance trades they had a virtual monopoly that they reinforced by giving rebates to shippers who were loyal to conference lines but cancelling such payments arbitrarily if a shipper dared to ship the smallest quantity in a non-conference ship. This stifling of competition was the subject of official enquiries and in the U.K. alone the government staged such investigations in 1909, 1923, and 1970 but on every occasion it was agreed that the advantage of conferences to merchants outweighed their disadvantages and they should not be outlawed.

The United Nations, on behalf of the world's developing nations, introduced a Code of Conduct for Liner Conferences. This was not so much to limit price-fixing but was an endeavour to ensure that the less developed countries, with their burgeoning national lines, would get a cargo share equal to the lines of the traditional maritime nations.

Paradoxically, by the time the UN Code became adopted as an international convention in 1982, containerisation had so altered the liner market that the conferences no longer enjoyed sufficient dominance in any trade and the Code became meaningless.

As has already been mentioned, prior to the advent of containers there was very little development in the basic design of liners, merely the natural evolution of propulsion machinery and hull design. The only real advance in shore-side practices was the reluctant acceptance by port labour of fork-lift trucks rather than hand barrows. There, was, therefore, no scope for any major reduction in freight rates.

Containers, however, provided room for massive economies of scale in a very short time, ship sizes increasing four-fold and with port times radically reduced voyage times were being halved. At about the same time the countries of South East Asia and the Far East were developing new merchant fleets. These were backed by their very high growth economies and large scale cheap ship building enabled shipowners from this region to enter liner trades, often outside the conference system. Even the most powerful conferences such as those for the Europe/Far East services found that these new operators, as well as new entrants from Europe, were competing successfully.

Conferences still exist in many trades and although they cannot exercise anything like the power they once had, they still strive to bring some order into liner routes. Their activities are constantly the subject of scrutiny by such anti-cartel regulatory bodies as the Federal Maritime Commission in the USA and the Directorate for Competition of the European Commission in Brussels.

Tariffs are still produced and regularly up-dated but in most trades a large measure of negotiation of freight rates is quite normal and these tend to be on a 'per box' structure irrespective of commodity.

6.4.1   Liner Consortium Agreements

Providing shippers with the frequency of sailings they require in a particular trade remains a problem as many lines cannot afford a large enough fleet to offer, say, a sailing on the same day every week. The solution these lines have found is to form joint services so that each line provides an agreed number of ships and then has a proportion of "slots" in every sailing regardless of whose ship it happens to be. There are cases where some consortium members may not contribute a vessel but as members still take a share of the slots available on each ship. These consortia emerge and disband according to the changes in the strength of the lines involved but the principle is now an integral part of container services.

6.4.2   Alliances

Consortia were originally formed by a group of lines operating in a particular trade such as Europe to the Far East. A line in that grouping might join with a total different set of partners in, say, the Europe to USA trade. With 'globalisation', the development of manufacturers selling to world wide markets in the last decade of the 20th Century, these customers sought to make agreements with carriers on a world-wide basis. This led to the formations of **alliances** where groups of lines come together on all three of the worlds major trade routes, USA/Europe, Europe/Far East and Far East/USA to provide an integral service.

6.4.3 Profile of a Typical Major Liner Operator

Today's liner operator probably involves:

1. Membership of a consortium, alliance and possibly a Conference.

2. Fixed day sailings

3. Network of own offices and/or agents supplying service to customers with intense publicity and sales activity.

4. Engaged in major East-West trade(s) with subsidiary trades either direct or through feeder services North-South.

5. Inland and distribution operations by rail, road or barge so as to provide a full door-to-door service.

6.5 LINER DOCUMENTATION

The most important document concerned with cargo in liner shipping is the **Bill of Lading (B/L)**. A B/L comprises the front, which has a series of blank sections to be completed in accordance with the shipment in question, and the reverse which is a mass of small print that gives details of the terms and conditions of the contract of carriage. The shipper supplies the line or its agent with all the cargo details when the booking is made in the form of Shipping Instructions; and this information is usually stored on a computer and can be incorporated into the Bill of Lading at the touch of button.

6.5.1 The Three Functions of a Bill of Lading

These have already been touched upon in the section on chartering when the importance and value of the Bill of Lading was stressed.

It is vital fix in one's mind that a B/L has three functions and if a mnemonic assists in this fixing process, think of a B/L being **RED**. A B/L is:

1. A Receipt for cargo

2. Evidence of contract

3. A Document of title

Appendix 12 is the face of a typical **Combined Transport Bill of Lading**. It acquired its name to differentiate it from the type of B/L which was used for break-bulk cargo and although the latter is now seldom encountered because of the predominance of containerisation, the name "combined transport" is still applied because it stresses the fact that this B/L can cover the transport of the cargo from shipper's domicile to consignee's premises and this may involve road or rail transport before or after the ocean voyage and may include shipment in a **feeder vessel** before or after the ocean voyage. The important fact with a combined transport B/L is that the carrier's responsibility covers all the different modes of transport that may be involved even though some of these may have to be provided by sub-contractors.

6.5.2 Receipt for Cargo

The B/Ls role as a **receipt** for cargo is easy to see because it sets out who is the shipper (consignor), who is the receiver (consignee) (ignore "Notify Party" at this stage) where the cargo is first received into the carrier's custody, the actual port of loading, where it is to be discharged and the final destination. Then there is a large amount of blank space in which to describe the cargo.

Below all this is space for the signature on behalf of the Master of the ship but above that space are some very important printed words reading "Received by the Carrier from the Shipper **in apparent good order and condition** – - – -" and then goes on to incorporate the terms printed on the back of the form. A Combined Transport B/L is issued when the goods are received by the carrier. This will often be at some inland point and only later will the goods be shipped on board the vessel. However, as will be seen later, contracts for the sale of goods often require the shipper to prove that the consignment has actually commenced the voyage to the buyer. This requires the B/L to give the actual date of shipment and in such cases the B/L is endorsed "Shipped on Board" with the date that occurred. Shipped on board B/Ls will also be issued for any goods which are received by the line at the port of shipment.

The B/L's function as a **receipt for cargo** is, therefore, twofold because it covers the **quantity** and the **condition** of the cargo and the consignee has the right to demand that he receives the same quantity in the same condition as it was when loaded.

With a **Full Container Load (FCL)** which has been **stuffed** by the shipper the description of the cargo will have the qualifying words "said to contain" so that the condition and quantity of the goods are outside the ship's control provided the exterior of the container is in good shape. In the case of **Less than Container Loads (LCL),** cargo where the container was stuffed by the line, the receipt as to condition and quantity are the same as for conventional cargo that is the actual number and type of packages.

Note that the expression for loading the goods into the container is **"stuffing"** in order to avoid confusion with **"loading"** which is the placing of the container in the ship. To avoid confusion with **"discharging"** which is taking the container off the ship, the expressions used for taking the goods out of the container are **"stripping"** or sometimes **"unstuffing"**.

6.5.3 Evidence of a Contract

Appendix 12 shows the reverse of the B/L which will be studied in a little more detail later in this lesson but at this stage it is sufficient to note that is comprises a mass of small print which gives details of the terms under which the goods are carried.

But the B/L is not the contract itself. It is not a document signed by both parties and in any case, the B/L is not drawn up until the custody of the goods passes from shipper to carrier. The actual contract, frequently no more than a simple verbal agreement, was made when the cargo was **booked** by the shipper with the line or the line's agent. Thus the B/L is the **evidence** of that contract.

Very rarely there will be a written contract for liner cargo and this will be in the form of a **booking note** an example of which may be found in **Appendix 13.** Booking notes are used in such instances as when a contractor for a major overseas civil engineering project wishes to arrange a fixed rate for all the materials involved rather than have the uncertainty of different rates for different materials, which could occur if the goods were shipped normally.

6.5.4 Document of Title

Title in this context is defined as **"the right to ownership of property with or without possession"** and this third function of a B/L is twofold.

"Right to ownership" simply means that whoever legally holds the B/L may claim the cargo and a unique feature of carriage in a ship, unlike surface transport is that once the cargo is shipped and the ship is at sea no one (except the crew of course) can get at the cargo. Thus, if the B/L changes hands lawfully the right to ownership changes at that moment. In other words the B/L is a **negotiable document**. This permits the initial transfer of ownership from the consignor to the consignee and also permits subsequent transfers of ownership by handing over the B/L, suitably endorsed, to the new buyer. If he so wished, the new buyer could resell the cargo and this could go on any number of times while the ship is still at sea until the eventual buyer presents the B/L to the line or the line's agent at the discharging port and claims physical possession of the goods.

It will be easily seen that the seller of the B/L can delay passing the right to ownership until payment has been made so that the B/L's other function as a document of title is as **security for payment;** this role is almost indispensable to international traders.

When one sells to an overseas buyer, only if the two parties are old and trusted friends can the matter of payment be an informal arrangement such as cash in advance or cash on delivery. Overseas trade is seldom like that and the problem is most often overcome by the system known as a **documentary credit**, often referred to as a **letter of credit.**

The buyer, having agreed price and other details with the seller, instructs his bank to arrange for a letter of credit to be made available at a bank in the shipper's country. When the cargo is shipped, the line or its agent gives a signed shipped B/L to the shipper who takes this to the bank holding the letter of credit together with all the other documents that the letter of credit may require. If the bank is satisfied that the documents comply exactly with the letter of credit the shipper is able to collect payment for the goods.

The bank in the shipper's country now has the B/L as security for payment by the buyer's bank to whom the B/L is now passed. Now the buyer's bank holds the B/L as security until the buyer has paid, at which point the buyer is in a position either to sell the cargo on, or to present the B/L to the line or its agent in order to claim the cargo.

Refer back to **Appendix 12** and look at the space just under the one marked "consignee", that box is titled **"notify address"** (some B/Ls show this as "notify party"). The point is that the bank involved does not wish to assume the position of actual consignee with all the responsibilities that may entail; the bank only wants the B/L as security. So, when a documentary credit is involved, the box marked "consignee" is completed with the one word **"Order"** which, after the shipper has endorsed it, makes the B/L 'open' (like a cheque drawn to 'cash'). The name of the buyer or his representative has been entered in the "notify" box so that the line or its agent knows who to communicate with even though that party will not have title to the goods until payment has been made to the bank and the B/L handed over.

Very rarely the buyer does not have the money and the bank is obliged to become the consignee rather than simply holding the B/L as security. It then disposes of the goods for as much cash as can be raised.

6.5.5   Sea Waybills

Today's more efficient liner services with just hours in port and high speed at sea present a new problem. The cargo can now arrive before the documents have filtered through the banking system because human hands and eyes still have to scrutinise the documents, that part cannot be rushed otherwise fraud would flourish.

One way to overcome this is for the buyer and the seller to agree to a different method of payment. If this is possible, and if the buyer has no intention to sell the goods on while the ship is on passage, a negotiable document is not necessary. In the circumstances a **Sea Waybill** can be used. Refer to **Appendix 14**

from which you will see that a Sea Waybill is similar to a B/L in almost all respects except it is NOT negotiable. A Sea Waybill is not a document of title so that it does not have to be presented at discharging port. The line or its agent simply has to satisfy itself that it has properly identified the consignee and then hand the cargo over.

6.5.6   Electronic Bills of Lading

All container lines now use sophisticated computer systems to handle the large volumes of B/Ls, Waybills, Freight Invoices. Manifests and other documents needed and in most cases this information is exchanged between the lines office and agents by electronic means, either through dedicated information system providers or the Internet and e-mail. Furthermore, many liner ports have integrated port-community computer systems which provide data sharing among interested parties. The line or its local agent inputs the data relative to their import or export vessel and this can be accessed by authorised port users such as Customs, Terminal Operators, Harbour Masters etc.

The part of the problem that still has to be overcome is that of replacing the 'negotiable' aspect of the B/L electronically. A pilot scheme is in progress initiated by a group working under the acronym **"BOLERO"** and this is being closely watched by all parties but especially the banks who fear the risk of fraud may be too high. Students should keep a watch on the shipping journals for more news of this system. In its annual report in March 2004, the TT Club (which owns half of the company which runs BOLERO) reduced its valuation of the shares because of the overall lack of interest in the system. There are some committed customers using it but it has definitely not been a runaway success.

6.6   BILL OF LADING TERMS AND CONDITIONS

Refer again to **Appendix 13** which is the reverse of a typical B/L. Read through all the clauses and endeavour to understand as much as possible but in particular note clauses dealing with **carrier's responsibility.** Almost all countries have adopted one of three international conventions concerning the carriage of goods under a bill of lading and incorporated it into its own law under a title such as **Carriage of Goods by Sea Act**. These conventions – Rules they are called – will be dealt with in more detail in the lesson concerned with the **law of carriage** but for this lesson is it sufficient to be aware of the fact that such rules strictly lay down the carrier's obligations especially the extent to which the carrier's liability for loss or damage can be limited. It is limited because there has to be a point where the contract states "this is where the carrier's insurance policy stops so this is where the merchant's insurance policy should start".

Such conventions are also in existence for the international carriage of goods by road and by rail. The responsibility clauses in a B/L explain that when combined transport is involved, if damage or loss takes place other than at sea the convention covering the mode of transport involved (road or rail) will apply. When it is not known where the problem arose then the convention covering sea transport will always apply.

(N.B. the documents in the appendices of this lesson are those devised and printed by the Baltic and International Maritime Council (BIMCO) and are included as examples only. Most regular lines have their own B/Ls with their own house style in the top right hand corner and their own clauses on the back of the form. Whilst these may differ from line to line the fundamentals are similar because so many of the clauses have to comply with whichever international "Rules" apply).

6.6.1   Differences Between Liner and Charter Party Bills of Lading

A bill of lading has the same three essential elements whether it is a liner bill of lading or a charter party Bill of Lading. The major difference between them is in the function as evidence of a contract. The liner bill contains the contract within the written clauses printed on the bill. There are no other documents, except perhaps a tariff for the freight amount payable, that would be needed for a court to decide what rights and responsibilities each party had under the contract. But a Bill of Lading issued under a charter party will contain a clause stating that it was issued in accordance with the charter party and contained all the terms and conditions therein. So in the case of a dispute the two parties would also have to produce the charter party before the courts could come to a decision.

Clearly any party who buys the goods covered by a liner Bill of Lading while they are at sea and who receives the Bill of Lading in exchange for payment, will be able to see immediately what the terms of the contract are. But when the same transaction occurs under a voyage charter, whilst the Bill of Lading may change hands it is unlikely that the c/p will so the new owner of the bill may not be fully aware of the terms of the c/p. The law recognises this and in some cases extends protection to the new owner of the bill that was not available to the original holder because of some clause in the charter party itself.

6.7   SELF-ASSESSMENT AND TEST QUESTIONS

Attempt the following and check your answers from the text:

1.   What are the dimensions of the most commonly used general purpose container?

2.   Which were the first two European container services?

3.   How many TEUs can the latest container ships carry?

4.   What do the initials FCL and LCL stand for?

Having completed Chapter 6 attempt the following and submit you answers to your tutor.

1.   Why has containerisation become the dominant method of liner cargo carrying in preference to other unitised methods or break-bulk?

2.   What are the roles of an NVOCC?

3.   Using a diagram to illustrate you answer, explain the progress of a Bill of Lading drawn to "order" from its blank state, via a documentary credit, to the completion of its life. Show also the progress of the goods themselves and of the funds used to pay for them.

4.   Distinguish between Conferences, Consortia and Alliances and discuss the importance of the role of each form of co-operation today.

Chapter 7

THE PRACTITIONERS IN SHIPPING BUSINESS

7.1 INTRODUCTION – THE SIX "DISCIPLINES"

The basic 'disciplines' or areas of activity in the commercial shipping world which are now accepted as falling under the term '**Shipbroking**' can be conveniently divided into six categories of professional expertise.

They can be visualised thus:

1. Buying (or selling) a ship – **Sale and Purchase Broking.**

2. Once purchased the ship has to be crewed, stored, maintained etc which involves **Ship Management,** after which it will require cargoes.

3. If the ship is a liner, the service must be marketed, the cargoes documented, arrangements made for loading and discharging these cargo all of which fall under the heading of **Liner Trades**, which will be carried out either within the liner operating company or by independent **Liner Agents.**

4. If the ship is a dry-cargo tramp, finding a cargo for the ship (or finding a ship for the cargo) will be the task of brokers in **Dry Cargo Chartering.**

5. A tanker will require a broker skilled in **Tanker Chartering.**

6. Whenever a dry-cargo tramp or a tanker calls at a port its interests will be entrusted to those who specialise in **Port Agency.**

There are, of course many other businesses involved in different aspects of commercial shipping. Two of these which interface most closely with the foregoing six 'disciplines' are the **exporters** and those that represent them, **freight forwarders**, both of these have their own professional institutes and are, therefore, outside the scope of this publication.

7.2 THE INSTITUTE OF CHARTERED SHIPBROKERS

In 1911, when the Institute was first formed, the world of shipping was a simpler place and the term 'shipbroker' in the United Kingdom referred to a person who arranged the chartering of ships, looked after them when they called in port and very occasionally became involved in sale and purchase negotiations. Liner services were in the hand of a relatively few major operators who used their own offices or exclusive 'loading brokers' to look after their business.

Since that time, the Institute has become a truly international organisation, retaining its title with all the tradition of professionalism it involves whilst fully recognising the way in which specialisation has created these six 'disciplines' within shipping business.

Furthermore it is recognised that the word 'shipbroker' means different things in different countries and in many there is a clear distinction made between brokers and agents. Indeed, several years ago the United Nations Conference on Trade and Development (UNCTAD) carried out a survey into the duties of the different intermediaries in shipping business in an attempt to find a single universal expression and eventually adopted the term "Shipping Agent" to cover everything including freight forwarders and forwarding agents. This survey was in connection with their devising a non-mandatory code of practice for shipping agents.

Although shipping business has become more specialised there are inevitably cases of overlapping with some people undertaking tasks which fall under more than one of the Institute's examination headings but in the interests of simplicity the six disciplines will be treated separately.

7.3 SHIP SALE AND PURCHASE

Almost all marine related property can be bought and sold – often for many millions of dollars – whether it be an order for a new vessel from a shipyard, an old ship to a scrapyard for demolition or a second-hand ship for further trading. It is this last named, the trade in second-hand ships, which forms the major part of the work of a ship Sale and Purchase broker.

Sale and Purchase broking is probably the most highly specialised sector of shipbroking, demanding as it does, all the usual attributes of a skilled negotiator with a wide range of knowledge of the technical aspects of ships.

It is customary for an S & P broker to be working specifically for one party or the other in a deal. When working for a potential buyer the broker has to be well versed in ship types as well as the vices and virtues of particular ship designs, builders and machinery in order to be able to advise clients appropriately. Advice on such matters as registration and classification even on sources of finance may even be called upon.

If working for a seller, the broker has to be able to place the ship before as many likely buyers via their brokers in the shortest possible time.

In both situations a thorough knowledge of the strength of the market is essential so that the buyer does not have to pay a penny more than the minimum necessary to secure the right ship and the seller gets the best price possible.

It is this market knowledge which enables leaders in the S & P field to act as **ship-valuers** when called upon for an expert opinion by such people as governments, financial institutions, insurance underwriters, probate lawyers, arbitrators and, of course, lawyers needing an expert witness.

As with many careers in shipbroking, ship Sale and Purchase demands many simultaneous skills. As well as an entrepreneurial flair and the technical knowledge the S & P broker needs a high degree of proficiency in gathering market information from every source possible. This has to include details of vessels in the market for sale and sales recently concluded as well as any factors such as freight market movements that might influence prices of ships. All this information has to be stored and in such a way that retrieval is rapid and accurate. Thus being up-to-date in the employment of computer technology is another vital faculty.

S & P brokers tend to specialise, some dealing exclusively in new ships where a close knowledge of the prices yards are quoting and the availability of building berths is needed together with knowing which yards are offering the best payment terms to buyers. Other brokers may operate at the opposite end of the scale and specialise in demolition when knowing which scrapyards are hungry for tonnage and which are over-stocked will dictate the prices available. Even among those working in the second hand for trading market may well specialise in tankers, or bulk carriers or in less regular areas such as oil exploration vessels, or smaller craft like dredgers or fishing vessels.

The sums of money involved in S & P are very great, but the ratio of deals which founder considerably outnumber those that succeed. An S & P broker must, therefore, be able to cope with a high level of frustration, although when a deal does succeed the rewards can be very attractive. S & P brokers' income arises from a commission on the price paid when the sale is concluded and all the brokers involved receive this commission from the seller. Rates of commission vary from $2\frac{1}{2}\%$ for very small ships, down to 1% for larger sizes.

An S & P Broker is only as strong as his records allow him to be so that impeccable data, constantly up-dated is essential. Support staff are, therefore, vital and many Sale and Purchase brokers started their careers pounding the keys of a desk-top computer.

7.4   SHIP MANAGEMENT

Maintaining a ship as an operational unit requires a variety of specialist services. In a large shipowning enterprise these are carried out within the company. Where an owner has only a few ships (few in this context probably being somewhere between 1 and 10) it may be found more economical to use the services of a ship management company.

Ship management companies fall into two main categories, one being a shipowning company that manages its own ships and offers the same service to other shipowners. The other type are companies that have no ships of their own and solely provide ship management services to shipowners.

Whichever type its is the function is the same and falls under five main headings:

(a)   Crewing

(b)   Storing

(c)   Technical

(d)   Insurance

(e)   Operations

Other services such as training and consultancy may also be offered.

Ship management appointments are individually negotiated according to the requirements of the principals but refer to **Appendix 15** which is a Standard Ship Management Agreement (Code named "Shipman") that sets out in greater detail all the different tasks a ship manager may be called upon to perform.

7.4.1   Crewing

It is not unusual for some shipowners to contract with a ship management company for crewing alone. This is particularly the trend among the traditional maritime nations where it is possible to register their ships under acceptable 'open registers'. One advantage of 'flagging out' (which is how this is often referred to) is that the national flag is retained but the regulations concerning the nationality of the ship's personnel are relaxed. Such shipowners, therefore, continue to carry out all other aspects of ship management but entrust the crewing to an offshore company. For the United Kingdom such places as the Isle of Man, Gibraltar and Bermuda have become popular, whilst several other countries – the Philippines is a typical example – provide a crew supply service as a form of 'invisible export'.

A crewing department will be responsible for checking the Certificates of Competency of the officers and take up references from previous employers. They will also ensure that the seamen are properly qualified for their positions in the ship.

Leave is often a significant factor in a seafarer's contract and the crewing department have to ensure that crew changes are carried out in such a way that ships are never delayed. All the travel arrangements for crew joining or leaving their ship will also be the responsibility of the crew department.

Last, but by no means least, ensuring all the crew receive their correct wages at the right time is a vital task for those in charge of crewing. Just as important (some might say more so) is ensuring that the portions of their wages to be sent to their dependents back home (called allotments) are promptly paid.

7.4.2 Storing

Stores fall into two classes, those items concerned with the crew and those concerned with the operation of the ship although some of the latter will be the responsibility of the technical department.

For the crew, the obvious items are food and drink. Still referred to a "victualling" by some traditionalists but now more usually called provisioning. This can be a demanding task as different nationalities have different food preferences, in many cases these are dictated as much by religious as by cultural needs. In many cases the ship's command has a high degree of control about buying supplies within budgetary limits but even in these cases close supervision is essential.

Other stores for the crew include such things as bed linen, cleaning materials, cooking utensils etc.

For the ship, one usually separates stores into two categories 'deck' and engine room'. Deck stores would include any materials needed for cargo operations such as ropes for lashing, timber for 'dunnage' etc. Specialist items such as tank cleaning and refrigeration materials as well as paints and other materials for routine maintenance also fall under the deck stores heading. Engine room stores will include such things as lubricants but spare parts are usually the responsibility of the technical people.

7.4.3 Technical

It is this department where one would be most likely to find former ship's officers with considerable sea-going experience. The technical department is often sub-divided into two sections, one under the management of the **marine superintendent**, who would be an ex-master mariner and the other managed by the **engineering superintendent,** who would be a former chief engineer.

The respective responsibilities of these two sections are probably self-evident. The engineers would be concerned with all the ship's machinery, probably including the cargo-handling equipment and possibly also the various electronic navigational devices. The marine superintendent would, in addition to his concern for the fabric of the ship, be responsible for keeping the classification surveys up to date.

The technical department also has one further vital rôle that is to respond instantly in the event of any ships under their control being involved in an accident. Technical department members are well accustomed to having to fly, perhaps to the other side of the world, at very short notice.

7.4.4 Insurance

Insurance is a shipowner's second biggest single item of cost so that the personnel dealing with this aspect need to be highly skilled. Marine insurance falls under two distinct headings. The first is the insuring of the ship itself, referred to as **hull and machinery insurance**. In view of the high value of ships today even a small reduction in the rate of premium can mean the saving of a substantial sum of money so that finding the best cover needs considerable expertise. The most famous provider of this type of insurance is **Lloyds of London** which is an organisation started in a City of London coffee house in the year 1687. Insurance with Lloyds is undertaken by individual **Underwriters** who group together in syndicates and can only be accessed through a **Lloyds broker.** Marine Insurance can also be arranged with insurance companies and it is for the ship manager's insurance department to ensure the best deal.

The other type of insurance is probably best described as **third party insurance** as it covers such things as claims against the ship by a port authority for damage done to a jetty; claims by ship's personnel for personal injury when negligence is alleged against the shipowner; claims made by cargo owners when their goods do not arrive in the same "apparent good order and condition" as it was when loaded. In other words any claim made against the ship by another person or company.

For reasons which go right back into history, Lloyds of London were reluctant to offer this type of insurance and so shipowners joined together into groups and formed mutual associations which to this day are still referred to a **"P & I Clubs"**, their more formal title is **Protection and Indemnity Associations**, "Protection" being the legal help given to fight off unfair claims and "indemnity" covers repayment to the owners for any third party claims which have been legitimately made and settled. As there are inevitably several third party claims "in the pipeline" the Insurance department is always busy.

7.4.5   Operations

This is the department that runs the ship. It communicates with the commercial people and plans the voyages, decides upon bunkering, appoints port agents and generally does all that is necessary to convert the work of the other departments into a trading entity on the high seas.

Constantly close links have to be kept with the other departments. It would be hopeless if, for example, the operations department planned a long voyage just when the technical department had committed the ship to a spell in drydock.

In some companies, the commercial people are an integral part of the operations department so that the ultimate decision as to what trade to undertake are taken here and the brokers seeking cargoes would obtain their authority to negotiate business from the commercial people in the operations department.

The jobs in ship management vary from undemanding tasks to highly specialised work and many of the technical positions are the natural choice for ships' officers when the time comes for them to forsake the sea.

There is no set fee or percentage commission for ship management, the manager's remuneration is a matter for negotiation at the time of the appointment.

7.4.6   ISM Code

Regardless of whether a ship is managed by its true owner or a third party, the standard of management will have a profound effect upon the condition of the ship and how safely and effectively it is operated.

Bad shipowners and managers will run bad ships and it is those ships that are most often involved in incidents that lead to loss of life, injury and major pollution incidents. Even companies that one would expect to operate to the highest standards can allow bad practices to creep into their standard procedures.

It was in recognition of this fact the IMO incorporated a section into the SOLAS convention that requires ship operators to comply with a code of practice designed to reduce the number of dangerous incidents, this code is know as the International Safe Management Code (ISM).

Under the code operators have to have their management procedures on shore and at sea, audited and approved by inspectors acting on behalf of the flag state. If they satisfy the inspectors the company will be issued with a document of compliance (DOC) for the shore office and each ship will also be audited and inspected before being issued with a Safe Management Certificate (SMC).

Passing the inspections is not a mere formality and the company and its ships must be able to demonstrate full compliance with SOLAS, MARPOL and local regulations governing conditions and training on board ships. All crew have to be properly trained for their jobs and in possession of appropriate certificates.

The ISM code was first introduced for companies operating passenger ships and tankers, bulkers followed soon after, and in July 2002 was extended to cover all ship types. Under the terms of the ISM code, every ship operator must appoint a **Designated Person Ashore (DPA)** whose role is to be a link between the ship and senior management. Usually the DPA is the senior superintendent but this is not cast in stone and individual companies may make their own arrangements. In very large management companies there may be several DPAs each dealing with a section of the fleet.

The ISPS Code

Or to give it its full name, the **International Ship and Port Facilities Security Code.** This is part of the SOLAS convention devised by the IMO as a response to concerns over security and terrorism.

The ISPS code is very much a reaction to the terrorist attacks on New York in September 2001 but it does include elements of two other problems – piracy and stowaways – that have been of concern for many years. Many within the shipping industry see the ISPS code as the product of politicians with little understanding of the way shipping works on a day-to-day basis. However it is a reality having come into force on July 1st 2004 although there are bound to be teething troubles in the early days.

As the full name suggests the ISPS code works on two levels – ships (but only those over 500GT) and ports. Governments and maritime administrations must appoint **Recognised Security Organisations (RSOs)** to certify the security arrangements that have been made in ports, on ships and in the shore offices of shipping companies. Exactly what sort of organisation can become an RSO is entirely at the discretion of national governments. Within the UK, only the Maritime and Coastguard Agency (MCA) has the power to vet ships but many flag states have delegated the work to classification societies while Panama has awarded a monopoly to a specialist security company founded by former US intelligence and military people.

To comply with the code, ships and ports have to be subjected to a risk assessment after which a security plan is drawn up. The plan is then reviewed by the RSO and after a successful inspection and audit of the port or ship, a certificate is issued. After the coming into force of the code, port states will be able to deny entry to any ship which does not have a certificate, as well as ships coming from ports which have not been certified as complying with the code.

What will happen in practice is very much a matter of guesswork, but the US has already declared that it intends to fully implement every aspect of the code from the coming into force date, a threat that the owners of ships trading to the US on a regular basis have taken seriously. The EU has made a similar statement but whether its members will bar non-compliant ships trading within the EU borders is yet to be established. The doubt arises because as this is being written, with less than 90 days to go before the deadline, so few ships and ports have completed the process that it would seem impossible for them all to do so in the time remaining. It is expected that an extended deadline of perhaps six months to a year will be allowed.

On a practical level both ports and ships will operate on a three stage security alert with the precautions taken dependant on the security threat assessed. This would mean that for the most part both would operate at the lowest level until some intelligence received makes a higher level desirable.

7.4.7   Liner Trades

The Institute refers to this sector of shipping business as Liner Trades rather than Liner Agency because whilst much of this work is carried out by independent liner agents, many liner operators now use departments in their own organisations to do this work. Whether "in house" or done by agents the work is the same and it will help if reference is made to **Appendix 16** which is a **Standard Liner Agency Agreement** a form devised by the international agents' association known as the **Federation of National Associations of Ship Brokers and Agents (FONASBA)** and recommended by the Baltic and International Maritime Council (BIMCO).

The agreement sets out in detail the duties of a liner agent, the important ones being:

(a)	Marketing and Sales	Sections	3.10 to 3.14
(b)	Documentation	"	3.15
(c)	Attending the Ship	"	3.20 to 3.29
(d)	Control of Equipment	"	3.30 to 3.38
(e)	Accounting and Finance	"	3.40 to 3.47

The Fonasba agreement is intentionally comprehensive in its summary of an agent's duties but there can be several variations. For example, the agent may only be called upon to deal with inward cargo arriving in the agent's territory or conversely only deal with outward cargo. The agent may even be involved only in sales and marketing (with no contact with the ship) which would be the case for an agent in, say, Switzerland, Austria, Zimbabwe or any other land-locked area; such agents are often referred to as **hinterland agents.**

Despite the rapid advance in electronic equipment, especially the computerisation of documentation and accounts, Liner work is the most labour-intensive sector of shipping business. That simple word "documentation" can involve the processing of many hundreds of separate consignments in a very short period of time. Each of these will involve several duties including, in the case of outward cargo, such items as taking cargo bookings including calculating the freight, checking the bills of lading, recording the container movement etc. With inward cargo there is the all-important task of ensuring the cargo is handed over to the legitimate bill of lading holder.

The prime advantage gained from containerisation was the reduction of the work to be done on the dockside but this inevitably meant radically increasing the amount of work in the liner agency office.

It will be seen from the foregoing that liner trades provides many types of work ranging from close links with the ship itself to jobs far remote from the dockside.

Independent liner agents' remuneration is a commission on the gross freight earned. In the days before containerisation there was a norm of 5% on outward freight (which was often considered to as 2½% for booking cargo and 2½% for handling cargo) and 2½% on inward freight. With the complex duties now involved with containers this simple formula has disappeared. It will be seen from the Schedule to the Standard Liner Agency Agreement that there can be negotiation around several aspects of the overall task of liner agency.

7.4.8 Dry Cargo Chartering

First assume that there is one broker representing the charterer looking for ships to carry his principal's cargoes and another broker representing the shipowner looking for cargoes to fill his principal's ships; this is not always so but is very often the case.

The brokers may be **exclusive brokers,** which means the principal channels all his business through that one broker whose job it is to advise the principal and to ensure the best possible deal in every case. Exclusivity may be total or may be exclusive to one part of the world so that the principal may use one broker in London another in New York another in Hong Kong and so on.

The other way is where the principal places his business through several brokers who are then referred to as **competitive brokers** because, of course, they compete with each other to bring suitable business to the principal.

There is another category that are referred to as **intermediate brokers** who may be part of a chain linking brokers on either side of them. This is far less common than it was because modern methods of communication make communication from one side of the world to another as easy as a local telephone call. An intermediate broker may also be used when that broker is the only one between the two principals.

The most exclusive broker is one who is part of the principal's company. This is quite common, for example almost all the 'London Greeks' have their own broking staff and many of the major grain companies have their own chartering departments.

When using an external broker the principal has what may be considered a dilemma. If using an exclusive broker, the principal will have a source of advice and service – a specific loyalty. In cynical terms that loyalty is motivated by the knowledge that the entire connection is at risk if a poor service is given. One may argue, however, that in a given time there is a limit to how much of the market one broker can cover. One the other hand by placing his business in the hands of many brokers, the principal may feel that the market has been fully saturated and the incentive is for the brokers to work as hard and as fast as they can so as to be the first to the principal with suitable business. This does mean, however, that the principal is going to receive less in the way of objective advice. For example, in a competitive situation a broker is unlikely to be keen to offer advice such as "the market will be more in your favour if your delay fixing for a few days" which is certainly the type of advice an exclusive broker would provide in such circumstances.

Whether exclusive, competitive or intermediate and whether working for the own or the charterer all have one duty in common they have to **know their market**. That does not simply mean knowing the trade they are in but recognising, for example, how a sudden demand in a different part of the world for a totally different commodity can trigger a rise in rates in their own trade sooner or later.

Although the face-to-face negotiations on the 'floor' of the Baltic Exchange have been overtaken by electronic advances in communication, chartering is still essentially a person to person activity. It, therefore, demands a highly developed ability to inspire confidence. Fellow brokers will be looking for someone whose word they can trust whilst principals will, additionally, be seeking speed, efficiency and sound advice. One might add that stamina is also a necessity. Chartering is essentially an international activity with shipping markets in different time zones. New York – five hours behind London – Tokyo finishing work just as Europe's working day is starting so that a chartering broker cannot expect a nine-to-five job.

A brokerage (commission) of $1\frac{1}{2}$% to each of the brokers involved in the fixture is usual in dry cargo chartering.

A chartering department does not consist entirely of brokers. Their back-up, generally referred to as the **post fixture department**, requires people who can translate the various notes, faxes, telexes etc into a written contract – the charter party – ready for principals to sign. Many brokers started their careers this way.

7.4.9   Tanker Chartering

Most of that which has been said about dry cargo chartering applies to tankers except that tanker chartering is highly specialised. Many of the ships are limited to one commodity and the charterers are often major oil companies. The broker is generally between the two principals both of whom have a profound knowledge of the trade.

Urgency seems endemic in the crude oil world, the time lapse between business coming in to the market and being fixed is usually very short. Thus the charterers tend to be more concerned with the sheer speed of finding the right ship. Exclusive brokers are rare in tankers and it has been said that the job requires something of a "fire brigade mentality".

There are, of course, many other liquids transported in tankers, each trade requiring its own particular expertise.

As with dry cargo chartering, $1\frac{1}{4}$% is the usual brokerage in tanker fixtures.

7.4.10 Port Agency

There is probably nowhere where the truth is more apparent that "time and tide wait for no man" than in Port Agency. It will be self evident that almost two thirds of all ships arrive and depart outside normal office hours. Nevertheless there is a special sort of job satisfaction in dealing physically with ships and their personnel.

When a tramp or a tanker calls at a port to load or discharge there s a considerable amount of work that has to be done before, during and after that call. The owner of the ship probably resides far away from the port concerned so that this work has to be entrusted to an agent who may be looked upon at the owner's 'extended right arm'.

The agent's first task will be to confer with the port authority who will demand payment (or a commitment to pay) large sums of money in dues for the use of the port and where appropriate, the dock. Duties may also include arranging a berth and will certainly entail liasing with the people involved in the actual loading or discharging who would be stevedores (dry cargo) or the jetty management (tankers). Then the tugs, pilot and mooring crew have to be ordered.

The agent usually meets the ship on arrival regardless of the time of day or night. In the past, except for a laconic exchange of radio telegrams, this would have been the first contact between the agent and the ship's Master (the Captain). Today, with the advances in radio-telephony, shipboard fax and telex machines, even mobile telephones there may have been several exchanges during which the arrangements made by the agent and the principal requirements of the ship will have been discussed. This first meeting is, however, an important one as there are several customs and immigration formalities to be dealt with. Important also will be the handing to the Captain the amount of cash he requires and almost as important, the handing over of the mail which will be eagerly awaited by the crew.

Delivery of stores and spares have to be arranged and cleared through customs, service engineers for ship's equipment may be needed and mundane tasks like organising laundry are all part of the agent's duties. Crew members may need medical or dental attention and it is even useful if the agent is skilled in the art of extricating from official custody any crew members who may have spent their time ashore unwisely. In fact there is no end to the activities in which the agent may be called upon to become involved and where the agent's local knowledge is invaluable.

Throughout this time the agent will be keeping the owner advised of the ship's progress and make any recommendations which might assist in the all-important task of turning the ship round in the shortest possible time.

The job is not finished when the ship has sailed. The parties will probably require a **Statement of Facts,** which is a record of how every minute of the ship's time in port was spent. From this the amount of demurrage or despatch, if any, will be calculated.

The final job, is to gather together all the accounts that have been paid on the ships behalf and compile the **disbursement account** for submission to the owner. A wise agent will have obtained substantial funds in advance and the disbursement account will denote what balance the agent requires or must refund to the owner.

The agent's remuneration is usually a fee, often based upon a tariff. These tariffs were at one time mandatory, some even had governmental support, but today in many countries any form of price-fixing is prohibited. The tariff is therefore no more than a guide and **Appendix 17** is an example of a scale of agency fees for dry cargo ships as currently produced by the Institute of Chartered Shipbrokers (this publication may eventually be disallowed by the European Commission). It will be seen that the scale tends to be based upon the size of the ship plus any more complex duties the agent may have to perform. Whilst the size of the ship may not determine the actual amount of work involved it has always been accepted that such scales reflect the concept that the larger the ship the greater the agent's responsibility, plus some element of 'what the traffic will bear'.

A problem a port agent may often face is that of conflict of interest. Quite frequently the charterers of a tramp or tanker will stipulate that the owner must appoint agents nominated by the charterers. For convenience in negotiations the is often referred to as **"charterers agents"** which gives an erroneous impression. In the eyes of the law the agent represents the owners of the ship (or the disponent owners if the ship is on time charter). It is perhaps easier to think in terms of the agent representing 'the ship'.

One may ask why charterers demand this right of nomination and there are several reasons. For example, in the case of tanker charterers there may be a combination of two reasons, first, is the need to maximise the efficient use of the oil jetty and having only one source of information about ships' positions from a known expert in whom they have confidence is valuable. Secondly, oil installations are extremely vulnerable places and limiting the number of people seeking access makes security easier. In other trades the owner might otherwise choose an agent with whom the charterer is anxious not to share knowledge of his business.

Not surprisingly in all cases of "charterers' agents" the charterer expects some *quid pro quo* from the agent in exchange for the nomination. The obvious one which in no way undermines the agent's loyalty to the owner is that the charterer will receive just as steady a stream of information about the ship's loading or discharging progress as the owner. Also the charterer can be confident that the handling of his cargo is in expert hands. Very occasionally the agent will be presented with a dilemma when a situation arises when the law of agency demands that the agent has to take the owner's side against the very people who insisted upon that agent being appointed. In such cases the agent's professionalism is rigorously tested.

As was mentioned earlier, the only occasion when the agent does not represent the owners of the ship is when the ship is on time charter when the agent represents the time charterer (the disponent owner) and under these circumstances the agent is expected to carry out all the normal duties for the ship. There are occasions when the owners want something extra done when it is quite usual for the owners to make an arrangement with the agent working for the time charterer to do this work which again is quite in order unless a conflict of interest is likely to arise.

There are rare occasions when the shipowner is simply not happy with the agent appointed by the charterer and in such circumstances the owner will appoint a **supervisory agent** sometimes called a **protecting agent** who will oversee the work done by the charterers appointed agents and will carry out any duties that the owner is not prepared to entrust to the charterers agent. You will see that the appointment of a supervisory agent is catered for in the scale of agency charges.

All the duties of a port agent are also carried out by a port-based liner agent and these are incorporated in the liner agency contract and are set out in clauses 3.20 to 3.29 of the Standard Liner Agency Agreement (**Appendix 16**).

Because of the essentially practical aspects of port agency work it can be the best possible basis for a career in any other branch of shipping business.

7.5   CONCLUSION

Except where any of the foregoing six 'disciplines' is carried out by a department in the principal's own office there is a principal/agent relationship and there have been occasional references to "the law of agency"; the legal aspects of this will be dealt with in a later lesson.

Reference has also been made at different times to "skill"; "the ability to inspire confidence"; "professionalism" which tend to emphasise the point that an agent is only of value to a principal so long as he or she can do the job more efficiently that the principal could do it himself and to do the job as well or better than any other agent in the same locality. It has often been said the "the world does not owe a shipbroker a living".

7.6 TEST QUESTIONS

Having completed Chapter Seven, attempt the following and submit you answers to your tutor:

1. Imagine you are a shipowning Principal wishing to appoint an Agent (or set up an in-house department) for one of the following tasks:

   (a) undertake Ship Sale and Purchase work

   (b) or undertake Ship Management

   (c) or provide Liner Trade services in a particular area

   (d) or act as your Chartering Broker

   (e) or act as your Tanker Broker or

   (f) or be your Port A

   gent at a particular port.

   Write an essay explaining what qualities you would be looking for.

2. Repeat the exercise for a completely different task.

Chapter 8

MARITIME GEOGRAPHY

8.1 INTRODUCTION

The previous seven Chapters have set out the pieces and moves in the commercial game of shipping, this Chapter deals with the board upon which the game is played.

Readers should have a simple atlas to hand for reference, the object of this Chapter is to highlight those elements which have an influence upon maritime matters.

In conventional geography the tendency is to study the land and to look up on the oceans as merely the blue areas that separate the land masses. In shipping, the interest is concentrated upon the seas, the coastal areas and any other geographical factors which impinge upon the life of persons in the business of shipping.

8.2 OCEANS AND SEAS

One often hears reference to "the seven seas" which is a misnomer because there are very many "seas" for example the North Sea, the Mediterranean Sea, South China Sea, Red Sea etc. The "seven" refers to the seven **oceans**. Study **Appendix 18** which is an outline map of the world. There will be seen the:

> North Atlantic Ocean
> South Atlantic Ocean
> North Pacific Ocean
> South Pacific Ocean
> Indian Ocean
> Arctic Ocean
> Antarctic or Southern Ocean

8.3 CONTINENTS

Note also there are seven main land masses or **continents** which in descending order of area are:

> Asia
> Africa
> North America
> South America
> Europe
> Antarctica
> Australia

8.3.1 Latitude and Longitude

It will be noted also on the outline map of the world that some straight lines have been drawn but in order to consider the significance of those lines it is important first of all to understand how a mariner identifies **position** anywhere on the earth.

To establish one's position on the surface of the earth it is necessary to refer to a universally accepted grid of lines which run East to West which are **Parallels of Latitude** and lines running North to South, from North Pole to South Pole, which are **Meridians of Longitude**.

There are 360 meridians of longitude each one being referred to as a **degree** and each degree is sub-divided into **60 minutes** and each minute into **60 seconds.** Refer now to the map and note the line running North to South cutting through England; it actually runs through a suburb of London called **Greenwich** where a famous astronomical observatory was once established. This line is nought degrees **(0°)** longitude and is referred to as the **Greenwich Meridian**. Longitude is therefore referred to as so many degrees, minutes and seconds East or West (of Greenwich).

The earth revolves on its axis once every twenty-four hours and mental arithmetic will reveal that the apparent movement of the sun in one hour will be 15° of longitude (360° ÷ 24hrs). This change of time with East-West travel will be referred to later when **time zones** are discussed.

It will be apparent that 180° West is the same as 180° East and further arithmetic will disclose that 180° of longitude is 12 hours (180 ÷ 15). This is why, on the map, there is another vertical line (although one which is not completely straight) this is the **International Date Line**. If one crosses this line from East to West the date is put back so that there are two consecutive days of the same name and thus if one crosses it in the reverse direction a day is apparently 'lost'. The reason why this line is 'bent' is to coincide with national boundaries so as to avoid confusion for the populations of those countries .

In the case of **latitude**, the 0° line is the **Equator** positions are referred to as so many degrees North or South; thus the North and South Poles are 90° North and South Latitude respectively. The parallels of latitude provide another purpose because it has been universally accepted that distances at sea should be referred to in **nautical miles**. A nautical mile is **one minute (1')** of latitude so that if one travels 60 miles due north or south one's latitude will have increased by one degree (1°).

It should be firmly established in one's mind that **speed** at sea is referred to as **knots** which is **nautical miles per hour.** (NEVER "knots per hour")

8.3.2 Charts

Because the earth is a sphere, depicting it on a flat page presented map-makers with a problem. There are several examples of solutions to this problem known as **projections**. The projection that one is most likely to encounter in shipping business is the **Mercator Projection,** named after the inventor, a sixteenth century geographer. Mercator's projection is based upon the idea of wrapping a cylinder of paper round the globe and projecting an image of the world's features on it. Its principal advantage is that it shows compass directions correctly which is vital for navigators, its disadvantage is the way that it distorts sizes because the further away from the equator, the larger things appear.

This is no problem for navigators because they measure distances according to the latitude scale, along the edge of the chart, which distorts at the same rate as other features.

8.3.3 Time

Reference was made earlier to the way the rotation of the earth means that the time of day varies according to where one is situated.

Appendix 19 shows the different **time zones**. Most time zone charts use as the datum, the time of noon on the Greenwich (London) meridian known as **Greenwich Mean Time (GMT)** and although, for convenience, seafarers personal time pieces are altered as time zones are crossed, navigation is always carried on the basis of GMT. This follows the tradition established in the pre-electronic age when the ship' chronometer (a very accurate clock) was set at GMT and never altered.

Countries such as those in Europe and North America, experience a significant change in the amount of daylight depending upon the season i.e. long nights and short days in winter and the reverse in the summer. These countries change their clocks by advancing them one hour in the spring, this is often referred to as "Daylight Saving Time"; the clocks are put back again in the Autumn (Fall). (Memory aid for changing clocks – "Spring forward, fall back")

Time zones and any clock changes are important considerations for those in shipping business especially if negotiating a charter with the time limits which are an essential part of offers and counter offers. For example, the New York shipping market is five hours later than the London market so that a London broker wishing to impart some interesting piece of market gossip to his friend in New York would be ill-advised to do so as soon as the Londoner gets into the office (say 0930 London time) because his opposite number in New York will be fast asleep (0430 New York Time). On the other hand the London broker's Japanese counterpart may be on his way home as it will be 1830 (6.30 pm) in Tokyo. A country like the USA has its own problems because it has five time zones within its own borders.

8.3.4 Tides and Currents

The rise and fall of the tide are often important in shipping. Tides rise and fall as a result of the gravitational pull of the moon acting in conjunction with the earth's own gravity. In most places in the world there are two high tides and two low tides in each day. The gravitational pull of the sun also has an effect and when the sun's pull is working with the moon, the high tides are very high and the low tides very low; the are called **spring tides**. When the sun and the moon are not pulling together the **tidal range** is at its least and these are called **neap tides**. Spring tide occur approximately twice each month.

The difference between high and low tides varies from place to place. For example, in London the tidal range is about 6.5 metres between high and low on spring tides and 4.3 metres range on neap tides. Compare this with the Bay of Fundy (the inlet between Nova Scotia and New Brunswick in Canada) where the spring tide range is over 15 metres between high and low tide. Conversely in the Mediterranean the greatest range between high and low tide is less than a metre.

As the time of the rotation of the moon round the earth is not an exact day, the times of tides vary. This can be calculated precisely so that almost all the world's ports publish **tide tables.** Such tables can be of vital interest to shipping because the rise and fall of tides determines how deep the water will be in the port area during the course of the day and so dictates when ships can reach the port and when the water is too shallow to accommodate the ship's draft.

In some ports, the draft is deep enough at high water to allow the ship to enter but when the tide falls the ship goes aground, hence the abbreviation mentioned in the chartering terms (**Appendix 8**) NAABSA – Not Always Afloat But Safe Aground. The effect of neap tides can have a serious effect on naabsa ports because a ship near the upper limit of the permitted draft may enter without difficulty on a reasonably high tide but may become trapped for several days if the neap tide occurs while the ship is at that berth.

One way that some ports have overcome the tidal problem and ensured that ships stay afloat throughout their stay is to construct **enclosed docks** which are large basins cut into the land which can be sealed from the tide by **lock gates.** Although this is an expensive solution the advantages outweigh the costs. Not only can large ships be accommodated without any risk of their going aground but as the water level within the dock is constant, the level of the ship relative to shore appliances also remains constant. The disadvantage is that the size of the dock and particularly the dimensions of the locks at its entrance impose a maximum size limitation which in many cases is far smaller than today's ships. It has been this tendency towards the ever-increasing size of ships that has caused many enclosed dock systems to become redundant.

Locks are simply short sections of canals with water-tight gates at each end. The water level is adjusted via sluice gates to match the level at the entrance side when that set of gates is opened. After the ship(s) have entered the lock, the gates are closed and the water level again adjusted, this time to match the level on the exit side when the exit gates are opened and the ships proceed. As well as being used to enter enclosed docks, locks can also be used to 'lift' ships over high ground in canal systems.

8.3.5 Currents

The effect of the flow of tides inevitably creates **currents**, that is the flow of water sometimes at appreciable speeds which can cause problems in estuaries (the wide entrances to rivers) and through narrow gaps between pieces of land. There is, for example, a gap called the Pentland Firth which is between the northern tip of the Scottish mainland and the Orkney Islands. The tidal current through this gap can flow at eight knots or more and some old small coasters in the past could find themselves making no headway against this flow.

There are other currents which are not related to tides but to the effect of prevailing winds. One of the most powerful of such currents is the **Gulf Stream** which flows diagonally across the Atlantic Ocean from South West (the Gulf of Mexico) to the North West corner of Europe. As this water is warm it has the effect of producing a mild climate in the British Isles and parts of North West Europe.

Various other factors play their part in the creation of ocean currents which can effect a navigator's task but fortunately the subject has been well researched and reference books produced which tell seafarers what currents to expect in any part of the world.

8.3.6 Wind and Weather

Far less predictable is the weather and even though modern ships are not dependent upon the wind as sailing ships were, very high winds and rough sea conditions are still responsible for delays, damage and actual loss of ships. Particularly severe are the tropical storms which have different names in different parts of the world but have the same devastating effect. In the area around the **Gulf of Mexico and the Caribbean Islands** they are called **hurricanes** which occur between June and November with the most severe time between August and October. In the **Far East** they are **typhoons** for which the season is May to January with maximum frequency between July and October. In the **Indian Ocean** they are **cyclones** which have various seasons in different parts of the region but the worst periods are during the middle and at the end of the year. When these cyclones reach the north-west corner of Australia they assume the somewhat whimsical name of "willy-willies".

These severe storms have been responsible for the loss of ships and in recent years, large bulk carriers have been the worst victims, a typical example being the bulk carrier "Derbyshire" which was loaded with iron ore and was lost with her entire crew in a typhoon. The disaster occurred so quickly that there was not even time for the ship to send a distress signal on the radio.

Even moderately strong winds and high seas can delay shipping and the strength of the wind is still referred to according to the **Beaufort Wind Scale** which was developed by Admiral Beaufort about 150 years ago. The Beaufort Scale is reproduced in **Appendix 20** from which it will be noted that the state of the sea at different wind strengths is also included.

The extent to which adverse weather can affect the performance of a ship can cause a problem when a time charter is involved. It will be recalled that the **speed and consumption** is an important term in a time charter because the time taken on a voyage and the amount of fuel consumed both have a considerable financial effect to the charterer. This has often been the cause of dispute between charterer and owner especially if the charterer has reason to doubt the accuracy of the entries in the ship's logbook. In more recent times disputes have been reduced by reference to meteorological specialists who maintain accurate records of weather conditions all over the world. Such **ocean routing** companies can be engaged to advise the best route to avoid severe weather and in certain time charters the owners insist on an ocean routing company being employed. The routing companies keep up a two-way communication with ships which enables the masters to be advised of any changes in course needed to avoid storms while the routing company receives feedback as to the actual weather conditions the ships are experiencing.

8.3.7 **Ice**

A hazard in some parts of the world, particularly the northern hemisphere is the risk of ships being immobilised through the sea freezing in winter. Most at risk are ports where timber is traditionally loaded in the Baltic Sea, White Sea and Gulf of Bothnia also ports in North West Russia. Another vulnerable area is the River St Lawrence and the whole of the Great Lakes. From time to time there is an air of concern verging on panic that some ships, which arrived late at Great Lakes ports, becoming trapped in the Great Lakes system because it is necessary to close the St Lawrence Seaway to avoid the lock gates being damaged by the formation of ice.

Port authorities in the Scandinavian region and in the St Lawrence River endeavour to keep some open water by the use of **ice breakers** which are specially designed ships some of which, notably those owned by the former Soviet Union, are nuclear powered. By this means some of the Scandinavian timber ports stay open all year round except during a particularly severe winter and in the St Lawrence, every effort is made to maintain access as far up river as Montreal.

Still a danger (although advance warnings and radar have lessened the hazard) are **icebergs.** These are pieces of the polar ice-cap which break free and can float into the shipping lanes. As in the days of the *"Titanic"* the North Atlantic is the area of greatest risk.

The Baltic and International Maritime Council (BIMCO) offer a service reporting weekly on the ice conditions. How to meet the problem of ice risk is covered in charter parties by an **ice clause** and an example of such a clause is shown in **Appendix 21.**

8.4 WATERWAYS

Two types of waterways are important in shipping, natural waterways such as rivers, estuaries and creeks and man-made waterways which are usually called canals.

Natural waterways provide the shelter from the weather that ships need when loading and discharging. Many major cities owe their very existence to the access afforded by a river. London is a typical example because it was founded by the Romans when they invaded Britain nearly two thousand years ago. London was as far up the river Thames that they could travel by ship and also the lowest point at which the river could be forded (crossed on foot).

Many other towns and cities began as ports, some typical examples are:

>   Buenos Aires – River Plate
>   Calcutta – Hooghly River
>   Hamburg – River Elbe
>   Lisbon – River Tagus
>   Montreal – River St Lawrence
>   Philadelphia – Delaware River

Man-made waterways are constructed for one of two reasons, either to reduce sailing time on a regularly used route – to cut off a corner so to speak – or to provide access to an inland region.

The most ambitious waterway to achieve access to a major inland region was the **St Lawrence Seaway (Appendix 22)**. Constructed in the 1950s, it enables ocean-going ships to penetrate North America as far west as Chicago and Duluth in the USA and Fort William in Canada which gives direct access to the vast grain producing areas in the centre of the North American Continent. Previously the St Lawrence was only navigable up to Montreal, although the Lachine Canal was dug which by-passed the Lachine Rapids and allowed small ships to reach Lake Ontario but the Niagara Falls prevented any further access. The Seaway, by a complex system of locks and canals opened up the Great Lakes to ocean ships with a draft limitation of 27 feet but many charters operate on the basis of loading to Seaway draft in the Lakes and then completing in Montreal.

A much older canal, constructed at the end of the 19th century, is the Manchester Ship Canal in North West England. This was principally designed to enable the ocean-going ships of the day to reach the industrial heartland of that part of the country. One of the main industries, due to its particularly humid climate and plentiful supplies of coal, was the spinning and weaving of cotton imported from the southern United States. The canal's size limitations no longer permit its use by deep sea liners but small ships still regularly call at ports along the canal as well as Manchester itself.

The first canal to reduce sailing time was the **Kiel Canal** which joins the North Sea to the Baltic sea **(Appendix 23)**. When it was first constructed in 1784 it was originally intended for use by the German navy which sought to avoid the stormy waters north of Denmark. In 1895 it was slightly re-routed and deepened to its present 11 metres and has since then been regularly used by commercial shipping.

Far more significant was the construction of the **Suez Canal** joining the Mediterranean Sea to the Red Sea **(Appendix 24).** Students will have read in another lesson what a tremendous change this shortening of the distance between Europe and South Asia had upon the trade with the Indian sub-continent and beyond, even to the extent of being the cause of the formation of first Liner Conference. Work on the Suez canal was commenced in 1859 and it was officially opened ten years later. Fortunately the difference in water levels between the Mediterranean and Red Seas never exceeds 1.25 metres so that there was no need to construct locks and thus it has been possible to widen and deepen the canal from time to time in tune with the increase in ship sizes.

More recent was the construction of the **Panama Canal** linking the Atlantic Ocean with the Pacific Ocean **(Appendix 25)**. People were toying with the idea of cutting through this very slim isthmus which links North America to South America as early as 1550 but it was not until 1908 that the United States Government obtained the concession to start construction and the canal was opened in 1914. Although the canal uses existing lakes and creeks for much of its length, there is a difference in sea levels between the two oceans. Furthermore the land rises considerably so that three sets of locks had to be constructed to raise and lower ships a total of 26 metres.

The Panama Canal is of vital importance for trade between Europe, America and the Far East as well, of course, for traffic between the East and West coasts of the USA itself.

8.5   PORTS

Ports form the beginning and end of a sea voyage and form the interface between the ship and the shore. Even today, ports vary widely in their degree of development and sophistication. Some are simply a reasonably sheltered inlet, creek or river mouth where a ship may lie at anchor and load or discharge into barges which ply between ship and shore. At the other end of the scale are highly developed systems of quays and terminals with the most technologically advanced systems of moving the cargo to or from the side of the ship and into or out of its holds or tanks. There are, of course an infinite variety of ports between those two extremes.

It is always interesting to discover why a port has developed in a particular location. In many cases, as was mentioned earlier in this lesson, a port and then a town grew up because of the geographical convenience of the position. A position sheltered from rough seas plus a good depth of water has often been the reason for a port to develop; Southampton on England's south coast is a typical example of this.

In many cases the original purpose of the port has long since disappeared but because its original use created a centre of population the town has remained and new uses have been found for the port. Several ports in the United Kingdom are like this because they were first developed simply as coal export outlets but remain as ports with several functions even though coal exporting has almost entirely disappeared.

Ports are still created as outlets for particular commodities and the exports of coal and iron ore from places like Australia have prompted the building of huge automated loading terminals in places which may have no population nearby but which have the right amount of shelter and depth of water and are conveniently located as near as possible to the mineral extraction.

Mineral extraction is not the only reason for creating a port even where there is little or no local trade. Containerisation has seen a massive increase in ship sizes which means a commensurate increase in daily running costs. This encourages shipowners to make their voyage distances as short as possible and to depend upon feeders or land transport to deliver cargo to many places rather than call at several ports. This has resulted in development of ports like Felixstowe in England which has an almost entirely agricultural hinterland but is well positioned to despatch containers all over the UK and to work with feeders to many places on the European mainland.

Singapore, similarly has a very limited land area behind it but its strategic position enables its trans-shipment traffic to keep it always among the top three container ports in the world. The port of Colombo in Sri Lanka, originally built to serve the local tea, rubber and coconut trades, now has ambitions to emulate Singapore as a trans-shipment port for the Indian sub-continent region.

The owner of a less specialised ship, the general purpose 'tramp' has many factors to consider when contemplating a port involved in charter negotiations as many of these affect the financial outcome, some may even deter him from accepting. Typical among such considerations would be:

1. The location of the loading port relating to the ship's present position (i.e how far would the ship have to sail in ballast to reach the loading port).

2. Limitations such as:
   (a) Depth of water on approaches and alongside.
   (b) Size of locks if any.
   (c) Tides.
   (d) Any adverse weather problems
   (e) Political problems

3. Costs, ports vary considerably in port, pilotage towage and other charges

4. Cargo handling systems and working schedules.

5. Facilities for repairs, and/or servicing of equipment.

6. Availability and cost of stores especially bunker fuel.

7. The location of discharging port relating to obtaining the ship's next cargo (again how far to sail in ballast).

8. A trustworthy agent.

8.6   GEOGRAPHY OF TRADE

8.6.1   Raw Materials

Students should endeavour to obtain copies of shipping journals which report on chartering "fixtures" (An example is in **Appendix 26**). These will quickly display the major routes for raw materials especially the basic commodities.

Note that **coal** moves from such places as:

USA (e.g. Hampton Roads in Virginia) to Europe and to Japan.

South Africa (e.g. Richards Bay) also to the Far East and to Europe.

Australia (e.g Newcastle – New South Wales and Hay Point – Queensland) particularly to Japan.

Grain is shipped from such places as:

Canada (e.g. the Great Lakes and Montreal) to Europe.

USA (e.g. Gulf of Mexico ports) to Europe and to the Far East.

West Coast North America (e.g. Vancouver) to Japan.

South America (e.g. Buenos Aires in Argentina) to Europe and to the Far East.

Iron Ore is shipped from such places as:

Canada (e.g. ports in the province of Quebec), to Europe.

South America (Brazilian ports) to Europe and the Far East

Australia (e.g Dampier – Western Australia) mainly to Japan.

Oil is shipped from such places as:

The Middle East, that is the countries around the Gulf between Iran and Saudi Arabia called by some the Arabian Gulf and by others the Persian Gulf and some the Middle East Gulf; politics influences the choice of name. These exports go to Europe, the Far East and many other places.

Latin America (e.g. Venezuela) to Europe and the Far East.

West Africa (Nigeria) mainly to Europe

United Kingdom (Sullom Voe in the Shetland Isles).

N.B. The oil from the North Sea oil fields (which are also drilled by the Netherlands and by Norway) produce a particularly light crude oil which provides quite different products and by-products from those derived from, for example the much heavier Middle East Crudes so that European oil-rich countries both export and import crude oil so that all the chemicals and other by-products can be produced in their refineries.

Other raw materials include:

Fertilizers	Timber	Other Forest Products
Agricultural Products	Cement	Minerals
Iron and Steel	Other Metals	Chemicals

These are examples and students should research into other seaborne trades specially those to and from their own locality.

8.6.2   Manufactured goods

The trade in manufactured or semi-manufactured goods – liner trades – follow quite different routes. Whilst the movements in raw materials tend to be predominantly North to South, general cargo routes are predominately East to West. For example Transatlantic between Europe and North America, Transpacific, e.g. West Coast USA to and from the Far East, and Europe to and from the Indian sub-continent, South East Asia and the Far East.

The world-wide container trade, which is almost entirely made up of manufactured or partly manufactured goods, is expected to reach one billion (1,000,000,000) tonnes per annum by the early years of the 21st century.

Cars and Trucks, carried in specially designed ships, are also now a global trade especially since motor manufacturers construct vehicles in other countries as well as their home base. The network of lines carrying cars and trucks is almost as complex as that of the container trade.

8.7   SELF-ASSESSMENT AND TEST QUESTIONS

Attempt the following and check your answers from the text:

1.   From an atlas locate at least ten "seas" apart from those mentioned in the text.

2.   The location of the headquarters of TutorShip is:

51° 30' 58" North Latitude and 0° 05' 01" West Longitude

Determine the longitude and latitude of your present location and check the answer with a knowledgeable local person.

3.   Try to tune your radio to a shipping weather forecast and listen particularly to reference to the force of the wind.

4.   Look in your newspaper and see if, alongside the weather forecast, there is a prediction of when high tides will be on that day

Having completed Chapter Eight, attempt the following and submit you assignment to your tutor.

1.   You have a bulk cargo to move from North West Europe to Australia. Taking as many factors as possible into consideration, discuss the advantages and disadvantages of the possible routes.

2.   Imagine you are a shipowner contemplating the carriage of a bulk raw material from the West Indies to Chicago. The charterer wants supplies spread evenly over the year. What problems do you envisage?

Chapter 9

ACCOUNTS

9.1 INTRODUCTION

The famous Greek shipowner, Aristotel Onassis, is once alleged to have said that "successful shipowning was 95% careful accounting". This view is perhaps reinforced when one considers how many prosperous Far East shipowners are, by background, financiers or bankers.

It is self-evident that if an enterprise spends more than it earns, it will not survive; unless, of course, it is subsidised from public funds such as a country bus service or an island ferry service which is run as a social service.

Whether intended as a profitable business or as a non-profit making undertaking it is necessary to produce records of income and expenditure more usually known as a "set of books". This lesson does not attempt to be a training course in accounting or bookkeeping but seeks to provide an introduction into the basics of accounting matters in a shipping business context.

9.2 ACCOUNTING

Accounting is the complete package of all the planning and managing of the company's financial affairs. Bookkeeping is a part of accounting, its particular objects being:

1. To have a permanent record of all mercantile transactions.

2. To show the effect of each transaction and the combined effect of all the transactions upon the financial position of the enterprise.

The rest of the accounting process involves many other things including, for example, deciding what commercial activities are viable (i.e. practicable from an economic point of view), deciding what capital items to purchase, raising money to purchase capital items, ensuring there is always sufficient money (cash) available to pay accounts at the correct time, investing surplus money so that it earns interest when not needed for immediate use. In fact anything which affects the financial position of the company comes under the heading of "accounts".

9.3 CAPITAL

Capital in bookkeeping terms is the total value of all the company's **fixed assets, investments,** and **cash,** these are called **assets.** Assets are divided into fixed assets and current assets

Capital is the money required to start a commercial enterprise and more may be required from time to time to maintain its momentum or to increase the range of its activities.

Capital is needed for two basic purposes, first to purchase any items of machinery or equipment i.e. anything which will become a **fixed asset** such as, for example, a ship. Capital is also required to run the company, to pay wages and salaries, to settle bills for rent etc this sort of capital is called **working capital**

Capital, for whatever purpose, has to be **raised**. This can be by means of letting other people become owners of part of the company which will be dealt with later in this lesson when the structure of companies is discussed. Or, capital can be raised by borrowing the money from a bank or other financial institution, this is often referred to as **loan capital** and the borrower has to pay the lender **interest** at an agreed percentage per annum as well as repay the loan in agreed instalments.

Interest is the percentage of the capital sum that the borrower pays the lender for the use of the money borrowed. Although borrowing among individuals may be frowned upon, borrowing and lending are an essential element of *commercial* life. A company may find it has, temporarily, more cash than it needs for its immediate purposes and will deposit this with a bank so that it earns interest rather than lying idle. On another occasion it may have a temporary shortage of ready cash which will require a short-term loan from the bank known as an **overdraft;** a well-run company can usually negotiate a substantial overdraft facility.

There is a special type of borrowing which is often used for buying such things as houses and **ships.** This is by means of a **mortgage** which is the name of the deed (agreement) signed by the owner of the ship which, in exchange for the loan of a substantial amount of its cost, pledges the ship as security for the loan. This means that if the owner, the borrower, cannot meet the loan repayments and interest charges the lender may **foreclose** on the mortgage which means the lender can take possession of the ship. It is important to note that it is the borrower who **gives** the mortgage to the lender so that the borrower, the shipowner, becomes the mortgag**or** and the bank or finance house who **takes** the mortgage becomes the mortgag**ee**.

A ship, or a building or a piece of machinery is capital and is classified as a **fixed asset.** Many companies invest in associated businesses, for example a shipping company might invest in part of terminal operating company. Such an investment, indeed any *long-term* investment, will also be classified as a fixed asset.

9.4   CREDIT

Goods and services in the commercial world are most frequently provided without immediate payment; the recipient of the goods is given **credit.** A most important function of bookkeeping is keeping track of this credit. When goods and/or services are supplied, an **account** is rendered, this may be called an **invoice**. This document gives details of the goods or service provided and the cost; there may be a reference on the invoice as to when payment should be made or the length of time permitted between supply and payment may be by mutual agreement between the two parties.

Those who have supplied goods or services and who are awaiting settlement of their invoices are **creditors.** When the accounts are paid, the outgoing money is referred to as **expenditure.**

Those who owe money against outstanding invoices are **debtors,** when they have settled their accounts the money received is referred to as **income** or **revenue.**

The function of bookkeeping is to record all outgoing and incoming accounts which are entered in **ledgers.** In years gone by these would have been large heavy books into which transactions were recorded in ink. Most major enterprises now keep all accounts by computer but the word "ledger" is still often use to refer to those parts of the system that record the issuing and/or receiving of invoices. The bookkeeping process then records when the invoices are settled and the traditional name for that record quite logically was the **cash book,** in computerised systems sometimes also referred to as **transaction lists.**

From time to time the totals of money received and money paid out and the totals of money owed by debtors and money owed to creditors are calculated and the result is either a **profit** or a **loss**. In most countries, such an account is simply called the **Profit and Loss Account** and such an account, covering the sum of all the transactions during the past year, has to be produced annually by limited companies, it has to be checked by an independent accountant called an **auditor** and then submitted to the government; it may eventually become available for public scrutiny.

At the same time as the Profit and Loss Account is published another account called the **Balance Sheet** also has to be produced. The Balance Sheet sets out the value of all the company's assets and liabilities at the end of that particular trading year. **Assets** as referred to earlier are the value of goods, investments, money due to be received from debtors and cash the company has at that moment in time. **Liabilities** include moneys due to be paid to creditors, loans which still have to be repaid and amounts due to the shareholders who subscribed the money with which the company was formed.

In the Balance Sheet assets are valued at the amount of money used to purchase them. Most fixed assets, such as cars and machinery, are worth substantially less than the original price once they are used. This progressive reduction in value has to be reflected in the company's accounts otherwise they would show a very misleading picture. The device used is to record a percentage of the value of such items as an expense each year under the heading of **depreciation** and the application of depreciation is referred to as **writing down** the asset.

Different rates of depreciation are applied to different types capital goods, a ship may be considered to have a life of 20 years and so be written down by 5% per year whilst an office desk may be written down at 25% per annum.

One cannot leave the subject of how the value of an asset is shown in the company's books without touching on the subject of **revaluation** of assets. In shipping, perhaps more than most industries, the market is constantly fluctuating and occasionally these fluctuations are very great. Such fluctuations go beyond simply affecting the rates of freight being paid and spread their influence into the ship sale and purchase market. It would, therefore, be ridiculous if one steadily reduced the valuation of a ship in the balance sheet in accordance with a depreciation schedule while in the real world that ship had, perhaps, doubled in value.

Sadly the converse applies, one would be lying to one's shareholders if a ship were shown in the books as only having reduced its value by, say, 10% when the recession was such that the ship had become worth only her value as scrap steel.

Revaluation of assets – up or down – is not carried out capriciously. A market trend has to be clearly expected to continue for a long time before any such action is taken and in may countries, company law has to be strictly observed.

To recapitulate, the Profit and Loss Account contains the sum of all the transactions over the previous year, the Balance Sheet show what the company is worth at that particular moment.

9.5 MANAGEMENT ACCOUNTING

Reference to accounting so far, whether for use by the company or for official publication, has tended to look at the company's finances from a historical point of view i.e. what has happened. Management accounting looks at what is currently happening and what the company intends (or hopes) will happen in the future so that plans can be made to ensure continued or, better still, increased profitability.

Reference to the immediate past is still vital, one will often encounter the expression "same period last year" when seeking a foundation upon which to set a guide as to the expenses this week, month or year. This forward estimation of expenses is a vital part of **budgeting** as, of course, is the parallel but often much more difficult job of estimating future income. Conscientiously using such systems of planning and checking is referred to as **budgetary control.**

Apart from all the obvious advantages of having as accurate an estimate as possible of the company's future fortunes, the ability to compare "actual" with "budget" at frequent intervals will give an early warning of anything going awry. In particular budgeting permits the company to forecast **cash flow** so that it can be sure it will have money actually available to pay expenses – from the smallest invoice to the highest salary, when they become due.

Most companies prepare management accounts several times a year, often monthly. They include a profit and loss account for the year to date and comparisons with both the budget and the previous year. They will also include cash flow forecasts.

9.6 CASH FLOW

Earlier in this Chapter it was shown how, by comparing money due to come in with money due to be paid out plus money actually in hand, the company's profitability can be estimated. However, it does not matter how profitable the company is on paper, if the money is not physically available to pay vital things such as loan repayments, rentals, salaries etc. the company will fail, "become broke", "go bankrupt" or whatever term is chosen to describe total collapse.

It will be recalled that **creditors** are the people to whom your company owes money so, effectively, your company has some of **their** money in **its** account. Similarly **debtors** are those who owe your company money thus they have some of **your** company's money in **their** accounts.

If debtors have more of the company's money in their accounts than it has creditor's money in the company's account it will fast approach the stage when it has insufficient cash to meet immediate commitments, in other words it will reach a **cash-flow crisis**. Many otherwise profitable companies have failed due to mismanagement of their cash flow.

This is NOT a recommendation that a company should deliberately delay paying its bills well beyond their due date; a reputation as a "slow payer" can be damaging to future prospects. It is, however, important to negotiate the best possible payment terms with one's suppliers and to avoid conceding long credit periods with one's customers. Also important is having a person (or department) with the special responsibility for **credit control** because slow payers can so easily become non-payers resulting in **bad debts.**

One might assume, if a company's accounts show a considerable surplus of creditors over debtors, that its cash-flow is in a healthy state. This may well be the case although such a situation could well be the precursor of a very unhealthy state of affairs such as falling sales which will produce a trading loss next year. One should not judge by a single detail in a company's accounts but always study all the different items.

Being able to show convincingly how healthy a company's future cash-flow position will be, is an exercise companies may often be called upon to do. If a bank or finance house is asked for a loan, the lender is primarily anxious to ensure that the borrower has the ability to repay the loan and meet the interest payments. Although a mortgage may be taken on, say, the ship as security for the loan, the finance house wants to "buy and sell money" not become a shipowner. Thus before the loan is agreed the lender will wish to study a **cash-flow forecast** or **cash-flow projection** which will have to persuade the lender that he can be confident the borrower will be able to earn enough in order to meet his obligations under the loan.

9.7 COSTS

A capital asset (e.g. a ship), once purchased, must be put to work in order to earn revenue and thus profit. To do so will require expenditure on a wide range of items, all of which will have to be forecast as accurately as possible for budgeting purposes. To assist in this process, costs are divided into two basic categories: **fixed costs** and **variable costs.**

In the case of a ship one may easily distinguish between the two because fixed costs, as the name implies, are those costs which would occur even if the ship were standing idle. Loan repayments and interest on the loan are certainly fixed costs (you will often hear this process referred to a **amortization**) and a cost which also continues regardless of what is happening is **depreciation** because, as an asset grows older, so its value decreases (subject to any revaluation of course).

The expression 'variable costs' is similarly self-explanatory. However, as your studies progress more deeply into the world of ship operations it will be seen that variable costs subdivide into **running costs** and **voyage costs.** Running costs are those that occur all the time a ship is operational, such as crews' wages, maintenance, insurance etc. Voyage costs are those that apply uniquely to the voyage being undertaken at the particular time and will include, bunker fuel, port costs, stevedoring, agency fees etc.

Whilst fixed costs are there to stay, variable costs give wide scope for the skills of those concerned with budgetary control; careful 'housekeeping' can make a considerable difference to the company's profitability.

9.8 DIFFERENT TYPES OF COMPANIES

9.8.1 Sole Traders and Partnerships

There is nothing to prevent an individual going into business on his or her own. In that way all the profit is retained (less what the Government takes as tax) but the individual has to raise all the money necessary to operate the business which may mean borrowing money against a security such as his or her own house. Furthermore all the risks fall on the individual with the ultimate risk of losing everything – bankruptcy.

Two or more people may decide to pool their resources of money and skills and thus form a partnership. Usually they draw up a **partnership agreement** which formalises the arrangement. The same benefits and risks apply to partnerships as to sole traders except, of course, they are shared according to the agreed terms. Note, however that if one partner is unable to fulfil his or her obligations, the other partner is obliged to bear full responsibility.

A partnership is usually referred to as a **firm** and partnerships are by no means always small affairs. Many firms of accountants, stock brokers and lawyers are very substantial but are still essentially partnerships.

9.8.2 Limited Companies

One way of avoiding some of the risks of sole trading or partnerships is to form a limited company. The thing that is limited is the **liability.** Those forming the company are **shareholders** rather than partners and their liability is limited to their shareholding; if the company collapses all they lose is what they paid for their shares.

Someone has to bear the rest of the loss and they are, of course, those to whom the company owed money. This seems hardly fair to any suppliers who provided goods on credit but it is a risk one runs when dealing with a limited company. However, this risk is lessened by the fact that limited companies are, in most countries, strictly controlled by law. They have to keep proper books of accounts and publish these each year via an official body (In the U.K. this is the **Registrar of Companies**).

Limited companies have to have **Directors** (at least two) who may or may not be major shareholders. The same set of laws that insist on accounts being published also set out certain terms of conduct to be adhered to by directors.

A limited company may be owned by a small group of shareholders in which case it is referred to as a **private company** and its name has to include certain prescribed words or initials after its name (the word 'Limited' or the initials 'Ltd' are used in the U.K.).

Larger companies owned by a substantial number of shareholders are known as **public companies** and a different name and/or initials have to appear after their names appear (in the U.K. the initials 'plc' standing for public limited company are used). As the name implies, public companies shares are available to anyone who wishes to buy them and they are traded on the stock exchange at whatever price the market puts on that company at the time of the sale or purchase.

Large companies may buy, or form, subsidiary companies which may themselves be quite huge but as they will only have a few actual shareholders they are still private limited companies (Ltd).

9.8.3 Conglomerates and Multi-national Companies

Large companies can become what are known as **conglomerates**, which means that in addition to having several branch offices and/or factories they buy or create a substantial number of subsidiary companies. These subsidiaries may be in a line of business related to that of the parent or in quite a different trade. One reason for forming a conglomeration is for **integration**, for example a shipowner may have in its group of companies a trucking company so that it does not have to buy inland transport from another company. It may well have other subsidiaries such as a chain of agency offices so that it uses its experience to gain income from others.

Other conglomerates may be a group of quite diverse operations such as a shipping company, an engineering division, a timber division and so on. They may trade with each other but this is not the main reason for this type of integration. The object is usually to spread the risk. One year shipping may be good but the building trade poor so that timber is not so profitable. Another year may be a boom time for engineering but the shipping market rather weak. In this way the total profitability is maintained because it does not depend on just one 'market'

A conglomerate which establishes branches and subsidiaries both in the country where the parent is registered and in other countries enables it to trade throughout the world but retain the trade and thus the profits from that trade within its own organization. This earns it the title of a **multi-national** and perhaps the best examples of such multi-nationals are the major oil companies as well as many of the liner shipping companies.

As referred to earlier in this Chapter, to run successfully a company needs **capital** which has to be raised. The principal way to raise capital is to sell **shares** in the company. The shareholders will only invest in the company if they are sure of receiving income in the form of **dividends** which is the term used to refer to the distribution of profits to the shareholders.

9.9 EXCHANGE RATES

Each country has its own currency and each currency has its value in comparison with the currency of another country. Furthermore these relative values fluctuate. Later in your studies you may encounter references to a country's **balance of trade** which is the difference between what a country earns abroad (with exports and/or services) and what it spends abroad on imports. One could look upon the balance of trade as the country's profit (or loss) and this measure of its prosperity will have a significant (but not the only) effect on the value of its currency against those of other countries. Other factors which impinge upon the complex foreign exchange markets are beyond the scope of this publication.

Those in shipping, being essentially an international business, constantly have to be aware of the effect that rates of exchange will have. For example one may have crews wages to pay in British Sterling, capital repayment in Japanese Yen, bunker and port costs in a wide variety of currencies and freight being earned in U.S. Dollars. Any of these currencies becoming either much stronger or weaker (worth more, respectively less, against your own currency) could have a profound effect upon one's profitability.

This effect is just as important to, say, a chartering broker whose own salary and communications costs are in the currency of its own country but as the freight is payable in, say, U.S. dollars the broker's commission (brokerage), being a percentage of the freight, will also be in dollars. There is, of course, the paradox that if one's own country is particularly prosperous just at that time and is enjoying a high rate of exchange in the world's markets, then the incoming dollar payment will yield less local currency than may have been hoped for at the time the deal was done.

When collecting freight on behalf of an overseas principal the effect of exchange rate fluctuations can cause a problem. If the agent in slow in remitting collected freight and the rate of exchange goes against the principal's country in the interim, the principal will suffer a loss, blame this on the agent's tardiness and demand recompense.

One can cite problem areas relating to exchange rates in all aspects of shipping business which means that it is a topic demanding constant vigilance.

9.10 COMPANY ACCOUNTS

Several references have been made to a company's "published accounts" and **Appendices 27 and 28** provide an example of how the basic elements of such a set of accounts might look. In practice a set of published accounts may also contain such things as a **Cash Flow Statement** as well as a list of **Explanatory Notes** which will include a description of the depreciation principles applied, the way in which assets have been valued and various other items.

Most of the terms used in the appendices should be self-evident but if there are any that are not clear please refer to Dictionary of Shipping International Business Trade Terms and Abbreviations (Published by Witherby's Publishing).

9.11 TEST QUESTIONS

Having completed Chapter Nine and having studied the Appendices, attempt the following and submit your answers to your Tutor.

1. From the Balance Sheet comment upon how well (badly) the XYZ Group is managing its cash-flow. Is this better or worse than last year?

2. Assuming no ships are bought or sold, very approximately how much would you expect to see shown in XYZ's balance sheet next year as the asset value of the ships (explain how you reached your estimation, assume a useful life of 20 years).

3. Based upon the data in the appendices discuss, in approximately 250 words, XYZ's trading performance this year as compared with last.

4. From sources outside this text find two examples used by other countries of the initials and words used to indicate a private limited company and two examples of a public limited company.

Chapter 10

LAW OF CARRIAGE

10.1   INTRODUCTION

In any area of business there are legal rules and there are legal remedies should any of the rules be transgressed or should any problems arise.

This is especially so in shipping business where many transactions are only able to take place because of long-established legal customs and practices. It is vital, therefore, that students should be aware of the fundamental elements of the law of carriage of goods by sea which now includes those additional factors which the door-to-door aspects of containerisation have introduced.

Among the fundamentals, this lesson will discuss the important principles governing agreements as well as liabilities arising even where there is no actual agreement or contract.

Different countries have different legal systems and it is beyond the scope of this course to examine closely those differences. A great deal of shipping law is, however, based upon **English Law** which will thus tend to dominate in this Chapter.

In any case, shipping is essentially an international business and the majority of the maritime nations of the world have agreed to conform to wide-ranging **International Conventions** by incorporating those conventions into their own legal systems.

10.2   FUNDAMENTALS OF ENGLISH LAW

English Law is a **Common Law** system which is to be contrasted with **Civil Law** systems which have all the law enacted as a set of codified legal principles. In a Common Law system, whilst there are, of course, many pieces of legislation enacted by the government, much of English Law is contained in a set of principles and rules taken from earlier decisions made by judges in court cases. Thus one often hears common law being referred to as **Case Law.**

Whenever one reads a report on a court case it is almost inevitable that there will be references to previous cases, perhaps even some going back to the nineteenth century. This is because no two cases are likely to be exactly similar and the judge, in reaching his decision, must consider the most comparable past cases in order to form a new decision.

10.2.1   The Civil Court Structure

In England there are three basic levels of courts.

1.   The courts of '**First Instance**' comprise (a) the **County Courts**, which deal in minor disputes, and (b) the **High Courts** for all other cases. The high courts have three divisions and the one dealing with commercial and maritime matters is called the **Queen's Bench Division.**

2.   Above the courts of first instance is the **Court of Appeal** to which the losing party may go if it feels the first judge was wrong in reaching the decision. The Court of Appeal decisions are binding upon the courts of first instance.

3.   The **House of Lords** is the ultimate court of appeal and only very controversial cases are decided at that level. House of Lords decisions are binding on all lower courts. It may overrule its own previous decisions although this rarely happens.

Also based in London is the **Judicial Committee of the Privy Council** which is the final court of appeal for the those United Kingdom dependent territories and those independent British Commonwealth countries which have retained this avenue of appeal upon achieving independence.

Those countries, including of course the United Kingdom, which are members of the **European Union** have a even higher court of appeal which is the **Court of Justice of the European Communities** whose purpose is to rule on any cases which may be held to violate the Community treaties.

10.2.2   Criminal Law

All the foregoing refers to civil law, that is disputes between individuals or groups of individuals. Quite separate from civil law is **Criminal Law** which deals with acts harmful to the population. Criminal law is beyond the scope of this course except to remark that some wrongful acts within shipping business, for example fraud, are crimes and would be dealt with in the criminal courts. The criminal courts have their own, tiered, structure similar to but quite separate from the civil courts.

10.3   ARBITRATION

Arbitration is a private means of settling a dispute. The parties choose their own arbitrator which may be a sole arbitrator if they are so agree or each party chooses his own arbitrator. Under some systems if the two arbitrators cannot agree they appoint an umpire. In other places the appointment of a third arbitrator to form a tribunal of three is automatic. There are several centres of maritime arbitration but the most active are London and New York.

Originally arbitration was a very cheap and speedy way of settling disputes with the arbitrators being themselves practising shipbrokers and their decisions being those of commercial men. Sadly, but perhaps inevitably, as the world has become a more complicated and more litigious place, arbitrations have involved professional lawyers arguing the case from both sides with the finer points of law appearing to be more important than a quick commercial settlement of an argument.

To overcome this problem and in an endeavour to regain arbitration's reputation for simplicity, both London and New York have introduced specific forms of arbitration which offer a quick and inexpensive alternative where the dispute is obviously suitable for a speedy solution.

Arbitration is not part of the country's public legal system although it is, of course, subject to governing legislation. With arbitration the parties are, in effect, "choosing their own judges". Arbitration awards are final and binding upon the parties, the only appeal to the courts would be for a judicial review on a question of law.

10.4   THE CONTRACT

Fundamental to any business act is a **contract** and it is vital to be clear as to what constitutes a legally binding contract and how it comes about. There are three distinct components to a contract:

(a)   The Offer

An offer is a specific expression of willingness to enter into a contract on specified terms.

(b)   Acceptance

The offer must be accepted on the exact stated terms. This converts to offer into an agreement.

(c) Consideration

For the agreement to become a contract there has to be a consideration. The person to whom the offer is made must give (or promise to give) something in return for the offer.

(d) Legality

In order to be valid a contract must also be legally enforceable; contracts cannot relate to an activity which is not in itself lawful

These four elements have to be technically present whether one is buying a bar of chocolate or chartering a 150,000 tonne tanker for twenty years. Furthermore, there need not be a physical object involved because (as will be discussed later in this lesson) one may enter into a contract to carry out a service such as a Port Agency.

Although there has to be a 'consideration' for a contract to exist, there are no rules as to how much must be involved. A contract to sell a vintage Rolls Royce for £100 would be just as valid as one for £100,000, provided the parties willingly agreed to it. Indeed there does not even have to be actual money involved, there are still some leases for property in existence for which the annual rent is one peppercorn.

The description of chartering negotiations set out in Lesson 4 are a perfect example of offer, acceptance and consideration (the freight rate).

10.5 REMEDIES FOR BREACH OF CONTRACT

If one party or the other in a contract does not perform in accordance to that which was agreed, a breach has been committed and the injured party may seek redress.

If the breach of contract is a major failure the injured party may simply withdraw from the contract and may seek damages. If the breach is a less important matter then the contract will continue to be valid but the injured party may seek damages.

Damages in this context mean the financial loss that has been suffered. In some cases, the amount of damages may be stipulated in the contract such as demurrage in a charter party in which case they are referred to as **liquidated damages.**

10.6 TORT

In the introduction it was mentioned that there may be liabilities even where no contract exists (and where no crime has been committed). Such a civil wrong is called a **tort** and it refers to an act or omission which causes another party damage in a situation where no contractual relationship exists. The party against whose person or property the tort was committed has the legal right to claim damages.

The type of tort which those in shipping business are most likely to encounter is **negligence** which is often described as a **failure of a duty of care.** A simple example would be where a ship allows an escape of oil which damages nearby property. The shipowner owed a duty of care to the nearby property owner, it was the oil spill that caused the damage and the property owner has the right to claim the cost of repairing that damage from the negligent shipowner.

Other torts include:

Trespass	–	physical damage to another's property.
Defamation	–	libel (written) or slander (spoken) statements which are held liable to damage a person's reputation.
Conversion	–	allowing the possession of goods to pass into the hands of the wrongful owner (this could also be the crime of theft).
Deceit	–	this would be fraud in a criminal case.

There are many instances in shipping business, for example, when an agent has control over what happens to goods even when they are not actually covered by a contract for which that agent is responsible, where a failure of a duty of care may occur and the agent may become liable for very heavy damages.

Another example could arise should a person be asked for information such as "You have done business with Mr So-and-So, is he all right financially?" If the answer given implies that Mr So-and-So is perfectly trustworthy financially without mentioning a suspicion that he is in fact a swindler, the enquirer could do business with Mr So-and-So and lose a lot of money. The enquirer could then have a legal case against the information provider who had a **duty of care** to give an honest and accurate reply.

Of course caution is needed here, the reply could have been "No, Mr So-and-So is a crook, have nothing to do with him" in which case the enquirer would not lose money but Mr So-and-So may get to hear what was said and sue the information giver for **defamation of character (slander or libel).**

The right way to deal with such a situation is of course to say something like "I had no trouble when I dealt with Mr So-and-So but you should make formal enquiries elsewhere"

One of the worst situations, which falls under the heading of the tort of **conversion,** is when the agent releases discharged cargo to the wrong party (i.e. one who did not present a valid bill of lading). In such a case the legitimate bill of lading holder can claim for the full value of the goods from the errant agent who will have no defence and no one else to turn to (unless he is very fully insured).

10.7 CONTRACTS RELATING TO THE CARRIAGE OF GOODS BY SEA

10.7.1 General

The way in which transport by sea is unique is that, whilst the ship is on passage, the goods loaded in her are:

(a) the ship's sole responsibility and

(b) inaccessible to anyone (except of course the crew).

A great deal of the smooth operation of international trade depends upon taking proper advantage of these two facts.

10.7.2 Charter Parties

It will be recalled from earlier lessons that there are two principal types of contracts for the carriage of goods by sea. Chapter four dealt with the **Charter Party**, which is a contract between **Charterer** and **Shipowner** with the rate and terms negotiated in an international market. Unless the parties choose specifically to incorporate any international conventions (such as the Hague-Visby Rules), a charterparty is a "stand-alone" contract in which virtually all the intentions of the parties are set out.

Chapter four covered the different types of charter with some detail about the standard forms used which, with any amendments and additions upon which the parties may agree, sets down in writing the full intentions of the parties which are legally referred to as the **express terms**.

There are, however, certain terms in a charter party which are implied under common law and are thus referred to as **implied terms.**

In the case of a voyage charter some basic implied terms are:

On the part of the shipowner:

  (a)   that the ship is seaworthy.
  (b)   that the ship will proceed "with reasonable despatch.
  (c)   that the ship will make no unjustifiable deviation. (deviation to save life is always justifiable).

On the part of the charterer:

  (d)   not to ship dangerous goods without the knowledge of the shipowner.

In the case of a time charter:

  (a)   that the timecharterer will only use the vessel between good and safe ports.
  (b)   that dangerous goods will not be shipped without the knowledge of the shipowner.

There are no international conventions covering ships under charter although the parties may choose to incorporate some such as:

  (a)   stipulating that bills of lading covering the cargo carried will be subject to the **Hague Rules** or the **Hague-Visby Rules.** See **Appendix 29.** The incorporating clause is often referred to as the **Clause Paramount (Appendix 30).**

  (b)   that **General Average** will be subject to the **York Antwerp Rules** which details how General Average should be applied and calculated.

        General Average is a centuries-old convention which agrees that if the ship takes action which avoids a peril or reduces the effects of a peril, all parties must contribute to the cost of this action (known as the "sacrifice") according to the value of their participation in the venture. The incorporating clause is often referred to as the **New Jason Clause. (Appendix 31)**

Other standard clauses which are not strictly speaking derived from international convention but have wide acceptance may also be included such as a **Both to Blame Collision Clause, (Appendix 32)** and/or a **War Risk Clause,** an example of such a clause is in **Appendix 33.**

10.8   LINER BILLS OF LADING

In the case of liner cargo, Chapter six explained how there is no equivalent of the charter party in the liner trade and whilst today there is often a degree of bargaining this tends almost always to be within the framework of the carrier's standard terms. Consequently it is rare for a written agreement to be produced for liner cargo and the vital document is the **Bill of Lading**. It was, therefore, stressed in Chapter six that the bill of lading was not an agreement but was **evidence of a contract;** the actual contract, very frequently only a verbal contract, having been made earlier.

Recall also from Chapter six the other functions of a Bill of Lading. It is a **receipt for goods** which covers both the **quantity** (which is set out in the body of the B/L) and the **quality** which is covered by the words "in apparent good order and condition". This enables the consignee to claim against the carrier if there is a shortage or if the cargo is damaged.

Today, most cargo is shipped in **containers** and in the case of Full Container Loads (FCLs) the question of quantity and quality is in the hands of the shipper and this part of the B/L will simply contain a Container number (together usually with the Seal number) and the words "said to contain" when describing the cargo. The consignee then has no claim against the carrier provided the container is undamaged and the seal is intact unless it can be proved that the contents had been damaged due to container having been badly handled.

With Less than Container Loads (LCL cargo) the carrier's responsibility as regards quantity and quality is the same as for break-bulk (conventional) cargo.

Note also in the case of break-bulk cargo, that technically, the B/L does not begin to operate until the cargo crosses the ship's rail at the time of loading. With container cargo, however, the receipt element of the B/L (and thus the carrier's liability) comes into effect much sooner, possibly at the shipper's premises. For this reason, it will be recalled, a container B/L states "Received" rather than "Shipped" above the carrier's signature and the B/L needs a further endorsement to say when shipment actually took place in order to become a "shipped on board" B/L.

Finally the B/L is a **document of title**; the definition of "title" in this context is *the right to ownership of property with or without actual possession*.

Refer back to the preamble to this section of the Chapter where it was pointed out that no one has access to the cargo whilst it is afloat. Therefore, during this time the B/L is able to be a **negotiable document** enabling a named consignee to sell the cargo and to pass title to the cargo by endorsing the B/L by signing it on the back. There is no limit to the number of times a B/L, and thus title to the cargo, can change hands in this manner so long as it takes place while the cargo is still on the ship.

Payment for the cargo may have been arranged via the banking system through the medium of a **documentary letter of credit** in which case the second part of the B/L's rôle as a document of title comes into play, this time as **security for payment.** In such a case, the B/L is not made out to a named consignee but in that part of the B/L the words **"To Order"** appear. Such a document has to be endorsed by the actual shipper and thereafter does not need any further endorsement because it is now 'open' and title to the goods belongs to anyone holding the B/L – theoretically he can claim the goods even if he found the B/L in the street. In the real world, shipping lines and their agents are very wary of handing goods to anyone who has obtained the B/L illegally. Most countries recognise the crime of stealing by finding.

Chapter six explains how the B/L is used in the letter of credit procedures.

Although title to the goods may be transferred from one to another, the actual contract remains between the original shipper and the carrier and a way had to be found to ensure that the rights and liabilities under the contract also pass to the new consignee (the endorsee). To achieve this the UK originally passed the *Bill of Lading Act 1855*. The evolution in liner shipping meant that this needed up-dating and it was replaced with the *Carriage of Goods by Sea Act 1992*.

Many find this title a misnomer because there is already a *Carriage of Goods by Sea Act 1971* which is the act with which the UK ratified the Hague/Visby rules. So it is vital to remember that the *1992 Act replaces the B/L Act of 1855 and does not affect the 1971 Act*.

The *Carriage of Goods by Sea Act 1992* (as did the 1855 B/L Act) empowers the consignee to sue the carrier and also subject the consignee to the liabilities in respect of the goods as if the contract had been made between the consignee and the carrier. The 1992 Act corrects various anomalies in the 1855 Act that the passage of time has revealed as well as taking Sea Waybills and Delivery orders into consideration.

10.9 THE HAGUE/VISBY RULES

Whereas there is some degree of equality of bargaining strength between an owner and a charterer which only varies according to the fluctuation of the market, liner shippers seldom have such power.

In the distant past, owners of ships carrying general cargo were able to exert their bargaining strength over shippers by imposing contract terms which allowed the shipowners to exempt themselves from all manner of negligence. Shippers rebelled and lobbied governments to introduce legislation in order to curb this abuse of shipowner power. This resulted in a hotch-potch of laws across the world which, in such an essentially international business as shipping created chaos.

Governments, therefore, came together to discuss the drafting of an international convention but it was not until 1921 that agreement was reached and the **Hague Rules** came into being. These were ratified by almost all the world's maritime nations; in the UK it was the *Carriage of Goods by Sea Act 1924*.

Then, largely due to the introduction of containerisation and changing values the Maritime Law Committee of the International Law Association agreed to amend the Hague Rules with the Brussels Protocol of 1958 and the amended Hague Rules became known as the **Hague/Visby Rules,** (refer again to **Appendix 29**) . These rules again found favour with most maritime nations and the UK ratified the rules with the *Carriage of Goods by Sea Act 1971* which replaced (repealed) the 1924 Act.

The Hague/Visby Rules only apply to goods carried under a Bill of Lading or similar document, they do not apply to a charter party unless specifically incorporated into it.

In the Rules the term "carrier" is used throughout so that it includes owner or charterer who enters into a contract of carriage with a shipper. In the simplest terms, the Rules set out:

(a) the duties of the carrier to provide a seaworthy (and 'cargoworthy') ship at the beginning of the voyage. This is not an absolute liability, if the ship becomes unseaworthy during the course of the voyage "want of due diligence" has to be proved.

(b) the carrier must provide a bill of lading or similar document.

(c) there must be no unjustifiable deviation (saving life or property is considered 'reasonable' under the rules).

(d) the shipper guarantees the accuracy of the details of the cargo supplied by him.

(e) there is a list of things for which the carrier shall not be liable, these are matters which are clearly not under the carrier's control.

(f) there is a limit to the amount of compensation the carrier has to pay in the event of loss or damage. This is the equivalent of saying "This is where my insurance stops so this is where yours should start". The maximum amount is "per package" and in the Hague/Visby Rules the definition of package when containerisation is involved has been covered

(g) there is a "Himalaya" clause incorporated in the rules (it was not in the original Hague Rules) which brings "a servant or agent of the carrier" under the protection of the bill of lading. (see below)

(h) a claim for loss or damage shall be time-barred "unless suit is brought within one year of delivery or the date when they should have been delivered"

Bear in mind that, now the vast majority of manufactured goods are being carried in containers, a Combined Transport B/L covers far more than simply carriage by sea. It now includes all the other ancillary transportation elements which comprise what is now termed **intermodalism.**

There are international conventions covering the carriage by road referred to as **The CMR Convention**. The initials stand for *Convention relative au contrat de transport des Marchandises par vois de Route.*

Similarly carriage by rail within Europe is covered by **The CIM Convention** and the translation in this case is *Convention International concernant le transport de Marchandises par chemin de fer.*

The details of these conventions are beyond the scope of this course but in Chapter six it was explained that the rules and limitations of liability of these modes of transport come into effect if loss or damage occurs on road respectively on rail but that if the precise place where the problem arose is unknown then the Hague Visby Rules shall apply.

10.9.1   "Himalaya" clause

Reference was made earlier that the Hague-Visby Rules include a "Himalaya Clause" which brings agents and other servants of the owner under the protection of the Bill of Lading's limits of liability. The clause gets its title from a passenger ship of that name which created a legal landmark in the shipping world in 1954. A lady passenger – Mrs Adler – was injured when descending a gangway from the ship; the gangway had been inadequately secured. She found that, under the contract evidenced by her passenger ticket, she could not claim damages from the shipowner but she successfully sued the ship's Master (Captain Dickson) in *tort* in that he had failed in his duty of care. Not only was this a classic example of the law of *tort* in action but it was also a demonstration of **vicarious liability.** Securing the gangway was not part of the captain's own duties but it was the job of someone under his command going about his normal duties. (The definition of vicarious is "acting or done for another").

This case (*Adler v Dickson 1954*) sent a shockwave through the whole shipping business world because it was realised that the same device could be used to circumvent the limits of liability which the Hague Rules conferred upon the bill of lading. Thus it was that bills of lading were hastily re-drafted to include a clause which extended the protection of the B/L to all those directly working for the owner.

The reasonableness of such a clause was generally accepted throughout the shipping world so that, when the time came to up-date the Hague Rules by producing the Hague-Visby Rules, the situation was fully covered by the inclusion of the fours clauses which comprise Article IV*bis* in the Rules. Note that Clause 4 in that article does not protect the servant or agent "if it is proved that the damage resulted from an act – – – – – done with the intent to cause damage or recklessly – – –".

10.10   THE HAMBURG RULES

The United Nations Commission for Trade and Development (UNCTAD) whose brief is principally to look after the affairs of less developed nations, held a meeting in Hamburg in 1978 to consider the carriage of goods by sea. The meeting produced a rival to the Hague/Visby Rules entitled the **Hamburg Rules**.

The object of these rules was to favour non-maritime nations which tend to be cargo-owning countries and this is apparent when you see the limited number of nations which have ratified the Hamburg Rules.

Some of the principal differences include:

(a)   Hague/Visby only operates as goods pass the ships rail in and out but Hamburg covers the whole period "during which the carrier is in charge of the goods" so for example applies before and after loading/discharge.

(b)   the carriage of live animals and deck cargo are completely excluded from the provisions of Hague/Visby but there is a qualified inclusion in Hamburg.

(d) there is no provision for loss due to delay in Hague/Visby but with Hamburg the carrier is liable for losses due to delay unless he can prove the delay was entirely beyond his control.

(e) the amount of compensation for loss or damage is much higher in Hamburg under limitation of liability provision.

(f) the time bar is two years under Hamburg against one year in Hague/Visby.

(g) Hague Rules apply to goods loaded in a signatory state. Hamburg rules apply when goods are loaded or discharged in a signatory state. This may lead to conflicts under the B/L where the loading port is Hague-Visby and the discharging port is under Hamburg Rules.

The full text of the Hamburg Rules will be found in **Appendix 34**

10.11 AGENCY

All the "disciplines" referred to in Chapter seven are forms of agency that is to say carrying out work on behalf of a principal except, of course, where the work is done by a department in the principal's own office. An agent's function is to bring his principal into contractual relationships with third parties.

10.11.1 Creation of a Relationship of Agency

An agency can be created:

(a) by express agreement.

(b) by implication/conduct

(c) by necessity, i.e. where a person is entrusted with another person's property and a definite and commercial necessity arises to deal with that property and it is impossible to obtain the property-owners's instructions.

10.11.2 Rights and Duties imposed as between Agent and Principal

Duties of an Agent:

(a) to exercise due diligence in performance of his duties.

(b) to apply any special skill which he professes to have.

(c) to render account.

(d) not to make a secret profit (doing so is a crime in many countries). An example could be where the agent agrees that the stevedore should inflate his account to the shipowner and pay the excess as a secret commission to the agent

Duties of a Principal:

(a) to remunerate the agent.

(b) to indemnify the agent for liabilities incurred in the execution of his authority. This not only includes reimbursing for expenses incurred on the principal's behalf but also protecting the agent against "mis-directed arrows" i.e. legal action directed against the agent when it should have been directed against the principal.

10.12 BREACH OF WARRANTY OF AUTHORITY

When a agent deals on behalf of his principal the agent is **warranting** to the third party that he has his principal's **authority** to do so. If he deals without that authority (actual, implicit or of necessity) then he is in breach of the warranty of authority.

The agent can be in breach **deliberately**, that is he knew he was doing so, or was **reckless** as to whether or not he was in breach. He can also be in breach through **negligence.** For example, misreading the terms upon which he was authorised to offer a ship for a cargo and the subsequent fixture is not on the terms the owner intended.

In either of these cases the agent, by warranting he had authority to do what he did, will be liable to the third party for any loss so caused; one pays for one's mistakes.

There is another way that breach of warranty of authority operates which is less easy to understand. Imagine that you are a broker negotiating with a charterer on behalf of an owner based in another country. Now suppose that the authority to make an offer to the charterer comes not directly from the owner but from a broker in the owner's country and it is **that** broker who misreads the authority and passes to you a firm offer with a mistake in it. In good faith you make this offer to the charterer *warranting you have to owner's authority to do so*. If a fixture is concluded with this error in it and the charterer sustains a loss he will seek recompense and the law says you have to pay.

This may seem unfair because you have made no mistake but the view the law takes is that it would be quite wrong for the charterer to suffer. It would be equally wrong for the charterer to have to proceed against the foreign broker who made the mistake as the charterer had no direct contact with that broker. No, the faulty offer came from you so you have to pay the charterer's damages, this is breach of warranty of authority **without negligence**. All you can do is proceed against the overseas broker who made the error to recover what you have had to pay out. Fortunately agents and brokers can insure (usually through their P & I Club – see below) against breach of warranty of authority, with or without negligence and in view of the way one cannot otherwise protect oneself against a 'without negligence' situation, such insurance is a wise precaution.

10.13 PROTECTION AND INDEMNITY ASSOCIATIONS

P & I Clubs as they are called are principally concerned with providing shipowners with insurance against third party risks. They originated in the 19th century because commercial insurers and underwriters were not prepared to offer the full cover for these risks because of their open ended nature. P & I cover is arranged on a basis of "mutuality" which is to say that the clubs are non-profit making entities whose funds are contributed by the members and are named "calls". Members present their claims for sums which they have settled with the third party and what they have paid is reimbursed to them; this is the "indemnity" element of the clubs. Should the claims on the club exceed the funds available, the club will make a **supplementary call** to obtain the necessary extra money from the members.

The "protection" element involves providing legal advice to members and fighting claims which are considered to be wrong or excessive.

The main P & I Clubs are those of shipowners and the third party claims where they may be involved include such things as personal injury claims by people working on the ships and damage to property such as colliding with a jetty but probably the most active section is that dealing with cargo claims when consignees claim short delivery or damage to their cargo.

There are also P & I Clubs for charterers and for shipbrokers, the latter are principally concerned with professional indemnity insurance that is insuring people in shipping business against claims made against them for negligence.

Recently there has been a tendency among some owners to return to commercial insurance cover for their third party risks.

10.14 SELF-ASSESSMENT AND TEST QUESTIONS

Attempt the following and check your answer from the text:

1. Ascertain where the different courts are in your locality.

   If you live outside England, ensure that you have a clear idea of the different levels of courts in your own country.

2. What four components are essential to comprise a contract?

3. Name five types of tort.

4. What are the names given to the clauses which incorporate into a charter party?

   (a) the Hague/Visby Rules.

   (b) the York Antwerp Rules

5. What are the three functions of a Bill of Lading?

6. What is the definition of "title".

7. What are the three ways an agency can be created?

8. What types of claims do the shipowners' P & I Club deal with?

Having completed Chapter Ten, attempt the following and submit your answers to your Tutor:

1. Propose a Breach of Warranty of Authority situation different from those used in the text.

2. An FCL container which in the B/L is said to contain ten air conditioning units each weighing 150 kgs is lost. Referring to **Appendix 29** calculate how much compensation the consignee can expect to be paid by the carrier. Explain how you arrive at your answer.

3. What is the advantage to an agent of the "Himalaya" clause incorporated in the Hague/Visby Rules?

APPENDICES

Forms marked * reproduced by kind permission of BIMCO

Lloyd's Register Page Extract 2003-2004

AMPHION

7903328 **AMPHION**
9HGD5 — ex Venita -1996 ex Mega Venita -1992
5321 — ex Venita -1990 ex Diana -1987
— Amphion Shipping Co. Ltd.
— Paralos Maritime Corp. S.A.
— Valletta — Malta
— SatCom: Inmarsat A
— MMSI: 249804000
- 53,898 / 23,425 / 87,549 T/cm / 88.4
- Class: NV (NK)
- 1980-07 Sasebo Heavy Industries Co. Ltd.-Sasebo Yard, Sasebo Yd No: 282
- Loa 243.01 Br ex 42.04 Dght 12.722
- Lbp 230.03 Br md 42.03 Dpth 19.82
- Welded, 1 dk
- **Crude Oil Tanker**
- COW IGS SBT
- Liq(Oil): 105,997
- Cargo Heating Coils
- 3 Cargo Pumps
- Manifold: Bow/CM: 122m
- **1 oil engine** driving 1 CP propeller
- Total Power: 11,700kW(15,906hp) 13.0kn
- MAN 12V48/60
- 1 x Vee 4 Stroke 12 Cy. 480 x 600 (new engine 1993)
- MAN B&W Diesel AG
- AuxGen: 1 x 560kW 450V 60Hz, 2 x 440kW 450V 60Hz
- Fuel: 281.0(d.o.) 2773.5(hvf) 53.0pd

8407890 **AMPHION**
SXZP — ex Grischuna -1999
573 — Panther Navigation Inc.
— Andriaki Shipping Co. Ltd.
— Andros — Greece
— MMSI: 239620000
- 37,031 / 24,287 / 64,442 T/cm / 65.8
- Class: AB
- 1987-10 Hyundai Heavy Industries Co., Ltd.-Ulsan Yd No: 359
- Loa 225.03 (BB) Br ex 32.26 Dght 13.101
- Lbp 215.65 Br md 32.21 Dpth 18.01
- Welded, 1 dk
- **Bulk Carrier**
- Str. heavy cargoes
- SERS(LR)
- Grain: 80,056
- Compartments: 7 Ho, ER
- 7 Ha: ER
- **1 oil engine** driving 1 FP propeller
- Total Power: 8,799kW(11,963hp) 15.0kn
- B&W 5L70MC
- 1 x 2 Stroke 5 Cy. 700 x 2,268
- Hyundai Engine & Machinery Co., Ltd.
- AuxGen: 3 x 525kW 440V 60Hz
- Fuel: 99.0(d.o.) 1890.0(hvf) 36.0pd

7226093 **AMPHITRITE**
UZCZ — ex Sovetskiy Sever -1998
712663 — ex Viktor Koryakin -1993
— Joint Stock Co "Amphitrite" (A/O "Amphitrite")
— Kherson — Ukraine
— MMSI: 272151000
- 2,478 / 917 / 3,135 T/cm
- Class: RS
- 1972 Sudostroitelnyy Zavod im. "Volodarskiy"-Rybinsk Yd No: 61
- Loa 113.90 Br ex 13.21 Dght 3.700
- Lbp 108.01 Br md - Dpth 5.54
- Welded, 1 dk
- **General Cargo Ship**
- Ice strengthened
- Bale: 4,125
- Compartments: 4 Ho, ER
- 4 Ha: (17.6 x 9.3) 3(18.1 x 9.3) ER
- **2 oil engines** driving 2 FP propellers
- Total Power: 485kW(1,320hp) 10.5kn
- S.K.L. 6NVD48A-U
- 1 x 4 Stroke 6 Cy. 320 x 480 485kW(660bhp)
- VEB Schwermaschinenbau "Karl Liebknecht" (SKL)
- S.K.L.
- 1 x 4 Stroke 6 Cy. 320 x 480 485kW(660bhp)
- VEB Schwermaschinenbau "Karl Liebknecht" (SKL)
- AuxGen: 2 x 75kW, 1 x 50kW
- Fuel: 94.0(d.o.)

7224368 **AMPLE HARVEST**
XU7MZ — ex Ample Route 1 -2001 ex Jin Tai -1999
0072334 — ex Jia Fa -1996 ex Ocean Mercury -1986
— ex Corona -1986 ex Finnmaster -1982
— Tian Hua Maritime Transportation Corp. Ltd.
— Phnom-Penh — Cambodia
- 4,275 / 2,400 / 5,919 T/cm
- Class: (CC) (NV)
- 1972 Kleven Mek. Verksted AS -Ulsteinvik Yd No: 23
- Loa 106.80 Br ex 17.07 Dght 7.070
- Lbp 100.36 Br md 17.00 Dpth 9.00
- Welded, 2 dks
- **General Cargo Ship**
- Grain: 8,546; Bale: 7,795
- TEU 173 C.Ho 93/20' C.Dk 80/20'(40')
- Compartments: 2 Ho, ER, 2 TwDk
- 2 Ha: 2(27.4 x 13.3) ER
- Cranes: 2x12.5t, 2x10t
- **1 oil engine** driving 1 FP propeller
- Total Power: 3,383kW(4,600hp) 14.0kn
- Werkspoor 8TM410
- 1 x 4 Stroke 8 Cy. 410 x 470
- Stork-Werkspoor Diesel B.V.
- AuxGen: 3 x 174kW 380V 60Hz
- Fuel: 236.0(d.o.) 386.0(hvf) 14.0pd

9013177 **AMPORELLE**
FQHN
425434 — Government of The Republic of France (Regie Departementale des Passages d'Eau de la Vendee)
— Ile d'Yeu — France
— MMSI: 227004400
- 345 / 258 / 100 T/cm
- Class: BV
- 1991-12 Soc. Francaise de Cons. Nav. -Villeneuve—la—Garenne Yd No: 869
- Loa 38.00 Br ex - Dght 1.350
- Lbp 33.50 Br md 7.75 Dpth 3.40
- Welded, 1 dk
- **Day-excursion Passenger Ship**
- Passengers: unberthed: 370
- **2 oil engines** with clutches, flexible couplings &sr geared to sc. shafts driving 2 Water jets
- Total Power: 3,398kW(4,620hp) 28.0kn
- MWM TBD604BV16
- 2 x Vee 4 Stroke 16 Cy. 170 x 195 each- 1,699kW(2,310bhp)
- Motoren Werke Mannheim AG (MWM)
- AuxGen: 2 x 60kW 380V 50Hz
- Fuel: 10.4(d.o.)

7102508 **AMR**
XUSF7 — ex Cherepovets -1998
9870089 — Quantel Shipping Ltd.
— Romalex Marine S.A.E.
— Phnom-Penh — Cambodia
— MMSI: 514166000
- 1,582 / 708 / 1,857 T/cm
- Class: (RS)
- 1970 Santierul Naval Constanta S.A. -Constanta Yd No: 339
- Loa 80.27 Br ex 11.94 Dght 4.900
- Lbp 71.49 Br md - Dpth 5.69
- Welded, 1 dk
- **General Cargo Ship**
- Ice strengthened
- Bale: 2,450
- Compartments: 3 Ho, ER
- 2 Ha: (3.5 x 5.8) 2(8.2 x 7.9) ER
- Cranes: 3x5t
- **1 oil engine** driving 1 FP propeller
- Total Power: 1,147kW(1,560hp) 12.0kn
- Sulzer 6TAD36
- 1 x 2 Stroke 6 Cy. 360 x 600
- Tvornica Dizel Motora "Jugoturbina"

5015294 **AMRADO**
— Government of The Republic of Ghana (Ports Authority)
— Takoradi — Ghana
- 201 T/cm
- Class: (LR) ✠ Classed LR until 10/48
- 1948-03 Ferguson Bros. (Port Glasgow) Ltd.-Port Glasgow Yd No: 384
- Loa 32.67 Br ex 7.47 Dght 3.277
- Lbp - Br md - Dpth -
- Welded,
- **Tug**
- **2 Steam Recip.** driving 2 FP propellers
- 2 x Steam Recip. Triple exp In-Line 6Cy. HP-(2) 283 IP1-(2) 445 & LP-(2) 737 x Stroke-559
- Ferguson Bros. (Port Glasgow) Ltd.

5138058 **AMREET**
YKBS — ex Al Schooner -1992 ex Rim -1988
39/LA — ex Mona Star -1978 ex Gullkrona -1976
— Nazih Sidawi, Hussni Ammoun, Abdul Mouem Markabi & Mohi Eldin Kaak
— Schooner Shipping
— Lattakia — Syria
- 999 / 504 / 1,408 T/cm
- Class: (LR) ✠ Classed LR until 7/1/83
- 1958-07 Valmet Oy -Helsinki Yd No: 191
- Loa 69.19 Br ex 10.83 Dght 4.242
- Lbp 62.62 Br md 10.80 Dpth 4.42
- Welded, 1 dk
- **General Cargo Ship**
- Ice strengthened
- Grain: 1,940; Bale: 1,743
- 2 Ha: (10.2 x 5.4) (16.2 x 6.0) ER
- Cranes: 2x3t
- **1 oil engine** driving 1 FP propeller
- Total Power: 706kW(960hp) 11.0kn
- Alpha 498R
- 1 x 2 Stroke 8 Cy. 290 x 490
- Alpha Diesel A/S
- Fuel: 71.0(d.o.)

9081746 **AMRIT KAUR**
VVXL
225 — Government of The Republic of India (Coast Guard)
— India
— SatCom: Inmarsat C
- 306 / 91 T/cm
- Class: (AB) (IR)
- 1993-03 Goa Shipyard Ltd. -Goa Yd No: 1150
- Loa 45.95 Br ex - Dght -
- Lbp 43.50 Br md 7.50 Dpth 4.30
- Welded, 1 dk
- **Patrol Vessel**
- Search & Rescue
- **2 oil engines** sr geared to sc. shaft driving 1 FP propeller
- Total Power: 2,960kW(4,024hp) 23.0kn
- M.T.U. 12V538TB82
- 2 x Vee 4 Stroke 12 Cy. 185 x 200 each- 1,480kW(2,012bhp)
- MTU Friedrichshafen GmbH
- AuxGen: 3 x 80kW 415V 50Hz

7102211 **AMRITA I**
YBYO
1172 — P.T. Pelayaran Lokal Karunrung
— Jakarta — Indonesia
- 173 / 10 T/cm
- Class: KI (GL)
- 1971 Handara Engineering & Shiprepairing Ltd.-Hong Kong Yd No: 22
- Loa 29.04 Br ex 7.73 Dght 3.210
- Lbp 26.80 Br md 7.40 Dpth 3.41
- Welded, 1 dk
- **Tug**
- **1 oil engine** driving 1 FP propeller
- Total Power: 588kW(800hp) 11.2kn
- Alpha 408-26VO
- 1 x 2 Stroke 8 Cy. 260 x 400
- Alpha Diesel A/S

5207615 **AMRO Z**
ODBX — ex Rabunion V -1992 ex Croesus -1975
B2795 — ex Berta -1973 ex Libertas -1972
— Amro Z Shipping Co. SARL
— Zeido Group
— Beirut — Lebanon
- 396 / 220 / 1,315 T/cm
- Class: (LR) ✠ Classed LR until 1/1/95
- 1958-09 E.J. Smit & Zoon's Scheepswerven N.V.-Westerbroek Yd No: 746
- Converted from: General Cargo Ship-1982
- Loa 64.85 Br ex 9.91 Dght 4.560
- Lbp 59.75 Br md 9.81 Dpth 5.80
- Riveted/Welded, 2 dks
- **Livestock Carrier**
- Ice strengthened
- Bale: 1,744
- Compartments: 2 Ho, ER
- 2 Ha: (8.0 x 4.0) (12.1 x 4.0) ER
- Derricks: 2x6t, 4x3t; Winches: 6
- **1 oil engine** driving 1 FP propeller
- Total Power: 552kW(750hp) 10.8kn
- Werkspoor TMAB396
- 1 x 4 Stroke 6 Cy. 390 x 680
- N.V. Werkspoor
- AuxGen: 3 x 25kW 110V d.c.

8401755 **AMRTA JAYA I**
3FVN2
14189-84CH — Admiral Three Star S.A.
— P.T. Pelayaran Samudera "Admiral Lines"
— Panama — Panama
— MMSI: 352112000
- 5,464 / 2,262 / 6,839 T/cm
- Class: NK
- 1984-05 Higaki Zosen K.K. -Imabari Yd No: 320
- Loa 98.18 (BB) Br ex 18.01 Dght 7.544
- Lbp 89.95 Br md 18.00 Dpth 13.01
- Welded, 1 dk
- **General Cargo Ship**
- Grain: 13,070; Bale: 12,097
- Compartments: 2 Ho, ER
- 2 Ha: (22.2 x 9.8) (24.7 x 9.8) ER
- Cranes: 4x20t
- **1 oil engine** driving 1 FP propeller
- Total Power: 2,427kW(3,300hp) 12.0kn
- Hanshin 6EL40
- 1 x 4 Stroke 6 Cy. 400 x 800
- The Hanshin Diesel Works Ltd.

8401834 **AMRTA JAYA II**
YFUS
— P.T. Pelayaran Samudera "Admiral Lines"
— Jakarta — Indonesia
- 5,498 / 3,836 / 6,840 T/cm
- Class: NK
- 1984-08 Nishi Zosen K.K. -Imabari Yd No: 327
- Loa 98.18 (BB) Br ex 18.04 Dght 7.544
- Lbp 89.95 Br md 18.00 Dpth 13.00
- Welded, 2 dks
- **General Cargo Ship**
- Grain: 13,070; Bale: 12,096
- Compartments: 2 Ho, ER
- 2 Ha: (22.2 x 9.8) (24.7 x 9.8) ER
- Derricks: 4x20t
- **1 oil engine** driving 1 FP propeller
- Total Power: 2,427kW(3,300hp) 12.0kn
- Hanshin 6EL40
- 1 x 4 Stroke 6 Cy. 400 x 800
- The Hanshin Diesel Works Ltd.
- AuxGen: 3 x 280kW a.c.

9003988 **AMRTA VII**
3EKN8 — ex Orient Queen -1997
19238-90C — Admiral Three Star S.A.
— P.T. Pelayaran Samudera "Admiral Lines"
— Panama — Panama
— SatCom: Inmarsat M
— MMSI: 353116000
- 5,473 / 1,999 / 7,018 T/cm
- Class: NK
- 1990-10 Murakami Hide Zosen K.K. -Hakata Yd No: 318
- Loa 99.92 (BB) Br ex 18.00 Dght 7.573
- Lbp 89.95 Br md 18.00 Dpth 13.00
- Welded,
- **General Cargo Ship**
- Grain: 13,285; Bale: 12,611
- Compartments: 2 Ho, ER, 2 TwDk
- 2 Ha: (21.7 x 9.8) (24.5 x 9.8) ER
- Derricks: 4x20t
- **1 oil engine** driving 1 FP propeller
- Total Power: 2,427kW(3,300hp) 11.6kn
- Akasaka A41
- 1 x 4 Stroke 6 Cy. 410 x 800
- Akasaka Tekkosho K.K. (Akasaka Diesels Ltd.)
- AuxGen: 4 x 167kW a.c.

9150080 **AMRUM TRADER**
V2LF — ex Seaboard Unity -1998
— launched as Amrum Trader -
— Dreiunddreissigste Grosse Bleichen Schiffahrtsgesellschaft mbH & Co. KG
— Hermann Buss GmbH & Cie.
— Leer — Antigua & Barbuda
- 5,941 / 2,777 / 8,081 T/cm
- Class: GL
- 1997-04 Peterswerft Wewelsfleth GmbH & Co.-Wewelsfleth Yd No: 659
- Loa 132.30 (BB) Br ex 19.50 Dght 6.921
- Lbp 123.40 Br md 19.20 Dpth 9.20
- Welded, 1 dk
- **Container Ship (Fully Cellular)**
- Grain: 9,259; Bale: 8,957
- TEU 624 C.Ho 170/20' (40') C.Dk 454/20' (40') incl. 80 ref C.
- Compartments: 3 Cell Ho, ER
- 3 Ha: ER
- **1 oil engine** with flexible couplings & reductiongeared to sc. shaft driving 1 FP propeller
- Total Power: 5,940kW(8,075hp)
- Wartsila 9R38
- 1 x 4 Stroke 9 Cy. 380 x 475
- Stork-Wartsila Diesel B.V.
- AuxGen: 2 x 320kW 400V 50Hz
- Thrusters: 1 Thwart. FP thruster (f)
- Fuel: 120.0(d.o.) 560.0(i.f.o.) 25.0pd

Deadweight Scale

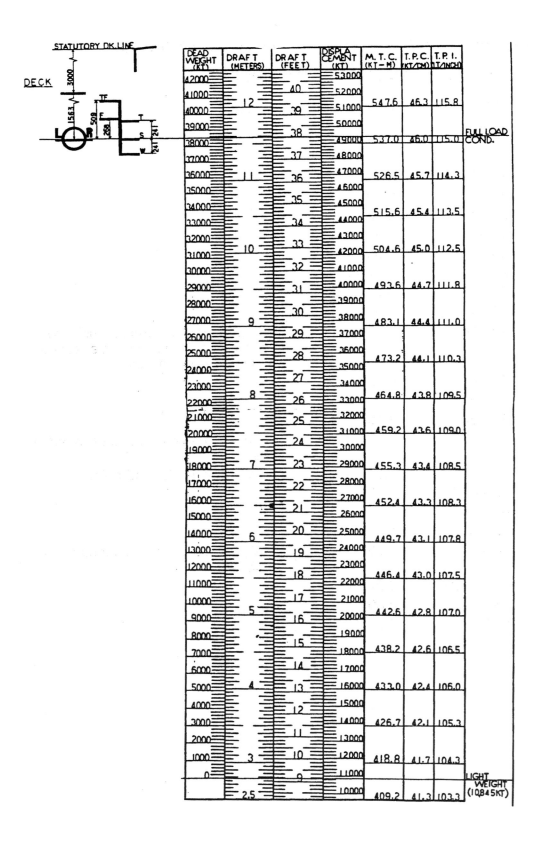

Stowage Factors

Imperial – 40 cubic feet (Ft³)/t ton Metric – 1 Cubic metre (M³)/tonne

Conversion – 1 M³/ Tonne = 35.314843 Ft³/ton

Commodity	Ft3/ton	M3/tonne	Remarks
Pig Iron	11	0.31	
Iron Ore	11 – 17	0.31 – 0 .47	
Bauxite	20 – 32	0.56 – 0 .89	
Sand	11 – 28	0.50 – 0.98	
Scrap Steel	20 – 40	0.56 – 1.11	
Salt	29 – 40	0.81 – 1.12	
Water	36	1.00	
Cement	23 – 29	0,67 – 0.99	
Sulphur	27 – 36	0.74 – 1.00	
China Clay	38 – 48	0.94 – 1.34	
Coal	40 – 58	1.11 – 1.53	If temperature exceeds 55°, head for nearest port. Do not use water at sea – use inert gas if available
Fertilizers	27 – 43	0.83 – 1.15	
Wheat in bulk	47 – 49	1.31 – 1.37	
Wheat in bags	52 – 54	1.45 – 1.50	
Urea	47 – 55	1.17 – 1.56	A form of fertilizer in granules, bead or prills
Petroleum Coke	48 – 55	1.25 – 1.67	Not hazardous if loaded below 54°
Canned Goods	55 – 60	1.53 – 1.61	
Oranges in cases	85 – 90	2.37 – 2.51	
Oranges in cartons	60 – 65	1.68 – 1.81	
Copra	70 – 78	1.95 – 2.18	Smell, infestation, risk of spontaneous combustion
Wood Chips	118 – 160	3.07 – 4.46	
Esparto Grass	180	4.00	
Cork	200	5.57	

Examples of Standard Forms of Charterparties

VOYAGE CHARTERPARTIES

Code Name

CEMENT

Standad Voyage Charterparty for the Transportation of Cement and Cement Clinker in Bulk — *CEMENTVOY

COAL

Americanised Welsh Coal Charter — **AMWELSH 93**

The Baltic & International Maritime Council Polish Coal Charter 1971 — *POLCOALVOY

Japan Shipping Exchange Coal Charter — **NIPPONCOAL**

FERTILIZERS

UK Chamber of Shipping Fertilizer Charter 1942 — **FERTICON**

North American Fertilizer Charter 1978 Amended 1988 — *FERTIVOY 88

Qatar Fertilizer Company Charter — **QAFCOCHARTER**

GENERAL

Baltic & International Maritime Council General Charter (Revised 1922, '74, '76, '94) — *GENCON

World Food Programme Charter — **WORLDFOOD**

GRAIN

Australian Wheat Charter 1990 — **AUSTWHEAT**

Continent Grain Charter (French) — **SYNACOMEX 90**

North American Grain Charter 1973 Amended 1989. Issued by Association of Ship Brokers & Agents (ASBA) U.S.A. — **NORGRAIN 89**

Grain Voyage Charter 1966 (Revised 1974) — *GRAINVOY

Examples of Standard Forms of Charterparties (continued)

ORE

Japan Shipping Exchange, Iron Ore Charter	**NIPPONORE**
Baltic & International Maritime Council Ore charter	***OREVOY**

STONE

UK Chamber of Shipping Stone Charter 1920 (Amended 1925, '59, '74, '95)	**PANSTONE**

WOOD

Baltic & International Maritime Council Baltic Wood Charter 1973 (Revised 1997)	***NUBALTWOOD**
Russian Wood Charter	***RUSSWOOD**
Japan Shipping Exchange, Charterparty for Logs	**NANYOZAI 1997**

TIME CHARTERPARTIES

Baltic & International Maritime Council Uniform Time Charter (Amended 1950, '74)	***BALTIME 1939**
Baltic & International Maritime Council Deep Sea Time Charter for Liners	***LINERTIME**
Baltic & International Maritime Council Time Charter for Container Ships	***BOXTIME**
New York Produce Exchange Time Charter	**NYPE 93**
Baltic & International Maritime Council Bareboat Charter	***BARECON 89**

N.B. This is a small selection of the many standard charterparty forms in circulation. All the above have either been Agreed or Adopted by The Baltic & International Maritime Council (BIMCO), those marked * actually compiled and published by BIMCO.

Baltime

1. Shipbroker	THE BALTIC AND INTERNATIONAL MARITIME CONFERENCE UNIFORM TIME-CHARTER (Box Layout 1974) CODE NAME: "BALTIME 1939"
	PART I
	2. Place and date
3. Owners/Place of business	4. Charterers/Place of business
5. Vessel's name	6. GRT/NRT
7. Class	8. Indicated horse power
9. Total tons d.w. (abt.) on Board of Trade summer freeboard	10. Cubic feet grain/bale capacity
11. Permanent bunkers (abt.)	
12. Speed capability in knots (abt.) on a consumption in tons (abt.) of	
13. Present position	
14. Period of hire (Cl. 1)	15. Port of delivery (Cl. 1)
	16. Time of delivery (Cl. 1)
17. (a) Trade limits (Cl. 2)	
(b) Cargo exclusions specially agreed	
18. Bunkers on re-delivery (state min. and max. quantity) (Cl. 5)	
19. Charter hire (Cl. 6)	20. Hire payment (state currency, method and place of payment; also beneficiary and bank account) (Cl. 6)
21. Place or range of re-delivery (Cl. 7)	22. War (only to be filled in if Section (C) agreed) (Cl. 21)
23. Cancelling date (Cl. 22)	24. Place of arbitration (only to be filled in if place other than London agreed) (Cl. 23)
25.. Brokerage commission and to whom payable (Cl. 25)	
	26. Numbers of additional clauses covering special provisions, if agreed

It is mutually agreed that this Contract shall be performed subject to the conditions contained in this Charter which shall include Part I as well as Part II. In the event of a conflict of conditions, the provisions of Part I shall prevail over those of Part II to the extent of such conflict.

Signature (Owners)	Signature (Charterers)

Appendix 5

PART II
"BALTIME 1939" Uniform Time-Charter (Box Layout 1974)

It is agreed between the party mentioned in Box 3 as Owners of the Vessel named in Box 5 of the gross/net Register tonnage indicated in Box 6, classed as stated in Box 7 and of indicated horse power as stated in Box 8, carrying about the number of tons deadweight indicated in Box 9 on Board of Trade summer freeboard inclusive of bunkers, stores, provisions and boiler water, having as per builder's plan a cubic-feet grain/bale capacity as stated in Box 10, exclusive of permanent bunkers, which contain about the number of tons stated in Box 11, and fully loaded capable of steaming about the number of knots indicated in Box 12 in good weather and smooth water on a consumption of about the number of tons best Welsh coal or oil-fuel stated in Box 12, now in position as stated in Box 13 and the party mentioned as Charterers in Box 4, as follows:

1. Period/Port of Delivery/Time of Delivery
The Owners let, and the Charterers hire the Vessel for a period of the number of calendar months indicated in Box 14 from the time (not a Sunday or a legal Holiday unless taken over) the Vessel is delivered and placed at the disposal of the Charterers between 9 a.m. and 6 p.m., or between 9 a.m. and 2 p.m. if on Saturday, at the port stated in Box 15 in such available berth where she can safely lie always afloat, as the Charterers may direct, she being in every way fitted for ordinary cargo service.
The Vessel to be delivered at the time indicated in Box 16.

2. Trade
The Vessel to be employed in lawful trades for the carriage of lawful merchandise only between good and safe ports or places where she can safely lie always afloat within the limits stated in Box 17.
No live stock nor injurious, inflammable or dangerous goods (such as acids, explosives, calcium carbide, ferro silicon, naphtha, motor spirit, tar, or any of their products) to be shipped.

3. Owners to Provide
The Owners to provide and pay for all provisions and wages, for insurance of the Vessel, for all deck and engine-room stores and maintain her in a thoroughly efficient state in hull and machinery during service.
The Owners to provide one winchman per hatch. If further winchmen are required, or if the stevedores refuse or are not permitted to work with the Crew, the Charterers to provide and pay qualified shore-winchmen.

4. Charterers to Provide
The Charterers to provide and pay for all coals, including galley coal, oil-fuel, water for boilers, port charges, pilotages (whether compulsory or not), canal steersmen, boatage, lights, tug-assistance, consular charges (except those pertaining to the Master, Officers and Crew), canal, dock and other dues and charges, including any foreign general municipality or state taxes, also all dock, harbour and tonnage dues at the ports of delivery and re-delivery (unless incurred through cargo carried before delivery or after re-delivery), agencies, commissions, also to arrange and pay for loading, trimming, stowing (including dunnage and shifting boards, excepting any already on board), unloading, weighing, tallying and delivery of cargoes, surveys on hatches, meals supplied to officials and men in their service and all other charges and expenses whatsoever including detention and expenses through quarantine (including cost of fumigation and disinfection).
All ropes, slings and special runners actually used for loading and discharging and any special gear, including special ropes, hawsers and chains required by the custom of the port for mooring to be for the Charterers' account. The Vessel to be fitted with winches, derricks, wheels and ordinary runners capable of handling lifts up to 2 tons.

5. Bunkers
The Charterers at port of delivery and the Owners at port of re-delivery to take over and pay for all coal or oil-fuel remaining in the Vessel's bunkers at current price at the respective ports.
The Vessel to be re-delivered with not less than the number of tons and not exceeding the number of tons of coal or oil-fuel in the Vessel's bunkers stated in Box 18.

6. Hire
The Charterers to pay as hire the rate stated in Box 19 per 30 days, commencing in accordance with Clause 1 until her re-delivery to the Owners.
Payment
Payment of hire to be made in cash, in the currency stated in Box 20, without discount, every 30 days, in advance, and in the manner prescribed in Box 20.
In default of payment the Owners to have the right of withdrawing the Vessel from the service of the Charterers, without noting any protest and without interference by any court or any other formality whatsoever and without prejudice to any claim the Owners may otherwise have on the Charterers under the Charter.

7. Re-delivery
The Vessel to be re-delivered on the expiration of the Charter in the same good order as when delivered to the Charterers (fair wear and tear excepted) at an ice-free port in the Charterers' option at the place or within the range stated in Box 21, between 9 a.m. and 6 p.m., and 9 a.m. and 2 p.m. on Saturday, but the day of re-delivery shall not be a Sunday or legal Holiday.
Notice
The Charterers to give the Owners not less than ten days' notice at which port and on about which day the Vessel will be re-delivered.
Should the Vessel be ordered on a voyage by which the Charter period will be exceeded the Charterers to have the use of the Vessel to enable them to complete the voyage, provided it could be reasonably calculated that the voyage would allow re-delivery about the time fixed for the termination of the Charter, but for any time exceeding the termination date the Charterers to pay the market rate if higher than the rate stipulated herein.

8. Cargo Space
The whole reach and burthen of the Vessel, including lawful deck-capacity to be at the Charterers' disposal, reserving proper and sufficient space for the Vessel's Master, Officers, Crew, tackle, apparel, furniture, provisions and stores.

9. Master
The Master to prosecute all voyages with the utmost despatch and to render customary assistance with the Vessel's Crew. The Master to be under the orders of the Charterers as regards employment, agency, or other arrangements. The Charterers to indemnify the Owners against all consequences or liabilities arising from the Master, Officers or Agents signing Bills of Lading or other documents or otherwise complying with such orders, as well as from any irregularity in the Vessel's papers or for overcarrying goods. The Owners not to be responsible for shortage, mixture, marks, nor for number of pieces or packages, nor for damage to or claims on cargo caused by bad stowage or otherwise.
If the Charterers have reason to be dissatisfied with the conduct of the Master, Officers, or Engineers, the Owners, on receiving particulars of the complaint, promptly to investigate the matter, and, if necessary and practicable, to make a change in the appointments.

10. Directions and Logs
The Charterers to furnish the Master with all instructions and sailing directions and the Master and Engineer to keep full and correct logs accessible to the Charterers or their Agents.

11. Suspension of Hire etc.
(A) In the event of drydocking or other necessary measures to maintain the efficiency of the Vessel, deficiency of men or Owners' stores, breakdown of machinery, damage to hull or other accident, either hindering or preventing the working of the Vessel and continuing for more than twentyfour consecutive hours, no hire to be paid in respect of any time lost thereby during the period in which the Vessel is unable to perform the service immediately required. Any hire paid in advance to be adjusted accordingly.
(B) In the event of the Vessel being driven into port or to anchorage through stress of weather, trading to shallow harbours or to rivers or ports with bars or suffering an accident to her cargo any detention of the Vessel and/or expenses resulting from such detention to be for the Charterers' account even if such detention and/or expenses, or the cause by reason of which either is incurred, be due to, or be contributed to by, the negligence of the Owners' servants.

12. Cleaning Boilers
Cleaning of boilers whenever possible to be done during service, but if impossible the Charterers to give the Owners necessary time for cleaning. Should the Vessel be detained beyond 48 hours hire to cease until again ready.

13. Responsibility and Exemption
The Owners only to be responsible for delay in delivery of the Vessel or for delay during the currency of the Charter and for loss or damage to goods onboard, if such delay or loss has been caused by want of due diligence on the part of the Owners or their Manager in making the Vessel seaworthy and fitted for the voyage or any other personal act or omission or default of the Owners or their Manager. The Owners not to be responsible in any other case nor for damage or delay whatsoever and howsoever caused even if caused by the neglect or default of their servants. The Owners not to be liable for loss or damage arising or resulting from strikes, lock-outs or stoppage or restraint of labour (including the Master, Officers or Crew) whether partial or general.
The Charterers to be responsible for loss or damage caused to the Vessel or to the Owners by goods being loaded contrary to the terms of the Charter or by improper or careless bunkering or loading, stowing or discharging of goods or any other improper or negligent act on their part or that of their servants.

14. Advances
The Charterers or their Agents to advance to the Master, if required, necessary funds for ordinary disbursements for the Vessel's account at any port charging only interest at 6 per cent. p. a., such advances to be deducted from hire.

15. Excluded Ports
The Vessel not to be ordered to nor bound to enter: a) any place where fever or epidemics are prevalent or to which the Master, Officers and Crew by law are not bound to follow the Vessel
Ice
b) any ice-bound place or any place where lights, lightships, marks and buoys are or are likely to be withdrawn by reason of ice on the Vessel's arrival or where there is risk that ordinarily the Vessel will not be able on account of ice to reach the place or to get out after having completed loading or discharging. The Vessel not to be obliged to force ice. If on account of ice the Master considers it dangerous to remain at the loading or discharging place for fear of the Vessel being frozen in and/or damaged, he has liberty to sail to a convenient open place and await the Charterers' fresh instructions.
Unforeseen detention through any of above causes to be for the Charterers' account.

16. Loss of Vessel
Should the Vessel be lost or missing, hire to cease from the date when she was lost. If the date of loss cannot be ascertained half hire to be paid from the date the Vessel was last reported until the calculated date of arrival at the destination. Any hire paid in advance to be adjusted accordingly.

17. Overtime
The Vessel to work day and night if required. The Charterers to refund the Owners their outlays for all overtime paid to Officers and Crew according to the hours and rates stated in the Vessel's articles.

18. Lien
The Owners to have a lien upon all cargoes and sub-freights belonging to the Time-Charterers and any Bill of Lading freight for all claims under this Charter, and the Charterers to have a lien on the Vessel for all moneys paid in advance and not earned.

19. Salvage
All salvage and assistance to other vessels to be for the Owners' and the Charterers' equal benefit after deducting the Master's and Crew's proportion and all legal and other expenses including hire paid under the charter for time lost in the salvage, also repairs of damage and coal or oil-fuel consumed. The Charterers to be bound by all measures taken by the Owners in order to secure payment of salvage and to fix its amount.

20. Sublet
The Charterers to have the option of subletting the Vessel, giving due notice to the Owners, but the original Charterers always to remain responsible to the Owners for due performance of the Charter.

21. War
(A) The Vessel unless the consent of the Owners be first obtained not to be ordered nor continue to any place or on any voyage nor be used on any service which will bring her within a zone which is dangerous as the result of any actual or threatened act of war, war hostilities, warlike operations, acts of piracy or of hostility or malicious damage against this or any other vessel or its cargo by any person, body or State whatsoever, revolution, civil war, civil commotion or the operation of international law, nor be exposed in any way to any risks or penalties whatsoever consequent upon the imposition of Sanctions, nor carry any goods that may in any way expose her to any risks of seizure, capture, penalties or any other interference of any kind whatsoever by the belligerent or fighting powers or parties or by any Government or Ruler.
(B) Should the Vessel approach or be brought or ordered within such zone, or be exposed in any way to the said risks, (1) the Owners to be entitled from time to time to insure their interests in the Vessel and/or hire against any of the risks likely to be involved thereby on such terms as they shall think fit, the Charterers to make a refund to the Owners of the premium on demand; and (2) notwithstanding the terms of Clause 11 hire to be paid for all time lost including any lost owing to loss of or injury to the Master, Officers, or Crew or to the action of the Crew in refusing to proceed to such zone or to be exposed to such risks.
(C) In the event of the wages of the Master, Officers and/or Crew or the cost of provisions and/or stores for deck and/or engine room and/or insurance premiums being increased by reason of or during the existence of any of the matters mentioned in section (A) the amount of any increase to be added to the hire and paid by the Charterers on production of the Owners' account therefor, such account being rendered monthly.
(D) The Vessel to have liberty to comply with any orders or directions as to departure, arrival, routes, ports of call, stoppages, destination, delivery or in any other wise whatsoever given by the Government of the nation under whose flag the Vessel sails or any other Government or any person (or body) acting or purporting to act with the authority of such Government or by any committee or person having under the terms of the war risks insurance on the Vessel the right to give any such orders or directions.
(E) In the event of the nation under whose flag the Vessel sails becoming involved in war, hostilities, warlike operations, revolution, or civil commotion, both the Owners and the Charterers may cancel the Charter and, unless otherwise agreed, the Vessel to be re-delivered to the Owners at the port of destination or, if prevented through the provisions of section (A) from reaching or entering it, then at a near open and safe port at the Owners' option, after discharge of any cargo on board.
(F) If in compliance with the provisions of this clause anything is done or is not done, such not to be deemed a deviation.
Section (C) is optional and should be considered deleted unless agreed according to Box 22.

22. Cancelling
Should the Vessel not be delivered by the date indicated in Box 23, the Charterers to have the option of cancelling.
If the Vessel cannot be delivered by the cancelling date, the Charterers, if required, to declare within 48 hours after receiving notice thereof whether they cancel or will take delivery of the Vessel.

23. Arbitration
Any dispute arising under the Charter to be referred to arbitration in London (or such other place as may be agreed according to Box 24) one Arbitrator to be nominated by the Owners and the other by the Charterers, and in case the Arbitrators shall not agree then to the decision of an Umpire to be appointed by them, the award of the Arbitrators or the Umpire to be final and binding upon both parties.

24. General Average
General Average to be settled according to York/Antwerp Rules, 1974. Hire not to contribute to General Average.

25. Commission
The Owners to pay a commission at the rate stated in Box 25 to the party mentioned in Box 25 on any hire paid under the Charter, but in no case less than is necessary to cover the actual expenses of the Brokers and a reasonable fee for their work. If the full hire is not paid owing to breach of Charter by either of the parties the party liable therefor to indemnify the Brokers against their loss of commission.
Should the parties agree to cancel the Charter, the Owners to indemnify the Brokers against any loss of commission but in such case the commission not to exceed the brokerage on one year's hire.

Appendix 6

Gencon

1. Shipbroker	**RECOMMENDED** **THE BALTIC AND INTERNATIONAL MARITIME COUNCIL** **UNIFORM GENERAL CHARTER (AS REVISED 1922, 1976 and 1994)** (To be used for trades for which no specially approved form is in force) **CODE NAME: "GENCON"** Part I
	2. Place and date
3. Owners/Place of business (Cl. 1)	4. Charterers/Place of business (Cl. 1)
5. Vessel's name (Cl. 1)	6. GT/NT (Cl. 1)
7. DWT all told on summer load line in metric tons (abt.) (Cl. 1)	8. Present position (Cl. 1)
9. Expected ready to load (abt.) (Cl. 1)	
10. Loading port or place (Cl. 1)	11. Discharging port or place (Cl. 1)
12. Cargo (also state quantity and margin in Owners' option, if agreed; if full and complete cargo not agreed state "part cargo" (Cl. 1)	
13. Freight rate (also state whether freight prepaid or payable on delivery) (Cl. 4)	14. Freight payment (state currency and method of payment: also beneficiary and bank account) (Cl. 4)
15. State if vessel's cargo handling gear shall not be used (Cl. 5)	16. Laytime (if separate laytime for load. and disch. is agreed, fill in a) and b). If total laytime for load. and disch., fill in c) only) (Cl. 6)
17. Shippers/Place of business (Cl. 6)	(a) Laytime for loading
18. Agents (loading) (Cl. 6)	(b) Laytime for discharging
19. Agents (discharging) (Cl. 6)	(c) Total laytime for loading and discharging
20. Demurrage rate and manner payable (loading and discharging) (Cl. 7)	21. Cancelling date (Cl. 9)
	22. General Average to be adjusted at (Cl. 12)
23. Freight Tax (state if for the Owners' account (Cl .13 (c))	24. Brokerage commission and to whom payable (Cl. 15)
25. Law and Arbitration (state 19 (a), 19 (b) or 19 (c) of Cl. 19; if 19 (c) agreed also state Place of Arbitration) (if not filled in 19 (a) shall apply) (Cl. 19)	
(a) State maximum amount for small claims/shortened arbitration (Cl. 19)	26. Additional clauses covering special provisions, if agreed

It is mutually agreed that this Contract shall be performed subject to the conditions contained in this Charter Party which shall include Part I as well as Part II. In the event of a conflict of conditions, the provisions of Part I shall prevail over those of Part II to the extent of such conflict.

Appendix 6

PART II
"Gencon" Charter (As Revised 1922, 1976 and 1994)

1. It is agreed between the party mentioned in Box 3 as the Owners of the Vessel named in Box 5, of the GT/NT indicated in Box 6 and carrying about the number of metric tons of deadweight capacity all told on summer loadline stated in Box 7, now in position as stated in Box 8 and expected ready to load under this Charter Party about the date indicated in Box 9, and the party mentioned as the Charterers in Box 4 that:
The said Vessel shall, as soon as her prior commitments have been completed, proceed to the loading port(s) or place(s) stated in Box 10 or so near thereto as she may safely get and lie always afloat, and there load a full and complete cargo (if shipment of deck cargo agreed same to be at the Charterers' risk and responsibility) as stated in Box 12, which the Charterers bind themselves to ship, and being so loaded the Vessel shall proceed to the discharging port(s) or place(s) stated in Box 11 as ordered on signing Bills of Lading, or so near thereto as she may safely get and lie always afloat, and there deliver the cargo.

2. Owners' Responsibility Clause
The Owners are to be responsible for loss of or damage to the goods or for delay in delivery of the goods only in case the loss, damage or delay has been caused by personal want of due diligence on the part of the Owners or their Manager to make the Vessel in all respects seaworthy and to secure that she is properly manned, equipped and supplied, or by the personal act or default of the Owners or their Manager.
And the Owners are not responsible for loss, damage or delay arising from any other cause whatsoever, even from the neglect or default of the Master or crew or some other person employed by the Owners on board or ashore for whose acts they would, but for this Clause, be responsible, or from unseaworthiness of the Vessel on loading or commencement of the voyage or at any time whatsoever.

3. Deviation Clause
The Vessel has liberty to call at any port or ports in any order, for any purpose, to sail without pilots, to tow and/or assist Vessels in all situations, and also to deviate for the purpose of saving life and/or property.

4. Payment of Freight
(a) The freight at the rate stated in Box 13 shall be paid in cash calculated on the intaken quantity of cargo.
(b) *Prepaid*. If according to Box 13 freight is to be paid on shipment, it shall be deemed earned and non-returnable, Vessel and/or cargo lost or not lost.
Neither the Owners nor their agents shall be required to sign or endorse bills of lading showing freight prepaid unless the freight due to the Owners has actually been paid.
(c) *On delivery*. If according to Box 13 freight, or part thereof, is payable at destination it shall not be deemed earned until the cargo is thus delivered. Notwithstanding the provisions under (a), if freight or part thereof is payable on delivery of the cargo the Charterers shall have the option of paying the freight on delivered weight/quantity provided such option is declared before breaking bulk and the weight/quantity can be ascertained by official weighing machine, joint draft survey or tally.
Cash for Vessel's ordinary disbursements at the port of loading to be advanced by the Charterers, if required, at highest current rate of exchange, subject to two (2) per cent to cover insurance and other expenses.

5. Loading/Discharging
(a) Costs/Risks
The cargo shall be brought into the holds, loaded, stowed and/or trimmed, tallied, lashed and/or secured and taken from the holds and discharged by the Charterers, free of any risk, liability and expense whatsoever to the Owners. The Charterers shall provide and lay all dunnage material as required for the proper stowage and protection of the cargo on board, the Owners allowing the use of all dunnage available on board. The Charterers shall be responsible for and pay the cost of removing their dunnage after discharge of the cargo under this Charter Party and time to count until dunnage has been removed.
(b) Cargo Handling Gear
Unless the Vessel is gearless or unless it has been agreed between the parties that the Vessel's gear shall not be used and stated as such in Box 15, the Owners shall throughout the duration of loading/discharging give free use of the Vessel's cargo handling gear and of sufficient motive power to operate all such cargo handling gear. All such equipment to be in good working order. Unless caused by negligence of the stevedores, time lost by breakdown of the Vessel's cargo handling gear or motive power – pro rata the total number of cranes/winches required at that time for the loading/discharging of cargo under this Charter Party – shall not count as laytime or time on demurrage.
On request the Owners shall provide free of charge cranemen/winchmen from the crew to operate the Vessel's cargo handling gear, unless local regulations prohibit this, in which latter event shore labourers shall be for the account of the Charterers. Cranemen/winchmen shall be under the Charterers' risk and responsibility and as stevedores to be deemed as their servants but shall always work under the supervision of the Master.
(c) Stevedore Damage
The Charterers shall be responsible for damage (beyond ordinary wear and tear) to any part of the Vessel caused by Stevedores. Such damage shall be notified as soon as reasonably possible by the Master to the Charterers or their agents and to their Stevedores, failing which the Charterers shall not be held responsible. The Master shall endeavour to obtain the Stevedores' written acknowledgement of liability.
The Charterers are obliged to repair any stevedore damage prior to completion of the voyage, but must repair stevedore damage affecting the Vessel's seaworthiness or class before the Vessel sails from the port where such damage was caused or found. All additional expenses incurred shall be for the account of the Charterers and any time lost shall be for the account of and shall be paid to the Owners by the Charterers at the demurrage rate.

6. Laytime
* *(a) Separate laytime for loading and discharging*
The cargo shall be loaded within the number of running days/hours as indicated in Box 16, weather permitting, Sundays and holidays excepted, unless used, in which event time used shall count.
The cargo shall be discharged within the number of running days/hours as indicated in Box 16, weather permitting, Sundays and holidays excepted, unless used, in which event time used shall count.
* *(b) Total laytime for loading and discharging*
The cargo shall be loaded and discharged within the number of total running days/hours as indicated in Box 16, weather permitting, Sundays and holidays excepted, unless used, in which event time used shall count.
(c) Commencement of laytime (loading and discharging)
Laytime for loading and discharging shall commence at 13.00 hours, if notice of readiness is given up to and including 12.00 hours, and at 06.00 hours next working day if notice given during office hours after 12.00 hours. Notice of readiness at loading port to be given to the Shippers named in Box 17 or if not named, to the Charterers or their agents named in Box 18. Notice of readiness at the discharging port to be given to the Receivers or, if not known, to the Charterers or their agents named in Box 19.
If the loading/discharging berth is not available on the Vessel's arrival at or off the port of loading/discharging, the Vessel shall be entitled to give notice of readiness within ordinary office hours on arrival there, whether in free pratique or not, whether customs cleared or not. Laytime or time on demurrage shall then count as if she were in berth and in all respects ready for loading/discharging provided that the Master warrants that she is in fact ready in all respects. Time used in moving from the place of waiting to the loading/discharging berth shall not count as laytime.
If, after inspection, the Vessel is found not to be ready in all respects to load/discharge time lost after the discovery thereof until the Vessel is again ready to load/discharge shall not count as laytime.
Time used before commencement of laytime shall count.
* *Indicate alternative (a) or (b) as agreed, in Box 16.*

7. Demurrage
Demurrage at the loading and discharging port is payable by the Charterers at the rate stated in Box 20 in the manner stated in Box 20 per day or pro rata for any part of a day. Demurrage shall fall due day by day and shall be payable upon receipt of the Owners' invoice.
In the event the demurrage is not paid in accordance with the above, the Owners shall give the Charterers 96 running hours written notice to rectify the failure. If the demurrage is not paid at the expiration of this time limit and if the vessel is in or at the loading port, the Owners are entitled at any time to terminate the Charter Party and claim damages for any losses caused thereby.

8. Lien Clause
The Owners shall have a lien on the cargo and on all sub-freights payable in respect of the cargo, for freight, deadfreight, demurrage, claims for damages and for all other amounts due under this Charter Party including costs of recovering same.

9. Cancelling Clause
(a) Should the Vessel not be ready to load (whether in berth or not) on the cancelling date indicated in Box 21, the Charterers shall have the option of cancelling this Charter Party.
(b) Should the Owners anticipate that, despite the exercise of due diligence, the Vessel will not be ready to load by the cancelling date, they shall notify the Charterers thereof without delay stating the expected date of the Vessel's readiness to load and asking whether the Charterers will exercise their option of cancelling the Charter Party, or agree to a new cancelling date.
Such option must be declared by the Charterers within 48 running hours after the receipt of the Owners' notice. If the Charterers do not exercise their option of cancelling, then this Charter Party shall be deemed to be amended such that the seventh day after the new readiness date stated in the Owners' notification to the Charterers shall be the new cancelling date.
The provisions of sub-clause (b) of this Clause shall operate only once, and in case of the Vessel's further delay, the Charterers shall have the option of cancelling the Charter Party as per sub-clause (a) of this Clause.

10. Bills of Lading
Bills of Lading shall be presented and signed by the Master as per the "Congenbill" Bill of Lading form, Edition 1994, without prejudice to this Charter Party, or by the Owners' agents provided written authority has been given by Owners to the agents, a copy of which is to be furnished to the Charterers. The Charterers shall indemnify the Owners against all consequences or liabilities that may arise from the signing of bills of lading as presented to the extent that the terms or contents of such bills of lading impose or result in the imposition of more onerous liabilities upon the Owners than those assumed by the Owners under this Charter Party.

11. Both-to-Blame Collision Clause
If the Vessel comes into collision with another vessel as a result of the negligence of the other vessel and any act, neglect or default of the Master, Mariner, Pilot or the servants of the Owners in the navigation or in the management of the Vessel, the owners of the cargo carried hereunder will indemnify the Owners against all loss or liability to the other or non-carrying vessel or her owners in so far as such loss or liability represents loss of, or damage to, or any claim whatsoever of the owners of said cargo, paid or payable by the other or non-carrying vessel or her owners to the owners of said cargo and set-off, recouped or recovered by the other or non-carrying vessel or her owners as part of their claim against the carrying Vessel or the Owners.
The foregoing provisions shall also apply where the owners, operators or those in charge of any vessel or vessels or objects other than, or in addition to, the colliding vessels or objects are at fault in respect of a collision or contact.

12. General Average and New Jason Clause
General Average shall be adjusted in London unless otherwise agreed in Box 22 according to York-Antwerp Rules 1994 and any subsequent modification thereof. Proprietors of cargo to pay the cargo's share in the general expenses even if same have been necessitated through neglect or default of the Owners' servants (see Clause 2).
If General Average is to be adjusted in accordance with the law and practice of the United States of America, the following Clause shall apply: "In the event of accident, danger, damage or disaster before or after the commencement of the voyage, resulting from any cause whatsoever, whether due to negligence or not, for which, or for the consequence of which, the Owners are not responsible, by statute, contract or otherwise, the cargo shippers, consignees or the owners of the cargo shall contribute with the Owners in General Average to the payment of any sacrifices, losses or expenses of a General Average nature that may be made or incurred and shall pay salvage and special charges incurred in respect of the cargo. If a salving vessel is owned or operated by the Owners, salvage shall be paid for as fully as if the said salving vessel or vessels belonged to strangers. Such deposit as the Owners, or their agents, may deem sufficient to cover the estimated contribution of the goods and any salvage and special charges thereon shall, if required, be made by the cargo, shippers, consignees or owners of the goods to the Owners before delivery.".

13. Taxes and Dues Clause
(a) *On Vessel* -The Owners shall pay all dues, charges and taxes customarily levied on the Vessel, howsoever the amount thereof may be assessed.
(b) *On cargo* -The Charterers shall pay all dues, charges, duties and taxes customarily levied on the cargo, howsoever the amount thereof may be assessed.
(c) *On freight* -Unless otherwise agreed in Box 23, taxes levied on the freight shall be for the Charterers' account.

Appendix 6

PART II
"Gencon" Charter (As Revised 1922, 1976 and 1994)

14. Agency

In every case the Owners shall appoint their own Agent both at the port of loading and the port of discharge.

15. Brokerage

A brokerage commission at the rate stated in Box 24 on the freight, dead-freight and demurrage earned is due to the party mentioned in Box 24.

In case of non-execution 1/3 of the brokerage on the estimated amount of freight to be paid by the party responsible for such non-execution to the Brokers as indemnity for the latter's expenses and work. In case of more voyages the amount of indemnity to be agreed.

16. General Strike Clause

(a) If there is a strike or lock-out affecting or preventing the actual loading of the cargo, or any part of it, when the Vessel is ready to proceed from her last port or at any time during the voyage to the port or ports of loading or after her arrival there, the Master or the Owners may ask the Charterers to declare, that they agree to reckon the laydays as if there were no strike or lock-out. Unless the Charterers have given such declaration in writing (by telegram, if necessary) within 24 hours, the Owners shall have the option of cancelling this Charter Party. If part cargo has already been loaded, the Owners must proceed with same, (freight payable on loaded quantity only) having liberty to complete with other cargo on the way for their own account.

(b) If there is a strike or lock-out affecting or preventing the actual discharging of the cargo on or after the Vessel's arrival at or off port of discharge and same has not been settled within 48 hours, the Charterers shall have the option of keeping the Vessel waiting until such strike or lock-out is at an end against paying half demurrage after expiration of the time provided for discharging until the strike or lock-out terminates and thereafter full demurrage shall be payable until the completion of discharging, or of ordering the Vessel to a safe port where she can safely discharge without risk of being detained by strike or lock-out. Such orders to be given within 48 hours after the Master or the Owners have given notice to the Charterers of the strike or lock-out affecting the discharge. On delivery of the cargo at such port, all conditions of this Charter Party and of the Bill of Lading shall apply and the Vessel shall receive the same freight as if she had discharged at the original port of destination, except that if the distance to the substituted port exceeds 100 nautical miles, the freight on the cargo delivered at the substituted port to be increased in proportion.

(c) Except for the obligations described above, neither the Charterers nor the Owners shall be responsible for the consequences of any strikes or lock-outs preventing or affecting the actual loading or discharging of the cargo.

17. War Risks ("Voywar 1993")

(1) For the purpose of this Clause, the words:

(a) The "Owners" shall include the shipowners, bareboat charterers, disponent owners, managers or other operators who are charged with the management of the Vessel, and the Master; and

(b) "War Risks" shall include any war (whether actual or threatened), act of war, civil war, hostilities, revolution, rebellion, civil commotion, warlike operations, the laying of mines (whether actual or reported), acts of piracy, acts of terrorists, acts of hostility or malicious damage, blockades (whether imposed against all Vessels or imposed selectively against Vessels of certain flags or ownership, or against certain cargoes or crews or otherwise howsoever), by any person, body, terrorist or political group, or the Government of any state whatsoever, which, in the reasonable judgement of the Master and/or the Owners, may be dangerous or are likely to be or to become dangerous to the Vessel, her cargo, crew or other persons on board the Vessel.

(2) If at any time before the Vessel commences loading, it appears that, in the reasonable judgement of the Master and/or the Owners, performance of the Contract of Carriage, or any part of it, may expose, or is likely to expose, the Vessel, her cargo, crew or other persons on board the Vessel to War Risks, the Owners may give notice to the Charterers cancelling this Contract of Carriage, or may refuse to perform such part of it as may expose, or may be likely to expose, the Vessel, her cargo, crew or other persons on board the Vessel to War Risks; provided always that if this Contract of Carriage provides that loading or discharging is to take place within a range of ports, and at the port or ports nominated by the Charterers the Vessel, her cargo, crew, or other persons onboard the Vessel may be exposed, or may be likely to be exposed, to War Risks, the Owners shall first require the Charterers to nominate any other safe port which lies within the range for loading or discharging, and may only cancel this Contract of Carriage if the Charterers shall not have nominated such safe port or ports within 48 hours of receipt of notice of such requirement.

(3) The Owners shall not be required to continue to load cargo for any voyage, or to sign Bills of Lading for any port or place, or to proceed or continue on any voyage, or on any part thereof, or to proceed through any canal or waterway, or to proceed to or remain at any port or place whatsoever, where it appears, either after the loading of the cargo commences, or at any stage of the voyage thereafter before the discharge of the cargo is completed, that, in the reasonable judgement of the Master and/or the Owners, the Vessel, her cargo (or any part thereof), crew or other persons on board the Vessel (or any one or more of them) may be, or are likely to be, exposed to War Risks. If it should so appear, the Owners may by notice request the Charterers to nominate a safe port for the discharge of the cargo or any part thereof, and if within 48 hours of the receipt of such notice, the Charterers shall not have nominated such a port, the Owners may discharge the cargo at any safe port of their choice (including the port of loading) in complete fulfilment of the Contract of Carriage. The Owners shall be entitled to recover from the Charterers the extra expenses of such discharge and, if the discharge takes place at any port other than the loading port, to receive the full freight as though the cargo had been carried to the discharging port and if the extra distance exceeds 100 miles, to additional freight which shall be the same percentage of the freight contracted for as the percentage which the extra distance represents to the distance of the normal and customary route, the Owners having a lien on the cargo for such expenses and freight.

(4) If at any stage of the voyage after the loading of the cargo commences, it appears that, in the reasonable judgement of the Master and/or the Owners, the Vessel, her cargo, crew or other persons on board the Vessel may be, or are likely to be, exposed to War Risks on any part of the route (including any canal or waterway) which is normally and customarily used in a voyage of the nature contracted for, and there is another longer route to the discharging port, the Owners shall give notice to the Charterers that this route will be taken. In this event the Owners shall be entitled, if the total extra distance exceeds 100 miles, to additional freight which shall be the same percentage of the freight contracted for as the percentage which the extra distance represents to the distance of the normal and customary route.

(5) The Vessel shall have liberty:-

(a) to comply with all orders, directions, recommendations or advice as to departure, arrival, routes, sailing in convoy, ports of call, stoppages, destinations, discharge of cargo, delivery or in any way whatsoever which are given by the Government of the Nation under whose flag the Vessel sails, or other Government to whose laws the Owners are subject, or any other Government which so requires, or any body or group acting with the power to compel compliance with their orders or directions;

(b) to comply with the orders, directions or recommendations of any war risks underwriters who have the authority to give the same under the terms of the war risks insurance;

(c) to comply with the terms of any resolution of the Security Council of the United Nations, any directives of the European Community, the effective orders of any other Supranational body which has the right to issue and give the same, and with national laws aimed at enforcing the same to which the Owners are subject, and to obey the orders and directions of those who are charged with their enforcement;

(d) to discharge at any other port any cargo or part thereof which may render the Vessel liable to confiscation as a contraband carrier;

(e) to call at any other port to change the crew or any part thereof or other persons on board the Vessel when there is reason to believe that they may be subject to internment, imprisonment or other sanctions;

(f) where cargo has not been loaded or has been discharged by the Owners under any provisions of this Clause, to load other cargo for the Owners' own benefit and carry it to any other port or ports whatsoever, whether backwards or forwards or in a contrary direction to the ordinary or customary route.

(6) If in compliance with any of the provisions of sub-clauses (2) to (5) of this Clause anything is done or not done, such shall not be deemed to be a deviation, but shall be considered as due fulfilment of the Contract of Carriage.

18. General Ice Clause

Port of loading

(a) In the event of the loading port being inaccessible by reason of ice when the Vessel is ready to proceed from her last port or at any time during the voyage or on the Vessel's arrival or in case frost sets in after the Vessel's arrival, the Master for fear of being frozen in is at liberty to leave without cargo, and this Charter Party shall be null and void.

(b) If during loading the Master, for fear of the Vessel being frozen in, deems it advisable to leave, he has liberty to do so with what cargo he has on board and to proceed to any other port or ports with option of completing cargo for the Owners' benefit for any port or ports including port of discharge. Any part cargo thus loaded under this Charter Party to be forwarded to destination at the Vessel's expense but against payment of freight, provided that no extra expenses be thereby caused to the Charterers, freight being paid on quantity delivered (in proportion if lumpsum), all other conditions as per this Charter Party.

(c) In case of more than one loading port, and if one or more of the ports are closed by ice, the Master or the Owners to be at liberty either to load the part cargo at the open port and fill up elsewhere for their own account as under section (b) or to declare the Charter Party null and void unless the Charterers agree to load full cargo at the open port.

Port of discharge

(a) Should ice prevent the Vessel from reaching port of discharge the Charterers shall have the option of keeping the Vessel waiting until the re-opening of navigation and paying demurrage or of ordering the Vessel to a safe and immediately accessible port where she can safely discharge without risk of detention by ice. Such orders to be given within 48 hours after the Master or the Owners have given notice to the Charterers of the impossibility of reaching port of destination.

(b) If during discharging the Master for fear of the Vessel being frozen in deems it advisable to leave, he has liberty to do so with what cargo he has on board and to proceed to the nearest accessible port where she can safely discharge.

(c) On delivery of the cargo at such port, all conditions of the Bill of Lading shall apply and the Vessel shall receive the same freight as if she had discharged at the original port of destination, except that if the distance of the substituted port exceeds 100 nautical miles, the freight on the cargo delivered at the substituted port to be increased in proportion.

19. Law and Arbitration

* (a) This Charter Party shall be governed by and construed in accordance with English law and any dispute arising out of this Charter Party shall be referred to arbitration in London in accordance with the Arbitration Acts 1950 and 1979 or any statutory modification or re-enactment thereof for the time being in force. Unless the parties agree upon a sole arbitrator, one arbitrator shall be appointed by each party and the arbitrators so appointed shall appoint a third arbitrator, the decision of the three-man tribunal thus constituted or any two of them, shall be final. On the receipt by one party of the nomination in writing of the other party's arbitrator, that party shall appoint their arbitrator within fourteen days, failing which the decision of the single arbitrator appointed shall be final.

For disputes where the total amount claimed by either party does not exceed the amount stated in Box 25** the arbitration shall be conducted in accordance with the Small Claims Procedure of the London Maritime Arbitrators Association.

* (b) This Charter Party shall be governed by and construed in accordance with Title 9 of the United States Code and the Maritime Law of the United States and should any dispute arise out of this Charter Party, the matter in dispute shall be referred to three persons at New York, one to be appointed by each of the parties hereto, and the third by the two so chosen; their decision or that of any two of them shall be final, and for purpose of enforcing any award, this agreement may be made a rule of the Court. The proceedings shall be conducted in accordance with the rules of the Society of Maritime Arbitrators, Inc..

For disputes where the total amount claimed by either party does not exceed the amount stated in Box 25** the arbitration shall be conducted in accordance with the Shortened Arbitration Procedure of the Society of Maritime Arbitrators, Inc..

* (c) Any dispute arising out of this Charter Party shall be referred to arbitration at the place indicated in Box 25, subject to the procedures applicable there. The laws of the place indicated in Box 25 shall govern this Charter Party.

(d) If Box 25 in Part I is not filled in, sub-clause (a) of this Clause shall apply.

* *(a), (b) and (c) are alternatives; indicate alternative agreed in Box 25.*

** *Where no figure is supplied in Box 25 in Part I, this provision only shall be void but the other provisions of this Clause shall have full force and remain in effect.*

Appendix 7

Principle Clauses

PRINCIPLE CLAUSES COMMON TO BOTH VOYAGE AND TIME CHARTER PARTIES

1. Titles of the contracting parties (name of Shipowner and name of Charterer).
2. Name of ship with description including tonnage, classification, present position etc.
3. Warranty of seaworthiness. (Often 'tight, staunch and strong").
4. Place of loading (of delivery in a time charter).
5. Type of cargo and quantity, (trading limits in a time charter).
6. Place of discharge (of redelivery in a time charter).
7. Rate of freight (of hire in a time charter).
8. When freight/hire to be paid (e.g. on loading or on discharge in a voyage charter, monthly or semi-monthly in a time charter).
9. Laydays/Cancelling.
10. Arbitration.
11. Exceptions and exemptions from liability clauses
12. Brokerages.

PRINCIPLE CLAUSES SPECIFIC TO VOYAGE CHARTERPARTIES

1. Rates of loading and discharging (tons per day or number of days/hours allowed).
2. When time commences to count including how and when notices of readiness to be given.
3. How laytime to be calculated e.g. SHEX.
4. Rate of demurrage (and despatch if any).
5. Who nominates port agents.

PRINCIPLE CLAUSES SPECIFIC TO TIME CHARTERPARTIES

1. Who pays for what especially fuel, fresh water, port charges etc.
2. Offhire clause (in case of breakdown, how soon hire ceases to become payable)
3. Owners option to drydock vessel during currency of charter.
4. Quantities of bunker fuel to be on board at time of delivery and redelivery.

Chartering Expressions and Abbreviations

Most chartering negotiations today will be conducted via some form of electronic written communication such as telex, fax, e-mail etc. Dating from the time when the only such medium was the telegraph many charterparty clauses were reduced to sets of initial letters. Because of their convenience they are still used.

It is vital that both parties in negotiations are fully aware of the meaning of these abbreviations and care should be taken to avoid ambiguity or misunderstanding.

Abbreviations concerning laytime

NOR   Notice of Readiness. The notice the ship gives to the shipper or receiver to say the ship is read to commence loading/discharging. This will determine when laytime commences to count.

SHEX   Sundays and Holidays excepted. Will follow the rate of loading/discharging and may be followed by 'uu' meaning 'unless used' or 'eiu' = 'even if used'. Would be FHEX (Fridays and Holidays) if Islamic countries involved.

SHINC   Sundays and Holidays included. Common when working at a dedicated bulk-cargo terminal which operates all day every day.

WWD   Weather Working Days ie days when bad weather does not interfere with loading/discharging.

Abbreviations concerning demurrage/dispatch

D1/2D   Despatch Half Demurrage may be followed by

BENDS   Meaning at Both Ends or

DLO   Despatch Loading Only or

DDO   Despatch Discharging Only

FD   Free of dispatch

Abbreviations concerning who pays for what

FIO   Free In and Out, means free of expense to the vessel, the shippers pay for loading and receivers pay for discharging.

FIOS   Free In and Out and Stowed. Shippers also pay for the stevedores working in the ship stowing the cargo in the holds.

FIOT   Free In and Out and Trimmed. With a bulk cargo the process of stowing, which will be that of levelling the material, is called trimming.

Gross Terms (or Liner Terms) means the ship pays all the cost of loading, stowing and discharging.

Appendix 8

Concerning the ship and cargo

DWAT	Deadweight All Told. The total weight of cargo, bunkers stores etc that the ship can carry.
DWCC	Deadweight Cargo Capacity. The total weight of cargo the ship can carry assuming an average quantity of bunkers and stores.
ETA	Estimated Time of Arrival.
ETD	Estimated Time of Departure.
ETS	Estimated Time of Sailing.
MOLOO	More of Less in Owners Option. Refers to the amount of cargo to be loaded where the owner seeks to allow the master some flexibility of depending upon the weight of fuel and stores he will have on board. The charterers may, however, insist on 'min/max' – an exact quantity.
aa	Always Afloat, the berth must be deep enough for the ship to be afloat at all states of the tide whether empty or loaded.
naabsa	Not Always Afloat But Safe Aground. At low tide there will not be enough water for the ship to be afloat but the bottom is sand or mud so the ship will not suffer damage.
SWAD	Salt Water Arrival Draft. The charterers cannot guarantee an accessible berth if the ship arrives on a deeper draft than stipulated.
Panamax	The dimensions of this ship are the maximum permissible for transmitting the Panama Canal. Usually about 60/80,000 tonnes dwat.
Capesize	Too large for Panama, usually over 100,000 dwat.
Handysize	An indeterminate size but currently around 30,000 dwat.
IWL	Institute Warranty Limits. The Institute in this case is the Institute of London Underwriters now called International Underwriters Association (IUA) who have published lists of geographical limits outside which the ship will not be insured unless additional premiums have been paid.
HHDW	Heavy Handy Deadweight. A method of referring to cargoes of scrap steel. As the name implies it will stow deadweight and there will be no awkward pieces.
HSS	Heavy grain/Sorghum/Soya refers to grain and gives charterers a range of options of types of grain to be loaded, typical method of chartering from the US Gulf.
TEU	Twenty Foot Equivalent Units, a way of describing the capacity of a ship intended for the container trade. Containers are either 20 feet or 40 feet long thus a 40 foot container is two Teus and known as an FEU.Beaufort Scale Wind Force Conversions.

Shellvoy Charter Party

Code word for this Charter Party
"SHELLVOY 5"

Issued July 1987

Voyage Charter Party
LONDON,   **19**

PREAMBLE

IT IS THIS DAY AGREED between

of   (hereinafter referred to as "Owners") being owners/disponent owners of the

motor/steam tank vessel called

(hereinafter referred to as "the vessel")

and   of

(hereinafter referred to as "Charterers")
that the service for which provision is herein made shall be subject to the terms and conditions of this charter which includes Part I and Part II. In the event of any conflict between the provisions of Part I and Part II hereof, the provisions of Part I shall prevail.

PART I

(A) Description of vessel

Owners guarantee that at the date hereof the vessel:-

(i) Is classed

(ii) Has a deadweight of   tonnes (1000 kg.) on a salt-water draft on assigned summer freeboard
of   m.

(iii) Has a capacity available for the cargo of   tonnes (1000 kg.) 5% more or less in Owners' option.

(iv) Is fully fitted with heating systems for all cargo tanks capable of maintaining cargo at a temperature of up to   degrees Celsius.

(v) Has tanks coated as follows:-

(vi) Is equipped with cranes/derricks capable of lifting to and supporting at the vessel's port and starboard manifolds submarine hoses of up to   tonnes (1000 kg.) in weight.

(vii) Has cargo pumps capable of discharging a full cargo within   hours or maintaining a back pressure of   at the vessel's manifold (provided shore facilities permit and the cargo does not have a kinematic viscosity exceeding 600 centistokes at the discharge temperature required by Charterers).

(viii) Has or will have carried the following three cargoes immediately prior to loading under this charter:-
Last
2.
3.

(ix) Has a crude oil washing system complying with the requirements of the International Convention for the Prevention of Pollution from Ships 1973 as modified by the Protocol of 1978 ("MARPOL 73/78").

(x) Has an operational inert gas system.

(xi) Has on board all papers and certificates required by any applicable law, in force as at the date of this charter, to enable the vessel to perform the charter service without any delay.

(xii) Is entered in   P&I Club.

(B) Position/ Readiness

Now   Expected ready to load

(C) Laydays

Commencing Noon Local Time on   (Commencement Date)
Terminating Noon Local Time on   (Termination Date)

Appendix 9

"SHELLVOY 5"

PART I

PAGE 2

(D) Loading
Port(s)/
Range

one or more ports at Charterers' option

(E) Discharging
Port(s)/
Range

one or more ports at Charterers' option

(F) Cargo
description

Charterers' option

Maximum temperature on loading

degrees Celsius

(G) Freight rate   At   % of the rate for the voyage as provided for in the Worldwide Tanker Nominal Freight Scale current at
the date of commencement of loading (hereinafter referred to as "Worldscale") per ton (2240lbs)/tonne
(1000Kg).

(H) Freight
payable to

(I) Laytime

running hours

(J) Demurrage
per day (or
pro rata)

(K) ETAs   All radio messages sent by the master to Charterers shall be addressed to

(L) Special
provisions

Signatures   IN WITNESS WHEREOF, the parties have caused this charter consisting of the Preamble, Parts I and II to be
executed as of the day and year first above written.

By

By

Appendix 9

Issued July 1987   **"SHELLVOY 5"**

PART II

Condition of vessel

1. Owners shall exercise due diligence to ensure that from the time when the obligation to proceed to the loading port(s) attaches and throughout the charter service -
   (a) the vessel and her hull, machinery, boilers, tanks, equipment and facilities are in good order and condition and in every way equipped and fit for the service required; and
   (b) the vessel has a full and efficient complement of master, officers and crew;
   and to ensure that before and at the commencement of any laden voyage the vessel is in all respects fit to carry the cargo specified in Part I(F).

Cleanliness of tanks

2. Whilst loading, carrying and discharging cargo the master shall at all times use due diligence to keep the tanks, lines and pumps of the vessel clean for the cargo specified in Part I(F). It shall be for the master alone to decide whether the vessel's tanks, lines and pumps are suitably clean. However, the decision of the master shall be without prejudice to the right of Charterers, should any contamination or damage subsequently be found, to contend that the same was caused by inadequate cleaning and/or some breach of this or any other Clause of this charter.

Voyage

3. Subject to the provisions of this charter the vessel shall perform her service with utmost despatch and shall proceed to such berths as Charterers may specify, in any port or ports within Part I(D) nominated by Charterers, or so near thereunto as she may safely get and there, always safely afloat, load a full cargo, but not in excess of the maximum quantity consistent with the International Load Line Convention for the time being in force and, being so loaded, proceed as ordered on signing bills of lading to such berths as Charterers may specify, in any port or ports within Part I(E) nominated by Charterers, or so near thereunto as she may safely get and there, always safely afloat, discharge the cargo.

Charterers shall nominate loading and discharging ports, and shall specify loading and discharging berths, in sufficient time to avoid delay or deviation to the vessel. Subject to the foregoing, and provided it does not cause delay or deviation to the vessel, Charterers shall have the option of ordering the vessel to safe areas at sea for wireless orders.

In this charter, "berth" means any berth, wharf, dock, anchorage, submarine line, a position alongside any vessel or lighter or any other loading or discharging point whatsoever to which Charterers are entitled to order the vessel hereunder, and "port" means any port or location at sea to which the vessel may proceed in accordance with the terms of this charter.

Safe berth

4. Charterers shall exercise due diligence to order the vessel only to ports and berths which are safe for the vessel and to ensure that transhipment operations conform to standards not less than those set out in the latest edition of ICS/OCIMF Ship-to-Ship Transfer Guide (Petroleum). Notwithstanding anything contained in this charter, Charterers do not warrant the safety of any port, berth or transhipment operation and Charterers shall not be liable for loss or damage arising from any unsafety if they can prove that due diligence was exercised in the giving of the order.

Freight

5. Freight shall be earned concurrently with delivery of cargo at the nominated discharging port or ports and shall be paid by Charterers to Owners without any deductions in United States Dollars at the rate(s) specified in Part I(G) on the gross Bill of Lading quantity as furnished by the shipper (subject to Clauses 8 and 40), upon receipt by Charterers of notice of completion of final discharge of cargo, provided that no freight shall be payable on any quantity in excess of the maximum quantity consistent with the International Load Line Convention for the time being in force.

If the vessel is ordered to proceed on a voyage for which a fixed differential is provided in Worldscale, such fixed differential shall be payable without applying the percentage referred to in Part I(G).

If cargo is carried between ports and/or by a route for which no freight rate is expressly quoted in Worldscale, then the parties shall, in the absence of agreement as to the appropriate freight rate, apply to Worldscale Association (London) Ltd., or Worldscale Association (NYC) Inc, for the determination of an appropriate Worldscale freight rate.

Save in respect of the time when freight is earned, the location of any transhipment at sea pursuant to Clause 26(2) shall not be an additional nominated port for the purposes of this charter (including this Clause 5) and the freight rate for the voyage shall be the same as if such transhipment had not taken place.

Dues and other charges

6. Dues and other charges upon the vessel, including those assessed by reference to the quantity of cargo loaded or discharged, and any taxes on freight whatsoever shall be paid by Owners, and dues and other charges upon the cargo shall be paid by Charterers. However, notwithstanding the foregoing, where under a provision of Worldscale a due or charge is expressly for the account of Owners or Charterers then such due or charge shall be payable in accordance with such provision.

Loading and discharging cargo

7. The cargo shall be loaded into the vessel at the expense of Charterers and, up to the vessel's permanent hose connections, at Charterers' risk. The cargo shall be discharged from the vessel at the expense of Owners and, up to the vessel's permanent hose connections, at Owners' risk. Owners shall, unless otherwise notified by Charterers or their agents, supply at Owners' expense all hands, equipment and facilities required on board for mooring and unmooring and connecting and disconnecting hoses for loading and discharging.

Deadfreight

8. Charterers need not supply a full cargo, but if they do not freight shall nevertheless be paid as if the vessel had been loaded with a full cargo.

The term "full cargo" as used throughout this charter means a cargo which, together with any collected washings (as defined in Clause 40) retained on board pursuant to the requirements of MARPOL 73/78, fills the vessel to either her applicable deadweight or her capacity stated in Part I(A)(iii), whichever is less, while leaving sufficient space in the tanks for the expansion of cargo.

Shifting

9. Charterers shall have the right to require the vessel to shift at ports of loading and/or discharging from a loading or discharging berth within port limits and back to the same or to another such berth once or more often on payment of all additional expenses incurred. For the purposes of freight payment and shifting the places

Appendix 9

grouped in Port and Terminal Combinations in Worldscale are to be considered as berths within a single port. If at any time before cargo operations are completed it becomes dangerous for the vessel to remain at the specified berth as a result of wind or water conditions, Charterers shall pay all additional expenses of shifting from any such berth and back to that or any other specified berth within port limits (except to the extent that any fault of the vessel contributed to such danger).

Subject to Clause 14(a) and (c) time spent shifting shall count against laytime or if the vessel is on demurrage for demurrage.

Charterers' failure to give orders

10. If the vessel is delayed due to Charterers' breach of Clause 3 Charterers shall, subject to the terms hereof, compensate Owners in accordance with Clause 15(1) and (2) as if such delay were time exceeding the laytime.

The period of such delay shall be calculated

(i) from 6 hours after Owners notify Charterers that the vessel is delayed awaiting nomination of loading port until such nomination has been received by Owners, or

(ii) from 6 hours after the vessel gives notice of readiness at the loading port until commencement of loading

as the case may be, subject always to the same exceptions as those set out in Clause 14. Any period of delay in respect of which Charterers pay compensation pursuant to this Clause 10 shall be excluded from any calculation of time for laytime or demurrage made under any other Clause of this charter.

Periods of delay hereunder shall be cumulative for each port, and Owners may demand compensation after the vessel has been delayed for a total of 20 running days, and thereafter after each succeeding 5 running days of delay and at the end of any delay. Each such demand shall show the period in respect of which compensation is claimed and the amount due. Charterers shall pay the full amount due within 14 days after receipt of Owners' demand. Should Charterers fail to make any such payments Owners shall have the right to terminate this charter by giving written notice to Charterers or their agents, without prejudice to any claims which Charterers or Owners may have against each other under this charter or otherwise.

Laydays/ Termination

11. Should the vessel not be ready to load by noon local time on the termination date set out in Part I(C) Charterers shall have the option of terminating this charter unless the vessel has been delayed due to Charterers' change of orders pursuant to Clause 26, in which case the laydays shall be extended by the period of such delay.

However, if Owners reasonably conclude that, despite the exercise of due diligence, the vessel will not be ready to load by noon on the termination date, Owners may, as soon as they are able to state with reasonable certainty a new date when the vessel will be ready, give notice to Charterers declaring the new readiness date and asking Charterers to elect whether or not to terminate this charter. Unless Charterers within 4 days after such notice or within 2 days after the termination date (whichever is earlier) declare this charter terminated, Part I(C) shall be deemed to be amended such that the new readiness date stated shall be the commencement date and the second day thereafter shall be the termination date.

The provisions of this Clause and the exercise or non-exercise by Charterers of their option to terminate shall not prejudice any claims which Charterers or Owners may have against each other.

Laytime

12. The laytime for loading, discharging and all other Charterers' purposes whatsoever shall be the number of running hours specified in Part I(I). Charterers shall have the right to load and discharge at all times, including night, provided that they shall pay for all extra expenses incurred ashore.

Notice of readiness/ Running time

13. (1) Subject to the provisions of Clauses 13(3) and 14, if the vessel loads or discharges cargo other than by transhipment at sea

(a) Time at each loading or discharging port shall commence to run 6 hours after the vessel is in all respects ready to load or discharge and written notice thereof has been tendered by the master or Owners' agents to Charterers or their agents and the vessel is securely moored at the specified loading or discharging berth. However, if the vessel does not proceed immediately to such berth time shall commence to run 6 hours after (i) the vessel is lying in the area where she was ordered to wait or, in the absence of any such specific order, in a usual waiting area and (ii) written notice of readiness has been tendered and (iii) the specified berth is accessible. A loading or discharging berth shall be deemed inaccessible only for so long as the vessel is or would be prevented from proceeding to it by bad weather, tidal conditions, ice, awaiting daylight pilot or tugs, or port traffic control requirements (except those requirements resulting from the unavailability of such berth or of the cargo).

If Charterers fail to specify a berth at any port, the first berth at which the vessel loads or discharges the cargo or any part thereof shall be deemed to be the specified berth at such port for the purposes of this Clause.

Notice shall not be tendered before commencement of laydays and notice tendered by radio shall qualify as written notice provided it is confirmed in writing as soon as reasonably possible.

(b) Time shall continue to run
(i) until cargo hoses have been disconnected, or

(ii) if the vessel is delayed for Charterers' purposes for more than one hour after disconnection of cargo hoses, until the termination of such delay provided that if the vessel waits at any place other than the berth, time on passage to such other place, from disconnecting of hoses to remooring/anchorage at such other place, shall not count.

(2) If the vessel loads or discharges cargo by transhipment at sea time shall count from the arrival of the vessel at the transhipment area or from commencement of the laydays, whichever is later, and, subject to Clause 14(c), shall run until transhipment has been completed and the vessels have separated.

(3) Notwithstanding anything else in this Clause 13, if Charterers start loading or discharging the vessel before time would otherwise start to run under this charter, time shall run from commencement of such

loading or discharging.

(4) For the purposes of this Clause 13 and of Clause 14 "time" shall mean laytime or time counting for demurrage, as the case may be.

Suspension of time

14. Time shall not count when

(a) spent on inward passage from the vessel's waiting area to the loading or discharging berth specified by Charterers, even if lightening occurred at such waiting area; or

(b) spent in handling ballast except to the extent that cargo operations are carried on concurrently and are not delayed thereby; or

(c) lost as a result of
    (i) breach of this Charter by Owners; or
    (ii) any cause attributable to the vessel, including breakdown or inefficiency of the vessel; or
    (iii) strike, lock-out, stoppage or restraint of labour of master, officers or crew of the vessel or tug boats or pilot.

Demurrage

15. (1) Charterers shall pay demurrage at the rate specified in Part I(J).

If the demurrage rate specified in Part I(J) is expressed as a percentage of Worldscale such percentage shall be applied to the demurrage rate applicable to vessels of a similar size to the vessel as provided in Worldscale or, for the purpose of clause 10 and/or if this charter is terminated prior to the commencement of loading, in the Worldwide Tanker Nominal Freight Scale current at the termination date specified in Part I(C).

Demurrage shall be paid per running day or pro rata for part thereof for all time which, under the provisions of this charter, counts against laytime or for demurrage and which exceeds the laytime specified in Part I(I).
Charterers' liability for exceeding the laytime shall be absolute and shall not in any case be subject to the provisions of Clause 32.

(2) If, however, all or part of such demurrage arises out of or results from fire or explosion at ports of loading and/or discharging in or about the plant of Charterers, shippers or consignees of the cargo (not being a fire or explosion caused by the negligence or wilful act or omission of Charterers, shippers or consignees of the cargo or their respective servants or agents), act of God, act of war, riot, civil commotion, or arrest or restraint of princes rulers or peoples, the rate of demurrage shall be reduced by half for such demurrage or such part thereof.

(3) Owners shall notify Charterers within 60 days after completion of discharge if demurrage has been incurred and any demurrage claim together with supporting documentation shall be submitted within 90 days after completion of discharge. If Owners fail to give notice of or to submit any such claim within the time limits aforesaid, Charterers' liability for such demurrage shall be extinguished.

Vessel inspection

16. Charterers shall have the right, but no duty, to have a representative attend on board the vessel at any loading and/or discharging ports (except locations at sea) and the master and Owners shall co-operate to facilitate his inspection of the vessel and observation of cargo operations. However, such right, and the exercise or non-exercise thereof, shall in no way reduce the master's or Owners' authority over, or responsibility to Charterers and third parties for, the vessel and every aspect of her operation, nor increase Charterers' responsibilities to Owners or third parties for the same.

Cargo inspection

17. Without prejudice to Clause 2 hereof, Charterers shall have the right to require inspection of the vessel's tanks at loading and/or discharging ports (except locations at sea) to ascertain the quantity and quality of the cargo, water and residues on board. Depressurisation of the tanks to permit inspection and/or ullaging shall be carried out in accordance with the recommendations in the latest edition of the International Safety Guide for Oil Tankers and Terminals. Charterers shall also have the right to inspect and take samples from the bunker tanks and other non-cargo spaces. Any delay to the vessel caused by such inspection and measurement or associated depressurising/repressurising of tanks shall count against laytime, or if the vessel is on demurrage, for demurrage.

Cargo measurement

18. The master shall ascertain the contents of all tanks before and after loading and before and after discharging, and shall prepare tank-by-tank ullage reports of the cargo, water and residues on board which shall be promptly made available to Charterers or their representative if requested. Each such ullage report shall show actual ullage/dips, and densities at observed and standard temperature (15 deg. Celsius). All quantities shall be expressed in cubic metres at both observed and standard temperature.

Inert gas

19. The vessel's inert gas system (if any) shall comply with Regulation 62, Chapter II-2 of the 1974 Safety of Life at Sea Convention as modified by the Protocol of 1978 and Owners warrant that such system shall be operated in accordance with the guidance given in the IMO publication "Inert Gas Systems (1983)". Should the inert gas system fail, Section 8 (Emergency Procedures) of the said IMO publication shall be strictly adhered to and time lost as a consequence of such failure shall not count against laytime or, if the vessel is on demurrage, for demurrage.

Crude oil washing

20. If the vessel is equipped for crude oil washing Charterers shall have the right to require the vessel to crude oil wash those tanks in which the cargo is carried. If crude oil washing is required by Charterers or any competent authority, any additional discharging time thereby incurred shall count against laytime or, if the vessel is on demurrage, for demurrage, and the number of hours specified in Part I(A)(vii) shall be increased by 0.75 hours per cargo tank washed.

Over age insurance

21. Any additional insurance on the cargo required because of the age of the vessel shall be for Owners' account.

Ice

22. The vessel shall not be required to force ice or to follow icebreakers. If the master finds that a nominated port is inaccessible due to ice, the master shall immediately notify Charterers requesting revised orders and shall remain outside the ice-bound area; and if after arrival at a nominated port there is danger of the vessel being frozen in, the vessel shall proceed to the nearest safe and ice free position and at the same time request Charterers to give revised orders.

In either case if the affected port is
(i) the first or only loading port and no cargo has been loaded, Charterers shall either nominate another port, or give notice cancelling this charter in which case they shall pay at the demurrage rate in Part I(J)

Appendix 9

for the time from the master's notification aforesaid or from notice of readiness on arrival, as the case may be, until the time such cancellation notice is given;

(ii)   a loading port and part of the cargo has been loaded, Charterers shall either nominate another port, or order the vessel to proceed on the voyage without completing loading in which case Charterers shall pay for any deadfreight arising therefrom;

(iii)   a discharging port, Charterers shall either nominate another port or order the vessel to proceed to or return to and discharge at the nominated port. If the vessel is ordered to proceed to or return to a nominated port, Charterers shall bear the risk of the vessel being damaged whilst proceeding to or returning to or at such port, and the whole period from the time when the master's request for revised orders is received by Charterers until the vessel can safely depart after completion of discharge shall count against laytime or, if the vessel is on demurrage, for demurrage.

If, as a consequence of Charterers revising orders pursuant to this clause, the nominated port(s) or the number or rotation of ports is changed, freight shall nevertheless be paid for the voyage which the vessel would otherwise have performed had the orders not been so revised, such freight to be increased or reduced by the amount by which, as a result of such revision of orders,

(a)   the time used including any time awaiting revised orders (which shall be valued at the demurrage rate in Part I(J)),

(b)   the bunkers consumed (which shall be valued at the bunker costs at the port at which bunkers were last taken) and

(c)   the port charges

for the voyage actually performed are greater or less than those that would have been incurred on the voyage which, but for the revised orders under this Clause, the vessel would have performed.

Quarantine   23.   Time lost due to quarantine shall not count against laytime or for demurrage unless such quarantine was in force at the time when the affected port was nominated by Charterers.

Agency   24.   The vessel's agents shall be nominated by Charterers at nominated ports of loading and discharging.

Such agents, although nominated by Charterers, shall be employed and paid by Owners.

Charterers' obligation at shallow draft port/ Lightening in port   25.   (1)   (a)   If the vessel, with the quantity of cargo then on board, is unable due to inadequate depth of water in the port safely to reach any specified discharging berth and discharge the cargo there always safely afloat, Charterers shall specify a location within port limits where the vessel can discharge sufficient cargo into vessels or lighters to enable the vessel safely to reach and discharge cargo at such discharging berth, and the vessel shall lighten at such location.

(b)   If the vessel is lightened pursuant to Clause 25(1)(a) then, for the purposes of the calculation of laytime and demurrage, the lightening place shall be treated as the first discharging berth within the port where such lightening occurs.

Charterers' orders/ Change of orders/ Part cargo transhipment   26.   (1)   If, after loading and/or discharging ports have been nominated, Charterers wish to vary such nominations or their rotation, Charterers may give revised orders subject to Part I(D) and/or (E), as the case may be. Charterers shall reimburse Owners at the demurrage rate provided in Part I(J) for any deviation or delay which may result therefrom and shall pay at replacement price for any extra bunkers consumed.

Charterers shall not be liable for any other loss or expense which is caused by such variation unless promptly on receipt of the revised orders Owners notify Charterers of the expectation of such loss or expense in which case, unless Charterers promptly revoke such orders, Charterers shall be liable to reimburse Owners for any such loss or expense proven.

(2)   Subject to Clause 33(6), Charterers may order the vessel to load and/or discharge any part of the cargo by transhipment at sea in the vicinity of any nominated port or en route between two nominated ports, in which case Charterers shall reimburse Owners at the demurrage rate specified in Part I(J) for any additional steaming time and/or delay which may be incurred as a consequence of proceeding to and from the location at sea of such transhipment and, in addition, Charterers shall pay at replacement price for any extra bunkers consumed.

Heating of cargo   27.   If Charterers require cargo heating the vessel shall, on passage to and whilst at discharging port(s), maintain the cargo at the loaded temperature or at the temperature stated in Part I(A)(iv), whichever is the lower. Charterers may request that the temperature of the cargo be raised above or lowered below that at which it was loaded, in which event Owners shall use their best endeavours to comply with such request and Charterers shall pay at replacement price for any additional bunkers consumed and any consequential delay to the vessel shall count against laytime or, if the vessel is on demurrage, for demurrage.

ETA   28.   Owners undertake that, unless Charterers require otherwise, the master shall:

(a)   advise Charterers by radio immediately on leaving the final port of call on the previous voyage or within 48 hours after the time and date of this charter, whichever is the later, of the time and date of the vessel's expected arrival at the first loading port or, if the loading range is in the Arabian Gulf, the time of her expected arrival off Quoin Island;

(b)   confirm or amend such advice not later than 72 hours and again not later than 24 hours before the vessel is due at the first loading port or, in the case of a loading range in the Arabian Gulf, off Quoin Island;

(c)   advise Charterers by radio immediately after departure from the final loading port, of the vessel's expected time of arrival at the first discharging port or the area at sea to which the vessel has been instructed to proceed for wireless orders, and confirm or amend such advice not later than 72 hours and again not later than 24 hours before the vessel is due at such port or area;

(d)   immediately radio any variation of more than six hours from expected times of arrival at loading or discharging ports, Quoin Island or such area at sea to Charterers;

(e)   address all radio messages in accordance with Part I(K).

Owners shall be responsible for any consequences or additional expenses arising as a result of non-compliance with this Clause.

Packed cargo   29.   Charterers have the option of shipping products and/or general cargo in available dry cargo space, the quantity being subject to the master's discretion. Freight shall be payable at the bulk rate in accordance with Clause 5 and Charterers shall pay in addition all expenses incurred solely as a result of the packed cargo being carried. Delay occasioned to the vessel by the exercise of such option shall count against laytime or, if the vessel is on demurrage, for demurrage.

Appendix 9

Subletting/ Assignment

30. Charterers shall have the option of sub-chartering the vessel and/or of assigning this charter to any person or persons, but Charterers shall always remain responsible for the due fulfilment of all the terms and conditions of this charter.

Liberty

31. The vessel shall be at liberty to tow or be towed, to assist vessels in all positions of distress, to call at any port or ports for bunkers, to sail without pilots, and to deviate for the purpose of saving life or property or for the purpose of embarking or disembarking persons spares or supplies by helicopter or for any other reasonable purpose.

Exceptions

32. (a) The vessel, her master and Owners shall not, unless otherwise in this charter expressly provided, be liable for any loss or damage or delay or failure arising or resulting from any act, neglect or default of the master, pilots, mariners or other servants of Owners in the navigation or management of the vessel; fire unless caused by the actual fault or privity of Owners; collision or stranding; dangers and accidents of the sea; explosion, bursting of boilers, breakage of shafts or any latent defect in hull, equipment or machinery; provided, however, that Part I(A) and Clauses I and 2 hereof shall be unaffected by the foregoing. Further, neither the vessel, her master or Owners, nor Charterers shall, unless otherwise in this charter expressly provided, be liable for any loss or damage or delay or failure in performance hereunder arising or resulting from act of God, act of war, act of public enemies, seizure under legal process, quarantine restrictions, strikes, lock-outs, restraints of labour, riots, civil commotions or arrest or restraint of princes rulers or people.

(b) Nothing in this charter shall be construed as in any way restricting, excluding or waiving the right of Owners or of any other relevant persons to limit their liability under any available legislation or law.

(c) Clause 32(a) shall not apply to or affect any liability of Owners or the vessel or any other relevant person in respect of
- (i) loss of or damage caused to any berth, jetty, dock, dolphin, buoy, mooring line, pipe or crane or other works or equipment whatsoever at or near any port to which the vessel may proceed under this charter, whether or not such works or equipment belong to Charterers. or
- (ii) any claim (whether brought by Charterers or any other person) arising out of any loss of or damage to or in connection with the cargo. Any such claim shall be subject to the Hague-Visby Rules or the Hague Rules, as the case may be, which ought pursuant to Clause 37 hereof to have been incorporated in the relevant bill of lading (whether or not such Rules were so incorporated), or, if no such bill of lading is issued, to the Hague-Visby Rules.

Bills of lading

33. (1) Subject to the provisions of this Clause Charterers may require the master to sign lawful bills of lading for any cargo in such form as Charterers direct.

(2) The signing of bills of lading shall be without prejudice to this charter and Charterers hereby indemnify Owners against all liabilities that may arise from signing bills of lading to the extent that the same impose liabilities upon Owners in excess of or beyond those imposed by this charter.

(3) All bills of lading presented to the master for signature, in addition to complying with the requirements of Clauses 35, 36 and 37, shall include or effectively incorporate clauses substantially similar to the terms of Clauses 22, 33(7) and 34.

(4) All bills of lading presented for signature hereunder shall show a named port of discharge. If when bills of lading are presented for signature discharging port(s) have been nominated hereunder, the discharging port(s) shown on such bills of lading shall be in conformity with the nominated port(s). If at the time of such presentation no such nomination has been made hereunder, the discharging port(s) shown on such bills of lading must be within Part I(E) and shall be deemed to have been nominated hereunder by virtue of such presentation.

(5) Article III Rules 3 and 5 of the Hague-Visby Rules shall apply to the particulars included in the bills of lading as if Charterers were the shippers, and the guarantee and indemnity therein contained shall apply to the description of the cargo furnished by or on behalf of Charterers.

(6) Notwithstanding any other provisions of this charter, Owners shall not be obliged to comply with any orders from Charterers to discharge all or part of the cargo
- (i) at any port other than that shown on the bills of lading (except as provided in Clauses 22 or 34) and/or
- (ii) without presentation of an original bill of lading

unless they have received from Charterers both written confirmation of such orders and an indemnity acceptable to Owners.

(7) The master shall not be required or bound to sign bills of lading for any blockaded port or for any port which the master or Owners in his or their discretion consider dangerous or impossible to enter or reach.

(8) Charterers hereby warrant that on each and every occasion that they issue orders under Clauses 22, 26, 34 or 38 they will have the authority of the holders of the bills of lading to give such orders, and that such bills of lading will not be transferred to any person who does not concur therein.

War risks

34. (1) If
- (a) any loading or discharging port to which the vessel may properly be ordered under the provisions of this charter or bills of lading issued pursuant to this charter be blockaded, or
- (b) owing to any war, hostilities, warlike operation, civil commotions, revolutions, or the operation of international law (i) entry to any such loading or discharging port or the loading or discharging of cargo at any such port be considered by the master or Owners in his or their discretion dangerous or prohibited or (ii) it be considered by the master or Owners in his or their discretion dangerous or impossible or prohibited for the vessel to reach any such loading or discharging port,

Charterers shall have the right to order the cargo or such part of it as may be affected to be loaded or discharged at any other loading or discharging port within the ranges specified in Part I(D) or (E) respectively (provided such other port is not blockaded and that entry thereto or loading or discharging of cargo thereat or reaching the same is not in the master's or Owners' opinion dangerous or impossible or prohibited).

(2) If no orders be received from Charterers within 48 hours after they or their agents have received from Owners a request for the nomination of a substitute port, then

    (a) if the affected port is the first or only loading port and no cargo has been loaded, this charter shall terminate forthwith;

    (b) if the affected port is a loading port and part of the cargo has already been loaded, the vessel may proceed on passage and Charterers shall pay for any deadfreight so incurred;

    (c) if the affected port is a discharging port, Owners shall be at liberty to discharge the cargo at any port which they or the master may in their or his discretion decide on (whether within the range specified in Part I(E) or not) and such discharging shall be deemed to be due fulfilment of the contract or contracts of affreightment so far as cargo so discharged is concerned.

(3) If in accordance with Clause 34(1) or (2) cargo is loaded or discharged at any such other port, freight shall be paid as for the voyage originally nominated, such freight to be increased or reduced by the amount by which, as a result of loading or discharging at such other port,

    (a) the time on voyage including any time awaiting revised orders (which shall be valued at the demurrage rate in Part I(J)),

    (b) the bunkers consumed (which shall be valued at the bunker costs at the port at which bunkers were last taken), and

    (c) the port charges

for the voyage actually performed are greater or less than those which would have been incurred on the voyage originally nominated. Save as aforesaid, the voyage actually performed shall be treated for the purpose of this Charter as if it were the voyage originally nominated.

(4) The vessel shall have liberty to comply with any directions or recommendations as to departure, arrival, routes, ports of call, stoppages, destinations, zones, waters, delivery or in any otherwise whatsoever given by the government of the nation under whose flag the vessel sails or any other government or local authority including any de facto government or local authority or by any person or body acting or purporting to act as or with the authority of any such government or authority or by any committee or person having under the terms of the war risks insurance on the vessel the right to give any such directions or recommendations. If by reason of or in compliance with any such directions or recommendations anything is done or is not done, such shall not be deemed a deviation.

If by reason of or in compliance with any such directions or recommendations the vessel does not proceed to the discharging port or ports originally nominated or to which she may have been properly ordered under the provisions of this charter or bills of lading issued pursuant to this charter, the vessel may proceed to any discharging port on which the master or Owners in his or their discretion may decide and there discharge the cargo. Such discharging shall be deemed to be due fulfilment of the contract or contracts of affreightment and Owners shall be entitled to freight as if discharging had been effected at the port or ports originally nominated or to which the vessel may have been properly ordered under the provisions of this charter or bills of lading issued pursuant to this charter. All extra expenses involved in reaching and discharging the cargo at any such other discharging port shall be paid by Charterers and Owners shall have a lien on the cargo for all such extra expenses.

Both to blame clause

35. If the liability for any collision in which the vessel is involved while performing this charter falls to be determined in accordance with the laws of the United States of America, the following clause, which shall be included in all bills of lading issued pursuant to this charter shall apply:-

"If the vessel comes into collision with another vessel as a result of the negligence of the other vessel and any act, neglect or default of the master, mariner, pilot or the servants of the Carrier in the navigation or in the management of the vessel, the owners of the cargo carried hereunder will indemnify the Carrier against all loss or liability to the other or non-carrying vessel or her owners in so far as such loss or liability represents loss of, or damage to, or any claim whatsoever of the owners of the said cargo, paid or payable by the other or non-carrying vessel or her owners to the owners of the said cargo and set off, recouped or recovered by the other or non-carrying vessel or her owners as part of their claim against the carrying vessel or the Carrier.

The foregoing provisions shall also apply where the owners, operators or those in charge of any vessel or vessels or objects other than, or in addition to, the colliding vessels or objects are at fault in respect of a collision or contact."

General average/ New Jason Clause

36. General average shall be payable according to the York/Antwerp Rules, 1974, and shall be adjusted in London, but should the adjustment be made in accordance with the law and practice of the United States of America, the following clause, which shall be included in all bills of lading issued pursuant to this charter, shall apply:-

"In the event of accident, danger, damage or disaster before or after the commencement of the voyage, resulting from any cause whatsoever, whether due to negligence or not, for which, or for the consequence of which, the Carrier is not responsible, by statute, contract or otherwise, the cargo, shippers, consignees or owners of the cargo shall contribute with the Carrier in general average to the payment of any sacrifices, losses or expenses of a general average nature that may be made or incurred and shall pay salvage and special charges incurred in respect of the cargo.

If a salving vessel is owned or operated by the Carrier, salvage shall be paid for as fully as if the said salving vessel or vessels belonged to strangers. Such deposit as the Carrier or its agents may deem sufficient to cover the estimated contribution of the cargo and any salvage and special charges thereon shall, if required, be made by the cargo, shippers, consignees or owners of the cargo to the Carrier before delivery."

Clause paramount

37. The following clause shall be included in all bills of lading issued pursuant to this charter:-

"CLAUSE PARAMOUNT

(1) Subject to sub-clause (2) hereof, this bill of lading shall be governed by, and have effect subject to, the rules contained in the International Convention for the Unification of Certain Rules relating to Bills of Lading signed at Brussels on 25th August 1924 (hereafter the "Hague Rules") as amended by the Protocol signed at Brussels on 23rd February 1968 (hereafter the "Hague-Visby Rules"). Nothing herein contained shall be deemed to be either a surrender by the Carrier of any of his rights or immunities or an increase of any of his responsibilities or liabilities under the Hague-Visby Rules.

Appendix 9

(2) If there is governing legislation which applies the Hague Rules compulsorily to this bill of lading, to the exclusion of the Hague-Visby Rules, then this bill of lading shall have effect subject to the Hague Rules. Nothing herein contained shall be deemed to be either a surrender by the Carrier of any of his rights or immunities or an increase of any of his responsibilities or liabilities under the Hague Rules.

(3) If any term of this bill of lading is repugnant to the Hague-Visby Rules, or the Hague Rules if applicable, such term shall be void to that extent but no further.

(4) Nothing in this bill of lading shall be construed as in any way restricting, excluding or waiving the right of any relevant party or person to limit his liability under any available legislation and/or law."

Back loading

38. Charterers may order the vessel to load a part cargo at any nominated discharging port, and to discharge such part cargo at a port(s) to be nominated by Charterers within the range specified in Part I(E) and within the rotation of the discharging ports previously nominated, provided that such part cargo is of the description specified in Part I(F) and that the master in his absolute discretion determines that this cargo can be loaded, segregated and discharged without risk of contamination by, or of, any other cargo remaining on board.

Charterers shall pay a lump sum freight in respect of such part cargo calculated at the demurrage rate specified in Part I(J) on any additional time used by the vessel as a result of loading, carrying or discharging such part cargo.

Any additional expenses, including port charges, incurred as a result of loading or discharging such part cargo shall be for Charterers' account.

Bunkers

39. Owners shall give Charterers or any other company in the Royal Dutch/Shell Group of Companies first option to quote for the supply of bunker requirements for the performance of this charter.

Oil pollution prevention

40. (1) Owners shall ensure that the master shall:-
  (a) comply with MARPOL 73/78 including in particular and without limitation Regulation 9, Chapter II of the International Convention for the Prevention of Pollution from Ships 1973;
  (b) collect the drainings and any tank washings into a suitable tank or tanks and, after maximum separation of free water, discharge the bulk of such water overboard, consistent with the above regulations; and
  (c) thereafter notify Charterers promptly of the amounts of oil and free water so retained on board and details of any other washings retained on board from earlier voyages (together called the "collected washings").

(2) On being so notified, Charterers, in accordance with their rights under this Clause (which shall include without limitation the right to determine the disposal of the collected washings), shall before the vessel's arrival at the loading berth (or if already arrived as soon as possible thereafter) give instructions as to how the collected washings shall be dealt with. Owners shall ensure that the master on the vessel's arrival at the loading berth (or if already arrived as soon as possible thereafter) shall arrange in conjunction with the cargo suppliers for the measurement of the quantity of the collected washings and shall record the same in the vessel's ullage record.

(3) Charterers may require the collected washings to be discharged ashore at the loading port, in which case no freight shall be payable on them.

(4) Alternatively Charterers may require either that the cargo be loaded on top of the collected washings and the collected washings be discharged with the cargo, or that they be kept separate from the cargo in which case Charterers shall pay for any deadfreight incurred thereby in accordance with Clause 8 and shall, if practicable, accept discharge of the collected washings at the discharging port or ports.

In either case, provided that the master has reduced the free water in the collected washings to a minimum consistent with the retention on board of the oil residues in them and consistent with sub-Clause (1)(a) above, freight in accordance with Clause 5 shall be payable on the quantity of the collected washings as if such quantity were included in a bill of lading and the figure therefor furnished by the shipper provided, however, that
  (i) if there is provision in this charter for a lower freight rate to apply to cargo in excess of an agreed quantity, freight on the collected washings shall be paid at such lower rate (provided such agreed quantity of cargo has been loaded) and
  (ii) if there is provision in this charter for a minimum cargo quantity which is less than a full cargo, then whether or not such minimum cargo quantity is furnished, freight on the collected washings shall be paid as if such minimum cargo quantity had been furnished, provided that no freight shall be payable in respect of any collected washings which are kept separate from the cargo and not discharged at the discharge port.

(5) Whenever Charterers require the collected washings to be discharged ashore pursuant to this Clause, Charterers shall provide and pay for the reception facilities, and the cost of any shifting therefor shall be for Charterers' account. Any time lost discharging the collected washings and/or shifting therefor shall count against laytime or, if the vessel is on demurrage, for demurrage.

TOVALOP

41. Owners warrant that the vessel:
  (i) is a tanker owned by a Participating Owner in TOVALOP
      and
  (ii) is entered in the P&I Club stated in Part I(A)(xii)
and will so remain during the currency of this charter.

When an escape or discharge of Oil occurs from the vessel and causes or threatens to cause Pollution Damage, or when there is the Threat of an escape or discharge of Oil (i.e. a grave and imminent danger of the escape or discharge of Oil which, if it occurred, would create a serious danger of Pollution Damage, whether or not an escape or discharge in fact subsequently occurs), then Charterers may, at their option upon notice to Owners or master, undertake such measures as are reasonably necessary to prevent or minimise such Pollution Damage or to remove the Threat, unless Owners promptly undertake the same. Charterers shall keep Owners advised of the nature and result of any such measures taken by them and, if time permits, the nature of the measures intended to be taken by them. Any of the aforementioned measures taken by Charterers shall be deemed taken on Owners' authority and as Owners' agents, and shall be at Owners' expense except to the extent

Appendix 9

that:

   (1)   any such escape or discharge or Threat was caused or contributed to by Charterers, or

   (2)   by reason of the exceptions set out in Article III, paragraph 2, of the 1969 International Convention on Civil Liability for Oil Pollution Damage or any protocol thereto, Owners are or, had the said Convention applied to such escape or discharge or to the Threat, would have been, exempt from liability for the same, or

   (3)   the cost of such measures together with all other liabilities, costs and expenses of Owners arising out of or in connection with such escape or discharge or Threat exceeds the maximum liability applicable to the vessel under TOVALOP as at the time of such escape or discharge or threat, save and insofar as Owners shall be entitled to recover such excess under either the 1971 International Convention on the Establishment of an International Fund for Compensation for Oil Pollution Damage or under CRISTAL

PROVIDED ALWAYS that if Owners in their absolute discretion consider said measures should be discontinued. Owners shall so notify Charterers and thereafter Charterers shall have no right to continue said measures under the provisions of this Clause and all further liability to Charterers under this Clause shall thereupon cease.

The above provisions are not in derogation of such other rights as Charterers or Owners may have under this charter or may otherwise have or acquire by law or any international convention or TOVALOP.

The term "TOVALOP" means the Tanker Owners' Voluntary Agreement Concerning Liability for Oil Pollution dated 7th January 1969, as amended from time to time, and the term "CRISTAL" means the Contract Regarding an Interim Supplement to Tanker Liability for Oil Pollution dated 14th January 1971, as amended from time to time. The terms "Participating Owner", "Oil" and, "Pollution Damage" shall for the purposes of this clause have the meanings ascribed to them in TOVALOP.

Lien   42. Owners shall have an absolute lien upon the cargo and all subfreights for all amounts due under this charter and the cost of recovery thereof including any expenses whatsoever arising from the exercise of such lien.

Law and litigation   43. (a) This charter shall be construed and the relations between the parties determined in accordance with the laws of England.

    (b) any dispute arising under this charter shall be decided by the English Courts to whose jurisdiction the parties hereby agree.

    (c) Notwithstanding the foregoing, but without prejudice to any party's right to arrest or maintain the arrest of any maritime property, either party may, by giving written notice of election to the other party, elect to have any such dispute referred to the arbitration of a single arbitrator in London in accordance with the provisions of the Arbitration Act 1950, or any statutory modification or re-enactment thereof for the time being in force.

       (i) A party shall lose its right to make such an election only if:
         (a) it receives from the other party a written notice of dispute which –
           (1) states expressly that a dispute has arisen out of this charter;
           (2) specifies the nature of the dispute; and
           (3) refers expressly to this clause 43(c) and;
         (b) it fails to give notice of election to have the dispute referred to arbitration not later than 30 days from the date of receipt of such notice of dispute.

       (ii) the parties hereby agree that either party may –
         (a) appeal to the High Court on any question of law arising out of an award;
         (b) apply to the High Court for an order that the arbitrator state the reasons for his award;
         (c) give notice to the arbitrator that a reasoned award is required; and
         (d) apply to the High Court to determine any question of law arising in the course of the reference.

    (d) It shall be a condition precedent to the right of any party to a stay of any legal proceedings in which maritime property has been, or may be, arrested in connection with a dispute under this charter, that that party furnishes to the other party security to which that other party would have been entitled in such legal proceedings in the absence of a stay.

Construction   44. The side headings have been included in this charter for convenience of reference only and shall in no way affect the construction hereof.

Typical Ship Structures

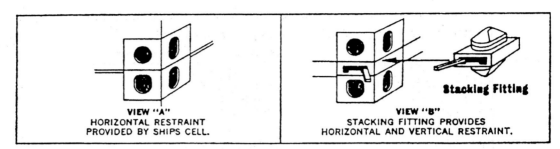

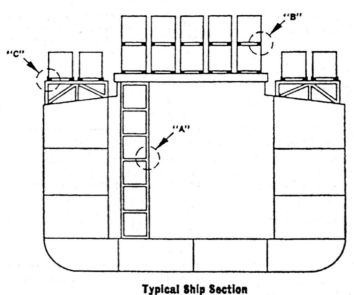

Typical Ship Section

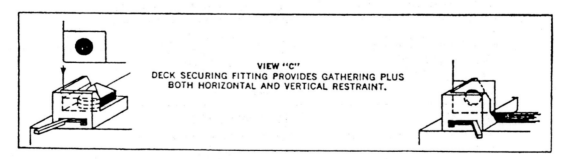

Typical use of corner fittings in shipload applications (in vertical container cells and on deck)

Containers

General Purpose Container 20'/40'

Ventilated-Container 20'

Especially for cargo which needs ventilation.

High Cube General Purpose Container 40'

Especially for light-weight, voluminous cargo.

Insulated Container 20'/40'

Especially for cargo which must be kept at a constant temperature. Temperature control via the ship's refrigeration plant, terminal refrigeration plant or a "clip-on" refrigeration unit.

Hardtop Container 20'/40'

With removable steel roof. Especially for heavy or excessively high cargo. For loading from above or from the door with door header swung out.

Reefer Container 20'/40'

With integrated refrigeration unit. Especially for cargo which must be kept at a constant temperature above or below freezing point.

Open Top Container

With removable tarpaulin. Especially for overheight cargo. Loading either from top side or door side by swung out header.

High Cube Reefer Container 40'

With integrated refrigeration unit. Especially for light weight, voluminous cargo which must be kept at a constant temperature above or below freezing point.

Flat 20'/40'

Especially for heavy cargo and especially wide cargo.

Bulk Container 20'

Especially for bulk cargo e.g. malt.

Platform 20'/40'

Especially for heavy loads and oversized cargo. Non-domestic shipments.

Tank Container 20'

Especially for liquid chemicals. Selected containers are used exclusively for the transport of liquid food stuffs.

Combined Transport Bill of Lading

Code Name: "COMBICONBILL"

Shipper

Reference No.

Negotiable

COMBINED TRANSPORT BILL OF LADING

Revised 1995

Consigned to order of

Notify party/address

Place of receipt

Ocean Vessel	Port of loading		
Port of discharge	Place of delivery	Freight payable at	Number of original Bills of Lading

Marks and Nos.	Quantity and description of goods	Gross weight, kg, Measurement, m³

Particulars above declared by Shipper

Freight and charges

RECEIVED the goods in apparent good order and condition and, as far as ascertained by reasonable means of checking, as specified above unless otherwise stated.

The Carrier, in accordance with and to the extent of the provisions contained in this Bill of Lading, and with liberty to sub-contract, undertakes to perform and/or in his own name to procure performance of the combined transport and the delivery of the goods, including all services related thereto, from the place and time of taking the goods in charge to the place and time of delivery and accepts responsibility for such transport and such services.

One of the Bills of Lading must be surrendered duly endorsed in exchange for the goods or delivery order.

IN WITNESS whereof TWO (2) original Bills of Lading have been signed, if not otherwise stated above, one of which being accomplished the other(s) to be void.

Shipper's declared value of ......

Place and date of issue

subject to payment of above extra charge.

Signed for

.... as Carrier

Note:

The Merchant's attention is called to the fact that according to Clauses 10 to 12 and Clause 24 of this Bill of Lading, the liability of the Carrier is, in most cases, limited in respect of loss of or damage to the goods and delay.

by ....

As agent(s) only to the Carrier

Appendix 12

COMBINED TRANSPORT BILL OF LADING

Adopted by The Baltic and International Maritime Council in January, 1971 (as revised 1995)

Code Name: "COMBICONBILL"

I. GENERAL PROVISIONS

1. **Applicability.**
Notwithstanding the heading "Combined Transport", the provisions set out and referred to in this Bill of Lading shall also apply, if the transport as described in this Bill of Lading is performed by one mode of transport only.

2. **Definitions.**
"Carrier" means the party on whose behalf this Bill of Lading has been signed.
"Merchant" includes the Shipper, the Receiver, the Consignor, the Consignee, the holder of this Bill of Lading and the owner of the goods.

3. **Carrier's Tariff.**
The terms of the Carrier's applicable Tariff at the date of shipment are incorporated herein. Copies of the relevant provisions of the applicable Tariff are available from the Carrier upon request. In the case of inconsistency between this Bill of Lading and the applicable Tariff, this Bill of Lading shall prevail.

4. **Time Bar.**
All liability whatsoever of the Carrier shall cease unless suit is brought within 9 months after delivery of the goods or the date when the goods should have been delivered.

5. **Law and Jurisdiction.**
Disputes arising under this Bill of Lading shall be determined by the courts and in accordance with the law at the place where the Carrier has his principal place of business.

II. PERFORMANCE OF THE CONTRACT

6. **Methods and Routes of Transportation.**
(1) The Carrier is entitled to perform the transport and all services related thereto in any reasonable manner and by any reasonable means, methods and routes.
(2) In accordance herewith, for instance, in the event of carriage by sea, vessels may sail with or without pilots, undergo repairs, adjust equipment, drydock and tow vessels in all situations.

7. **Optional Stowage.**
(1) Goods may be stowed by the Carrier by means of containers, trailers, transportable tanks, flats, pallets, or similar articles of transport used to consolidate goods.
(2) Containers, trailers, transportable tanks and covered flats, whether stowed by the Carrier or received by him in a stowed condition from the Merchant, may be carried on or under deck without notice to the Merchant.

8. **Hindrances etc. Affecting Performance.**
(1) The Carrier shall use reasonable endeavours to complete the transport and to deliver the goods at the place designated for delivery.
(2) If at any time the performance of the contract as evidenced by this Bill of Lading is or will be affected by any hindrance, risk, delay, difficulty or disadvantage of whatsoever kind, and if by virtue of sub-clause 8 (1) the Carrier has no duty to complete the performance of the contract, the Carrier (whether or not the transport is commenced) may elect to:
(a) treat the performance of this Contract as terminated and place the goods at the Merchant's disposal at any place which the Carrier shall deem safe and convenient; or
(b) deliver the goods at the place designated for delivery.
(3) If the goods are not taken delivery of by the Merchant within a reasonable time after the Carrier has called upon him to take delivery, the Carrier shall be at liberty to put the goods in safe custody on behalf of the Merchant at the latter's risk and expense.
(4) In any event the Carrier shall be entitled to full freight for goods received for transportation and additional compensation for extra costs resulting from the circumstances referred to above.

III. CARRIER'S LIABILITY

9. **Basic Liability.**
(1) The Carrier shall be liable for loss of or damage to the goods occurring between the time when he receives the goods into his charge and the time of delivery.
(2) The Carrier shall be responsible for the acts and omissions of any person of whose services he makes use for the performance of the contract of carriage evidenced by this Bill of Lading.
(3) The Carrier shall, however, be relieved of liability for any loss or damage if such loss or damage arose or resulted from:
(a) The wrongful act or neglect of the Merchant.
(b) Compliance with the instructions of the person entitled to give them.
(c) The lack of, or defective conditions of packing in the case of goods which, by their nature, are liable to wastage or to be damaged when not packed or when not properly packed.
(d) Handling, loading, stowage or unloading of the goods by or on behalf of the Merchant.
(e) Inherent vice of the goods.
(f) Insufficiency or inadequacy of marks or numbers on the goods, covering, or unit loads.
(g) Strikes or lock-outs or stoppages or restraints of labour from whatever cause whether partial or general.
(h) Any cause or event which the Carrier could not avoid and the consequence whereof he could not prevent by the exercise of reasonable diligence.
(4) Where under sub-clause 9 (3) the Carrier is not under any liability in respect of some of the factors causing the loss or damage, he shall only be liable to the extent that those factors for which he is liable under this Clause have contributed to the loss or damage.
(5) The burden of proving that the loss or damage was due to one or more of the causes or events, specified in (a), (b) and (h) of sub-clause 9 (3) shall rest upon the Carrier.
(6) When the Carrier establishes that in the circumstances of the case, the loss or damage could be attributed to one or more of the causes or events, specified in (c) to (g) of sub-clause 9 (3), it shall be presumed that it was so caused. The Merchant shall, however, be entitled to prove that the loss or damage was not, in fact, caused either wholly or partly by one or more of the causes or events.

10. **Amount of Compensation**
(1) When the Carrier is liable for compensation in respect of loss of or damage to the goods, such compensation shall be calculated by reference to the value of such goods at the place and time they are delivered to the Merchant in accordance with the contract or should have been so delivered.
(2) The value of the goods shall be fixed according to the commodity exchange price or, if there be no such price, according to the current market price or, if there be no commodity exchange price or current market price, by reference to the normal value of goods of the same kind and quality.
(3) Compensation shall not, however, exceed two Special Drawing Rights per kilogramme of gross weight of the goods lost or damaged.
(4) Higher compensation may be claimed only when, with the consent of the Carrier, the value for the goods declared by the Shipper which exceeds the limits laid down in this Clause has been stated on the face of this Bill of Lading at the place indicated. In that case the amount of the declared value shall be substituted for that limit.

11. **Special Provisions for Liability and Compensation**
(1) Notwithstanding anything provided for in Clauses 9 and 10 of this Bill of Lading, if it can be proved where the loss or damage occurred, the Carrier and the Merchant shall, as to the liability of the Carrier, be entitled to require such liability to be determined by the provisions contained in any international convention or national law, which provisions:
(a) cannot be departed from by private contract, to the detriment of the claimant, and
(b) would have applied if the Merchant had made a separate and direct contract with the Carrier in respect of the particular stage of transport where the loss or damage occurred and received as evidence thereof any particular document which must be issued if such international convention or national law shall apply.
(2) Insofar as there is no mandatory law applying to carriage by sea by virtue of the provisions of sub-clause 11 (1), the liability of the Carrier in respect of any carriage by sea shall be determined by the International Brussels Convention 1924 as amended by the Protocol signed at Brussels on February 23rd 1968 – The Hague/Visby Rules. The Hague/Visby Rules shall also determine the liability of the Carrier in respect of carriage by inland waterways as if such carriage were carriage by sea. Furthermore, they shall apply to all goods, whether carried on deck or under deck.

12. **Delay, Consequential Loss, etc.**
If the Carrier is held liable in respect of delay, consequential loss or damage other than loss of or damage to the goods, the liability of the Carrier shall be limited to the freight for the transport covered by this Bill of Lading, or to the value of the goods as determined in Clause 10, whichever is the lesser.

13. **Notice of Loss of or Damage to the Goods**
(1) Unless notice of loss of or damage to the goods, specifying the general nature of such loss or damage, is given in writing by the Merchant to the Carrier when the goods are handed over to the Merchant, such handing over is *prima facie* evidence of the Delivery by the Carrier of the goods as described in this Bill of Lading.
(2) Where the loss or damage is not apparent, the same *prima facie* effect shall apply if notice in writing is not given within three (3) consecutive days after the day when the goods were handed over to the Merchant.

14. **Defences and Limits for the Carrier, Servants, etc.**
(1) The defences and limits of liability provided for in this Bill of Lading shall apply in any action against the Carrier for loss or damage to the goods whether the action can be founded in contract or in tort.
(2) The Carrier shall not be entitled to the benefit of the limitation of liability provided for in sub-clause 10 (3), if it is proved that the loss or damage resulted from a personal act or omission of the Carrier done with intent to cause such loss or damage or recklessly and with knowledge that damage would probably result.
(3) The Merchant undertakes that no claim shall be made against any servant, agent or other persons whose services the Carrier has used in order to perform this Contract and if any claim should nevertheless be made, to indemnify the Carrier against all consequences thereof.
(4) However, the provisions of this Bill of Lading apply whenever claims relating to the performance of this Contract are made against any servant, agent or other person whose services the Carrier has used in order to perform this Contract, whether such claims are founded in contract or in tort. In entering into this Contract, the Carrier, to the extent of such provisions, does so not only on his own behalf but also as agent or trustee for such persons. The aggregate liability of the Carrier and such persons shall not exceed the limits in Clauses 10, 11 and 24, respectively.

IV. DESCRIPTION OF GOODS

15. **Carrier's Responsibility.**
The information in this Bill of Lading shall be *prima facie* evidence of the taking in charge by the Carrier of the goods as described by such information unless a contrary indication, such as "shipper's weight, load and count", "Shipper-packed container" or similar expressions, have been made in the printed text or superimposed on the Bill of Lading. Proof to the contrary shall not be admissible when the Bill of Lading has been transferred, or the equivalent electronic data interchange message has been transmitted to and acknowledged by the Consignee who in good faith has relied and acted thereon.

16. **Shipper's Responsibility.**
The Shipper shall be deemed to have guaranteed to the Carrier the accuracy, at the time the goods were taken in charge by the Carrier, of the description of the goods, marks, number, quantity and weight, as furnished by him, and the Shipper shall defend, indemnify and hold harmless the Carrier against all loss, damage and expenses arising or resulting from inaccuracies in or inadequacy of such particulars. The right of the Carrier to such indemnity shall in no way limit his responsibility and liability under this Bill of Lading to any person other than the Shipper. The Shipper shall remain liable even if the Bill of Lading has been transferred by him.

17. **Shipper-packed Containers, etc.**
(1) If a container has not been filled, packed or stowed by the Carrier, the Carrier shall not be liable for any loss of or damage to its contents and the Merchant shall cover any loss or expense incurred by the Carrier, if such loss, damage or expense has been caused by:
(a) negligent filling, packing or stowing of the container;
(b) the contents being unsuitable for carriage in container; or
(c) the unsuitability or defective condition of the container unless the container has been supplied by the Carrier and the unsuitability or defective condition would not have been apparent upon reasonable inspection at or prior to the time when the container was filled, packed or stowed.
(2) The provisions of sub-clause (1) of this Clause also apply with respect to trailers, transportable tanks, flats and pallets which have not been filled, packed or stowed by the Carrier.
(3) The Carrier does not accept liability for damage due to the unsuitability or defective condition of reefer equipment or trailers supplied by the Merchant.

18. **Dangerous Goods.**
(1) The Merchant shall comply with all internationally recognised requirements and all rules which apply according to national law or by reason of international Convention, relating to the carriage of goods of a dangerous nature, and shall in any event inform the Carrier in writing of the exact nature of the danger before goods of a dangerous nature are taken into charge by the Carrier and indicate to him, if need be, the precautions to be taken.
(2) Goods of a dangerous nature which the Carrier did not know were dangerous, may, at any time or place, be unloaded, destroyed, or rendered harmless, without compensation; further, the Merchant shall be liable for all expenses, loss or damage arising out of their handing over for carriage or of their carriage.
(3) If any goods shipped with the knowledge of the Carrier as to their dangerous nature shall become a danger to any person or property, they may in like manner be landed at any place or destroyed or rendered innocuous by the Carrier without liability on the part of the Carrier except to General Average, if any.

19. **Return of Containers**
(1) For the purpose of this Clause the Consignor shall mean the person who concludes this Contract with the Carrier and the Consignee shall mean the person entitled to receive the goods from the Carrier.
(2) Containers, pallets or similar articles of transport supplied by or on behalf of the Carrier shall be returned to the Carrier in the same order and condition as handed over to the Merchant, normal wear and tear excepted, with interiors clean and within the time prescribed in the Carrier's tariff or elsewhere.
(3) (a) The Consignor shall be liable for any loss of, damage to, or delay, including demurrage, of such articles, incurred during the period between handing over to the Consignor and return to the Carrier for carriage.
(b) The Consignor and the Consignee shall be jointly and severally liable for any loss of, damage to, or delay, including demurrage, of such articles, incurred during the period between handing over to the Consignee and return to the Carrier.

V. FREIGHT AND LIEN

20. **Freight.**
(1) Freight shall be deemed earned when the goods have been taken in charge by the Carrier and shall be paid in any event.
(2) The Merchant's attention is drawn to the stipulations concerning currency in which the freight and charges are to be paid, rate of exchange, devaluation and other contingencies relative to freight and charges in the relevant tariff conditions. If no such stipulation as to devaluation exists or is applicable the following shall apply:
If the currency in which freight and charges are quoted is devalued between the date of the freight agreement and the date when the freight and charges are paid, then all freight and charges shall be automatically and immediately increased in proportion to the extent of the devaluation of the said currency.
(3) For the purpose of verifying the freight basis, the Carrier reserves the right to have the contents of containers, trailers or similar articles of tranport inspected in order to ascertain the weight, measurement, value, or nature of the goods.

21. **Lien.**
The Carrier shall have a lien on the goods for any amount due under this Contract and for the costs of recovering the same, and may enforce such lien in any reasonable manner, including sale or disposal of the goods.

VI. MISCELLANEOUS PROVISIONS

22. **General Average.**
(1) General Average shall be adjusted at any port or place at the Carrier's option, and to be settled according to the York-Antwerp Rules 1994, or any modification thereof, this covering all goods, whether carried on or under deck. The New Jason Clause as approved by BIMCO to be considered as incorporated herein.
(2) Such security including a cash deposit as the Carrier may deem sufficient to cover the estimated contribution of the goods and any salvage and special charges thereon, shall, if required, be submitted to the Carrier prior to delivery of the goods.

23. **Both-to-Blame Collision Clause.**
The Both-to-Blame Collision Clause as adopted by BIMCO shall be considered incorporated herein.

24. **U.S. Trade**
(1) In case the contract evidenced by this Bill of Lading is subject to the Carriage of Goods by Sea Act of the United States of America, 1936 (U.S. COGSA), then the provisions stated in the said Act shall govern before loading and after discharge and throughout the entire time the goods are in the Carrier's custody.
(2) If the U.S. COGSA applies, and unless the nature and value of the goods have been declared by the shipper before the goods have been handed over to the Carrier and inserted in this Bill of Lading, the Carrier shall in no event be or become liable for any loss of or damage to the goods in an amount exceeding USD 500 per package or customary freight unit.

Liner Booking Note

Shipper (if known at time of booking)	**BIMCO BLANK BACK FORM OF LINER BOOKING NOTE**
	Place and date
Consignee (if known at time of booking)	Name of Merchant effecting the booking
	Name of Carrier
Notify address at place of delivery	Merchant's representatives at loading port
	Time for shipment (about)
Place of receipt by pre-carrier*	It is hereby agreed that this Contract shall be performed subject to the terms contained in this Booking Note and in the Carrier's Standard Conditions of Carriage, which shall prevail over any previous arrangements and which shall in turn be superseded (except as to deadfreight and demurrage) by the terms of the Bill of Lading. Copies of Carrier's Standard Conditions of Carriage, if any, can be obtained upon request from the Carrier or his agents.
Vessel Port of loading**	
Port of discharge Place of delivery by on-carrier*	

Marks and Nos. (if available)	Description of goods	Gross weight (if available)	Measurement (if available)

Freight details, charges, etc.	Special terms, if agreed	
Daily demurrage rate (if agreed)	Freight (state prepayable or payable at destination)	Signature (Merchant)
	Number of original Bs/L required	Signature (Carrier)

*Applicable only when Through Transport foreseen

**(or so near thereunto as the vessel may safely get and lie always afloat)

Appendix 14

Sea Waybill

Consignee (not to order)
_____

Notify address
_____

Pre-carriage by*	Place of receipt by pre-carrier*

Vessel	Port of loading

Port of discharge	Place of delivery by on-carrier*

Marks and Nos.	Number and kind of packages; description of goods	Gross weight	Measurement

Particulars furnished by the Merchant

Freight details, charges etc.	
	RECEIVED for carriage the goods as specified above according to Shipper's declaration in apparent good order and condition – unless otherwise stated herein – weight, measure, marks, numbers, quality, contents and value unknown.
	The goods shipped under this Liner Waybill will be delivered to the Party named as Consignee or its authorised agent, on production of proof of identity without any documentary formalities. Carrier to excercise due care ensuring that delivery is made to the proper party. However, in case of incorrect delivery, no responsibility will be accepted unless due to fault or neglect on the part of the Carrier.
	This Liner Waybill which is not a document of title to the goods is deemed to be a contract of carriage which is subject to the exeptions, limitations, conditions and liberties (including those relating to pre-carriage and on-carriage) set out in the Carrier's Standard Conditions of Carriage applicable to the voyage covered by this Liner Waybill and operative on its date of issue. If the Carrier does not have Standard Conditions of Carriage, this Liner Waybill is subject to the exceptions, limitations, conditions and liberties as set out on Page 1 of the "Conlinebill" Liner Bill of Lading operative on its date of issue.
	The "Conlinebill" Liner Bill of Lading and the Carrier's Standard Conditions of Carriage incorporate or are deemed to incorporate the Hague Rules contained in the Brussels Convention dated 25th August 1924 and any compulsorily applicable national enactment of either the Hague Rules as such or as amended by the Hague-Visby Rules contained in the Brussels Protocol dated 23rd February 1968.
	A copy of the Carrier's Standard Conditions of Carriage applicable hereto may be inspected or will be supplied on request at the office of the Carrier or the Carrier's Principal agents.
	Every reference in the Carrier's Standard Conditions of Carriage or in the "Conlinebill" Liner Bill of Lading to the words "Bill of Lading" shall be read and construed as a reference to the words "Non-Negotiable Liner Waybill" and the terms and conditions thereof shall be read and construed accordingly.

Daily demurrage rate (if agreed)	Freight payable at	Place and date of issue
		Signature

* Applicable only when document used as a Through Liner Waybill

Appendix 15

Ship Management Agreement

1. Date of Agreement	THE BALTIC AND INTERNATIONAL MARITIME COUNCIL (BIMCO) STANDARD SHIP MANAGEMENT AGREEMENT CODE NAME: "SHIPMAN 98"
2. Owners (name, place of registered office and law of registry) (Cl. 1) Name Place of registered office Law of registry	3. Managers (name, place of registered office and law of registry) (Cl. 1) Name Place of registered office Law of registry
4. Day and year of commencement of Agreement (Cl. 2)	
5. Crew Management (state "yes" or "no" as agreed) (Cl. 3.1)	6. Technical Management (state "yes" or "no" as agreed) (Cl. 3.2)
7. Commercial Management (state "yes" or "no" as agreed) (Cl. 3.3)	8. Insurance Arrangements (state "yes" or "no" as agreed) (Cl. 3.4)
9. Accounting Services (state "yes" or "no" as agreed) (Cl. 3.5)	10. Sale or purchase of the Vessel (state "yes" or "no" as agreed) (Cl. 3.6)
11. Provisions (state "yes" or "no" as agreed) (Cl. 3.7)	12. Bunkering (state "yes" or "no" as agreed) (Cl. 3.8)
13. Chartering Services Period (only to be filled in if "yes" stated in Box 7) (Cl. 3.3(i))	14. Owners' Insurance (state alternative (i), (ii) or (iii) of Cl. 6.3)
15. Annual Management Fee (state annual amount) (Cl. 8.1)	16. Severance Costs (state maximum amount) (Cl. 8.4(ii))
17. Day and year of termination of Agreement (Cl. 17)	18 Law and Arbitration (state alternative 19.1, 19.2 or 19.3; if 19.3 place of arbitration must be stated) (Cl. 19)
19. Notices (state postal and cable address, telex and telefax number for serving notice and communication to the Owners) (Cl. 20)	20. Notices (state postal and cable address, telex and telefax number for serving notice and communication to the Managers) (Cl. 20)

It is mutually agreed between the party stated in Box 2 and the party stated in Box 3 that this Agreement consisting of PART I and PART II as well as Annexes "A" (Details of Vessel), "B" (Details of Crew), "C" (Budget) and "D" (Associated vessels) attached hereto, shall be performed subject to the conditions contained herein. In the event of a conflict of conditions, the provisions of PART I and Annexes "A", "B", "C" and "D" shall prevail over those of PART II to the extent of such conflict but no further.

Signature(s) (Owners)	Signature(s) (Managers)

Appendix 15

PART II
"Shipman 98" Standard Ship Management Agreement

1. Definitions

In this Agreement save where the context otherwise requires, the following words and expressions shall have the meanings hereby assigned to them.

"Owners" means the party identified in Box 2.

"Managers" means the party identified in Box 3.

"Vessel" means the vessel or vessels details of which are set out in Annex "A" attached hereto.

"Crew" means the Master, officers and ratings of the numbers, rank and nationality specified in Annex "B" attached hereto.

"Crew Support Costs" means all expenses of a general nature which are not particularly referable to any individual vessel for the time being managed by the Managers and which are incurred by the Managers for the purpose of providing an efficient and economic management service and, without prejudice to the generality of the foregoing, shall include the cost of crew standby pay, training schemes for officers and ratings, cadet training schemes, sick pay, study pay, recruitment and interviews.

"Severance Costs" means the costs which the employers are legally obliged to pay to or in respect of the Crew as a result of the early termination of any employment contract for service on the Vessel.

"Crew Insurances" means insurances against crew risks which shall include but not be limited to death, sickness, repatriation, injury, shipwreck unemployment indemnity and loss of personal effects.

"Management Services" means the services specified in sub-clauses 3.1 to 3.8 as indicated affirmatively in Boxes 5 to 12.

"ISM Code" means the International Management Code for the Safe Operation of Ships and for Pollution Prevention as adopted by the International Maritime Organization (IMO) by resolution A.741(18) or any subsequent amendment thereto.

"STCW 95" means the International Convention on Standards of Training, Certification and Watchkeeping for Seafarers, 1978, as amended in 1995 or any subsequent amendment thereto.

2. Appointment of Managers

With effect from the day and year stated in Box 4 and continuing unless and until terminated as provided herein, the Owners hereby appoint the Managers and the Managers hereby agree to act as the Managers of the Vessel.

3. Basis of Agreement

Subject to the terms and conditions herein provided, during the period of this Agreement, the Managers shall carry out Management Services in respect of the Vessel as agents for and on behalf of the Owners. The Managers shall have authority to take such actions as they may from time to time in their absolute discretion consider to be necessary to enable them to perform this Agreement in accordance with sound ship management practice.

3.1 Crew Management

(only applicable if agreed according to Box 5)

The Managers shall provide suitably qualified Crew for the Vessel as required by the Owners in accordance with the STCW 95 requirements, provision of which includes but is not limited to the following functions:

(i) selecting and engaging the Vessel's Crew, including payroll arrangements, pension administration, and insurances for the Crew other than those mentioned in Clause 6;

(ii) ensuring that the applicable requirements of the law of the flag of the Vessel are satisfied in respect of manning levels, rank, qualification and certification of the Crew and employment regulations including Crew's tax, social insurance, discipline and other requirements;

(iii) ensuring that all members of the Crew have passed a medical examination with a qualified doctor certifying that they are fit for the duties for which they are engaged and are in possession of valid medical certificates issued in accordance with appropriate flag State requirements. In the absence of applicable flag State requirements the medical certificate shall be dated not more than three months prior to the respective Crew members leaving their country of domicile and maintained for the duration of their service on board the Vessel;

(iv) ensuring that the Crew shall have a command of the English language of a sufficient standard to enable them to perform their duties safely;

(v) arranging transportation of the Crew, including repatriation;

(vi) training of the Crew and supervising their efficiency;

(vii) conducting union negotiations;

(viii) operating the Managers' drug and alcohol policy unless otherwise agreed.

3.2 Technical Management

(only applicable if agreed according to Box 6)

The Managers shall provide technical management which includes, but is not limited to, the following functions:

(i) provision of competent personnel to supervise the maintenance and general efficiency of the Vessel;

(ii) arrangement and supervision of dry dockings, repairs, alterations and the upkeep of the Vessel to the standards required by the Owners provided that the Managers shall be entitled to incur the necessary expenditure to ensure that the Vessel will comply with the law of the flag of the Vessel and of the places where she trades, and all requirements and recommendations of the classification society;

(iii) arrangement of the supply of necessary stores, spares and lubricating oil;

(iv) appointment of surveyors and technical consultants as the Managers may consider from time to time to be necessary;

(v) development, implementation and maintenance of a Safety Management System (SMS) in accordance with the ISM Code (see sub-clauses 4.2 and 5.3).

3.3 Commercial Management

(only applicable if agreed according to Box 7)

The Managers shall provide the commercial operation of the Vessel, as required by the Owners, which includes, but is not limited to, the following functions:

(i) providing chartering services in accordance with the Owners' instructions which include, but are not limited to, seeking and negotiating employment for the Vessel and the conclusion (including the execution thereof) of charter parties or other contracts relating to the employment of the Vessel. If such a contract exceeds the period stated in Box 13, consent thereto in writing shall first be obtained from the Owners.

(ii) arranging of the proper payment to Owners or their nominees of all hire and/or freight revenues or other moneys of whatsoever nature to which Owners may be entitled arising out of the employment of or otherwise in connection with the Vessel.

(iii) providing voyage estimates and accounts and calculating of hire, freights, demurrage and/or despatch moneys due from or due to the charterers of the Vessel;

(iv) issuing of voyage instructions;

(v) appointing agents;

(vi) appointing stevedores;

(vii) arranging surveys associated with the commercial operation of the Vessel.

3.4 Insurance Arrangements

(only applicable if agreed according to Box 8)

The Managers shall arrange insurances in accordance with Clause 6, on such terms and conditions as the Owners shall have instructed or agreed, in particular regarding conditions, insured values, deductibles and franchises.

3.5 Accounting Services

(only applicable if agreed according to Box 9)

The Managers shall:

(i) establish an accounting system which meets the requirements of the Owners and provide regular accounting services, supply regular reports and records,

(ii) maintain the records of all costs and expenditure incurred as well as data necessary or proper for the settlement of accounts between the parties.

3.6 Sale or Purchase of the Vessel

(only applicable if agreed according to Box 10)

The Managers shall, in accordance with the Owners' instructions, supervise the sale or purchase of the Vessel, including the

Appendix 15

PART II
"Shipman 98" Standard Ship Management Agreement

performance of any sale or purchase agreement, but not negotiation of the same.

3.7 Provisions *(only applicable if agreed according to Box 11)*
The Managers shall arrange for the supply of provisions.

3.8 Bunkering *(only applicable if agreed according to Box 12)*
The Managers shall arrange for the provision of bunker fuel of the quality specified by the Owners as required for the Vessel's trade.

4. Managers' Obligations
4.1 The Managers undertake to use their best endeavours to provide the agreed Management Services as agents for and on behalf of the Owners in accordance with sound ship management practice and to protect and promote the interests of the Owners in all matters relating to the provision of services hereunder.
Provided, however, that the Managers in the performance of their management responsibilities under this Agreement shall be entitled to have regard to their overall responsibility in relation to all vessels as may from time to time be entrusted to their management and in particular, but without prejudice to the generality of the foregoing, the Managers shall be entitled to allocate available supplies, manpower and services in such manner as in the prevailing circumstances the Managers in their absolute discretion consider to be fair and reasonable.
4.2 Where the Managers are providing Technical Management in accordance with sub-clause 3.2, they shall procure that the requirements of the law of the flag of the Vessel are satisfied and they shall in particular be deemed to be the "Company" as defined by the ISM Code, assuming the responsibility for the operation of the Vessel and taking over the duties and responsibilities imposed by the ISM Code when applicable.

5. Owners' Obligations
5.1 The Owners shall pay all sums due to the Managers punctually in accordance with the terms of this Agreement.
5.2 Where the Managers are providing Technical Management in accordance with sub-clause 3.2, the Owners shall:
(i) procure that all officers and ratings supplied by them or on their behalf comply with the requirements of STCW 95;
(ii) instruct such officers and ratings to obey all reasonable orders of the Managers in connection with the operation of the Managers' safety management system.
5.3 Where the Managers are not providing Technical Management in accordance with sub-clause 3.2, the Owners shall procure that the requirements of the law of the flag of the Vessel are satisfied and that they, or such other entity as may be appointed by them and identified to the Managers, shall be deemed to be the "Company" as defined by the ISM Code assuming the responsibility for the operation of the Vessel and taking over the duties and responsibilities imposed by the ISM Code when applicable.

6. Insurance Policies
The Owners shall procure, whether by instructing the Managers under sub-clause 3.4 or otherwise, that throughout the period of this Agreement:
6.1 at the Owners' expense, the Vessel is insured for not less than her sound market value or entered for her full gross tonnage, as the case may be for:
(i) usual hull and machinery marine risks (including crew negligence) and excess liabilities;
(ii) protection and indemnity risks (including pollution risks and Crew Insurances); and
(iii) war risks (including protection and indemnity and crew risks) in accordance with the best practice of prudent owners of vessels of a similar type to the Vessel, with first class insurance companies, underwriters or associations ("the Owners' Insurances");
6.2 all premiums and calls on the Owners' Insurances are paid promptly by their due date,
6.3 the Owners' Insurances name the Managers and, subject to underwriters' agreement, any third party designated by the Managers as a joint assured, with full cover, with the Owners obtaining cover in respect of each of the insurances specified in sub-clause 6.1:
(i) on terms whereby the Managers and any such third party are liable in respect of premiums or calls arising in connection

with the Owners' Insurances; or
(ii) if reasonably obtainable, on terms such that neither the Managers nor any such third party shall be under any liability in respect of premiums or calls arising in connection with the Owners' Insurances; or
(iii) on such other terms as may be agreed in writing.
Indicate alternative (i), (ii) or (iii) in Box 14. If Box 14 is left blank then (i) applies.
6.4 written evidence is provided, to the reasonable satisfaction of the Managers, of their compliance with their obligations under Clause 6 within a reasonable time of the commencement of the Agreement, and of each renewal date and, if specifically requested, of each payment date of the Owners' Insurances.

7. Income Collected and Expenses Paid on Behalf of Owners
7.1 All moneys collected by the Managers under the terms of this Agreement (other than moneys payable by the Owners to the Managers) and any interest thereon shall be held to the credit of the Owners in a separate bank account.
7.2 All expenses incurred by the Managers under the terms of this Agreement on behalf of the Owners (including expenses as provided in Clause 8) may be debited against the Owners in the account referred to under sub-clause 7.1 but shall in any event remain payable by the Owners to the Managers on demand.

8. Management Fee
8.1 The Owners shall pay to the Managers for their services as Managers under this Agreement an annual management fee as stated in Box 15 which shall be payable by equal monthly instalments in advance, the first instalment being payable on the commencement of this Agreement (see Clause 2 and Box 4) and subsequent instalments being payable every month.
8.2 The management fee shall be subject to an annual review on the anniversary date of the Agreement and the proposed fee shall be presented in the annual budget referred to in sub-clause 9.1.
8.3 The Managers shall, at no extra cost to the Owners, provide their own office accommodation, office staff, facilities and stationery. Without limiting the generality of Clause 7 the Owners shall reimburse the Managers for postage and communication expenses, travelling expenses, and other out of pocket expenses properly incurred by the Managers in pursuance of the Management Services.
8.4 In the event of the appointment of the Managers being terminated by the Owners or the Managers in accordance with the provisions of Clauses 17 and 18 other than by reason of default by the Managers, or if the Vessel is lost, sold or otherwise disposed of, the "management fee" payable to the Managers according to the provisions of sub-clause 8.1, shall continue to be payable for a further period of three calendar months as from the termination date. In addition, provided that the Managers provide Crew for the Vessel in accordance with sub-clause 3.1:
(i) the Owners shall continue to pay Crew Support Costs during the said further period of three calendar months and
(ii) the Owners shall pay an equitable proportion of any Severance Costs which may materialize, not exceeding the amount stated in Box 16.
8.5 If the Owners decide to lay-up the Vessel whilst this Agreement remains in force and such lay-up lasts for more than three months, an appropriate reduction of the management fee for the period exceeding three months until one month before the Vessel is again put into service shall be mutually agreed between the parties.
8.6 Unless otherwise agreed in writing all discounts and commissions obtained by the Managers in the course of the management of the Vessel shall be credited to the Owners.

9. Budgets and Management of Funds
9.1 The Managers shall present to the Owners annually a budget for the following twelve months in such form as the Owners require. The budget for the first year hereof is set out in Annex "C" hereto. Subsequent annual budgets shall be prepared by the Managers and submitted to the Owners not less than three months before the anniversary date of the

Appendix 15

PART II
"Shipman 98" Standard Ship Management Agreement

commencement of this Agreement (see Clause 2 and Box 4).

9.2 The Owners shall indicate to the Managers their acceptance and approval of the annual budget within one month of presentation and in the absence of any such indication the Managers shall be entitled to assume that the Owners have accepted the proposed budget.

9.3 Following the agreement of the budget, the Managers shall prepare and present to the Owners their estimate of the working capital requirement of the Vessel and the Managers shall each month up-date this estimate. Based thereon, the Managers shall each month request the Owners in writing for the funds required to run the Vessel for the ensuing month, including the payment of any occasional or extraordinary item of expenditure, such as emergency repair costs, additional insurance premiums, bunkers or provisions. Such funds shall be received by the Managers within ten running days after the receipt by the Owners of the Managers' written request and shall be held to the credit of the Owners in a separate bank account.

9.4 The Managers shall produce a comparison between budgeted and actual income and expenditure of the Vessel in such form as required by the Owners monthly or at such other intervals as mutually agreed.

9.5 Notwithstanding anything contained herein to the contrary, the Managers shall in no circumstances be required to use or commit their own funds to finance the provision of the Management Services.

10. Managers' Right to Sub-Contract

The Managers shall not have the right to sub-contract any of their obligations hereunder, including those mentioned in sub-clause 3.1, without the prior written consent of the Owners which shall not be unreasonably withheld. In the event of such a sub-contract the Managers shall remain fully liable for the due performance of their obligations under this Agreement.

11. Responsibilities

11.1 *Force Majeure* - Neither the Owners nor the Managers shall be under any liability for any failure to perform any of their obligations hereunder by reason of any cause whatsoever of any nature or kind beyond their reasonable control.

11.2 *Liability to Owners* - **(i)** Without prejudice to sub-clause 11.1, the Managers shall be under no liability whatsoever to the Owners for any loss, damage, delay or expense of whatsoever nature, whether direct or indirect, (including but not limited to loss of profit arising out of or in connection with detention of or delay to the Vessel) and howsoever arising in the course of performance of the Management Services **UNLESS** same is proved to have resulted solely from the negligence, gross negligence or wilful default of the Managers or their employees, or agents or sub-contractors employed by them in connection with the Vessel, in which case (save where loss, damage, delay or expense has resulted from the Managers' personal act or omission committed with the intent to cause same or recklessly and with knowledge that such loss, damage, delay or expense would probably result) the Managers' liability for each incident or series of incidents giving rise to a claim or claims shall never exceed a total of ten times the annual management fee payable hereunder.

(ii) Notwithstanding anything that may appear to the contrary in this Agreement, the Managers shall not be liable for any of the actions of the Crew, even if such actions are negligent, grossly negligent or wilful, except only to the extent that they are shown to have resulted from a failure by the Managers to discharge their obligations under sub-clause 3.1, in which case their liability shall be limited in accordance with the terms of this Clause 11.

11.3 *Indemnity* - Except to the extent and solely for the amount therein set out that the Managers would be liable under sub-clause 11.2, the Owners hereby undertake to keep the Managers and their employees, agents and sub-contractors indemnified and to hold them harmless against all actions, proceedings, claims, demands or liabilities whatsoever or howsoever arising which may be brought against them or incurred or suffered by them arising out of or in connection with the performance of the Agreement, and against and in respect of all costs, losses, damages and expenses (including legal costs and expenses on a full indemnity basis) which the Managers may suffer or incur (either directly or indirectly) in the course of the performance of this Agreement.

11.4 *"Himalaya"* - It is hereby expressly agreed that no employee or agent of the Managers (including every sub-contractor from time to time employed by the Managers) shall in any circumstances whatsoever be under any liability whatsoever to the Owners for any loss, damage or delay of whatsoever kind arising or resulting directly or indirectly from any act, neglect or default on his part while acting in the course of or in connection with his employment and, without prejudice to the generality of the foregoing provisions in this Clause 11, every exemption, limitation, condition and liberty herein contained and every right, exemption from liability, defence and immunity of whatsoever nature applicable to the Managers or to which the Managers are entitled hereunder shall also be available and shall extend to protect every such employee or agent of the Managers acting as aforesaid and for the purpose of all the foregoing provisions of this Clause 11 the Managers are or shall be deemed to be acting as agent or trustee on behalf of and for the benefit of all persons who are or might be their servants or agents from time to time (including sub-contractors as aforesaid) and all such persons shall to this extent be or be deemed to be parties to this Agreement.

12. Documentation

Where the Managers are providing Technical Management in accordance with sub-clause 3.2 and/or Crew Management in accordance with sub-clause 3.1, they shall make available, upon Owners' request, all documentation and records related to the Safety Management System (SMS) and/or the Crew which the Owners need in order to demonstrate compliance with the ISM Code and STCW 95 or to defend a claim against a third party.

13. General Administration

13.1 The Managers shall handle and settle all claims arising out of the Management Services hereunder and keep the Owners informed regarding any incident of which the Managers become aware which gives or may give rise to claims or disputes involving third parties.

13.2 The Managers shall, as instructed by the Owners, bring or defend actions, suits or proceedings in connection with matters entrusted to the Managers according to this Agreement.

13.3 The Managers shall also have power to obtain legal or technical or other outside expert advice in relation to the handling and settlement of claims and disputes or all other matters affecting the interests of the Owners in respect of the Vessel.

13.4 The Owners shall arrange for the provision of any necessary guarantee bond or other security.

13.5 Any costs reasonably incurred by the Managers in carrying out their obligations according to Clause 13 shall be reimbursed by the Owners.

14. Auditing

The Managers shall at all times maintain and keep true and correct accounts and shall make the same available for inspection and auditing by the Owners at such times as may be mutually agreed. On the termination, for whatever reasons, of this Agreement, the Managers shall release to the Owners, if so requested, the originals where possible, or otherwise certified copies, of all such accounts and all documents specifically relating to the Vessel and her operation.

15. Inspection of Vessel

The Owners shall have the right at any time after giving reasonable notice to the Managers to inspect the Vessel for any reason they consider necessary.

16. Compliance with Laws and Regulations

The Managers will not do or permit to be done anything which might cause any breach or infringement of the laws and regulations of the Vessel's flag, or of the places where she trades.

17. Duration of the Agreement

This Agreement shall come into effect on the day and year stated in Box 4 and shall continue until the date stated in Box 17. Thereafter it shall continue until terminated by either party giving to the other notice in writing, in which event the Agreement shall

Appendix 15

terminate upon the expiration of a period of two months from the date upon which such notice was given.

18. Termination

18.1 *Owners' default*

(i) The Managers shall be entitled to terminate the Agreement with immediate effect by notice in writing if any moneys payable by the Owners under this Agreement and/or the owners of any associated vessel, details of which are listed in Annex "D", shall not have been received in the Managers' nominated account within ten running days of receipt by the Owners of the Managers written request or if the Vessel is repossessed by the Mortgagees.

(ii) If the Owners:

(a) fail to meet their obligations under sub-clauses 5.2 and 5.3 of this Agreement for any reason within their control, or

(b) proceed with the employment of or continue to employ the Vessel in the carriage of contraband, blockade running, or in an unlawful trade, or on a voyage which in the reasonable opinion of the Managers is unduly hazardous or improper,

the Managers may give notice of the default to the Owners, requiring them to remedy it as soon as practically possible. In the event that the Owners fail to remedy it within a reasonable time to the satisfaction of the Managers, the Managers shall be entitled to terminate the Agreement with immediate effect by notice in writing.

18.2 *Managers' Default*

If the Managers fail to meet their obligations under Clauses 3 and 4 of this Agreement for any reason within the control of the Managers, the Owners may give notice to the Managers of the default, requiring them to remedy it as soon as practically possible. In the event that the Managers fail to remedy it within a reasonable time to the satisfaction of the Owners, the Owners shall be entitled to terminate the Agreement with immediate effect by notice in writing.

18.3 *Extraordinary Termination*

This Agreement shall be deemed to be terminated in the case of the sale of the Vessel or if the Vessel becomes a total loss or is declared as a constructive or compromised or arranged total loss or is requisitioned.

18.4 For the purpose of sub-clause 18.3 hereof

(i) the date upon which the Vessel is to be treated as having been sold or otherwise disposed of shall be the date on which the Owners cease to be registered as Owners of the Vessel;

(ii) the Vessel shall not be deemed to be lost unless either she has become an actual total loss or agreement has been reached with her underwriters in respect of her constructive, compromised or arranged total loss or if such agreement with her underwriters is not reached it is adjudged by a competent tribunal that a constructive loss of the Vessel has occurred.

18.5 This Agreement shall terminate forthwith in the event of an order being made or resolution passed for the winding up, dissolution, liquidation or bankruptcy of either party (otherwise than for the purpose of reconstruction or amalgamation) or if a receiver is appointed, or if it suspends payment, ceases to carry on business or makes any special arrangement or composition with its creditors.

18.6 The termination of this Agreement shall be without prejudice to all rights accrued due between the parties prior to the date of termination.

19. Law and Arbitration

19.1 This Agreement shall be governed by and construed in accordance with English law and any dispute arising out of or in connection with this Agreement shall be referred to arbitration in London in accordance with the Arbitration Act 1996 or any statutory modification or re-enactment thereof save to the extent necessary to give effect to the provisions of this Clause.

The arbitration shall be conducted in accordance with the London Maritime Arbitrators Association (LMAA) Terms current at the time when the arbitration proceedings are commenced.

The reference shall be to three arbitrators. A party wishing to refer a dispute to arbitration shall appoint its arbitrator and send notice of such appointment in writing to the other party requiring the other party to appoint its own arbitrator within 14 calendar days of that notice and stating that it will appoint its arbitrator as sole arbitrator unless the other party appoints its own arbitrator and gives notice that it has done so within the 14 days specified. If the other party does not appoint its own arbitrator and give notice that it has done so within the 14 days specified, the party referring a dispute to arbitration may, without the requirement of any further prior notice to the other party, appoint its arbitrator as sole arbitrator and shall advise the other party accordingly. The award of a sole arbitrator shall be binding on both parties as if he had been appointed by agreement.

Nothing herein shall prevent the parties agreeing in writing to vary these provisions to provide for the appointment of a sole arbitrator.

In cases where neither the claim nor any counterclaim exceeds the sum of USD50,000 (or such other sum as the parties may agree) the arbitration shall be conducted in accordance with the LMAA Small Claims Procedure current at the time when the arbitration proceedings are commenced.

19.2 This Agreement shall be governed by and construed in accordance with Title 9 of the United States Code and the Maritime Law of the United States and any dispute arising out of or in connection with this Agreement shall be referred to three persons at New York, one to be appointed by each of the parties hereto, and the third by the two so chosen; their decision or that of any two of them shall be final, and for the purposes of enforcing any award, judgement may be entered on an award by any court of competent jurisdiction. The proceedings shall be conducted in accordance with the rules of the Society of Maritime Arbitrators, Inc.

In cases where neither the claim nor any counterclaim exceeds the sum of USD50,000 (or such other sum as the parties may agree) the arbitration shall be conducted in accordance with the Shortened Arbitration Procedure of the Society of Maritime Arbitrators, Inc. current at the time when the arbitration proceedings are commenced.

19.3 This Agreement shall be governed by and construed in accordance with the laws of the place mutually agreed by the parties and any dispute arising out of or in connection with this Agreement shall be referred to arbitration at a mutually agreed place, subject to the procedures applicable there.

19.4 If Box 18 in Part I is not appropriately filled in, sub-clause 19.1 of this Clause shall apply.

Note: 19.1, 19.2 and 19.3 are alternatives; indicate alternative agreed in Box 18.

20. Notices

20.1 Any notice to be given by either party to the other party shall be in writing and may be sent by fax, telex, registered or recorded mail or by personal service.

20.2 The address of the Parties for service of such communication shall be as stated in Boxes 19 and 20, respectively.

Appendix 16

Standard Liner and General Agency Agreement

The Federation of National Associations of Ship Brokers and Agents

STANDARD LINER AND GENERAL AGENCY AGREEMENT

Revised and adopted 2001

Approved by BIMCO 2001

It is hereby agreed between:

....of..(hereinafter referred to as the Principal)

and

....of..(hereinafter referred to as the Agent)

on the ....day of ....20.........

that:

1.00   The Principal hereby appoints the Agent as its Liner Agent for all its owned and/or chartered vessels including any space or slot charter agreement serving the trade between .... and ....

1.01   This Agreement shall come into effect on ....and shall continue until......................
Thereafter it shall continue until terminated by either party giving to the other notice in writing, in which event the Agreement shall terminate upon the expiration of a period of .....months from the date upon which such notice was given.

1.02   The territory in which the Agent shall perform its duties under the Agreement shall be...............
hereinafter referred to as the "Territory".

1.03   This Agreement covers the activities described in section 3...............................

1.04   The Agent undertakes not to accept the representation of other shipping companies nor to engage in NVOCC or such freight forwarding activities in the Territory, which are in direct competition to any of the Principal's transportation activities, without prior written consent, which shall not unreasonably be withheld.

1.05   The Principal undertakes not to appoint any other party in the Agent's Territory for the services defined in this Agreement.

1.06   The established custom of the trade and/or port shall apply and form part of this Agreement.

1.07   In countries where the position of the agent is in any way legally protected or regulated, the Agent shall have the benefit of such protection or regulation.

1.08   All aspects of the Principal's business are to be treated confidentially and all files and records pertaining to this business are the property of the Principal.

2.0   Duties of the Agent

2.01   To represent the Principal in the Territory, using his best endeavours to comply at all times with any reasonable specific instructions which the Principal may give, including the use of Principal's documentation, terms and conditions.

2.02   In consultation with the Principal to recommend and/or appoint on the Principal's behalf and account, Sub-Agents.

2.03   In consultation with the Principal to recommend and/or to appoint on the Principal's behalf and account, Stevedores, Watchmen, Tallymen, Terminal Operators, Hauliers and all kinds of suppliers.

2.04   The Agent will not be responsible for the negligent acts or defaults of the Sub-Agent or Sub-Contractor unless the Agent fails to exercise due care in the appointment and supervision of such Sub-Agent or Sub-Contractor. Notwithstanding the foregoing the Agent shall be responsible for the acts of his subsidiary companies appointed within the context of this Clause.

2.05   The Agent will always strictly observe the shipping laws and regulations of the country and will indemnify the Principal for fines, penalties, expenses or restrictions that may arise due to the failure of the Agent to comply herewith.

Activities of Agent(Delete those which do not apply)

3.1   Marketing and Sales

3.11   To provide marketing and sales activities in the Territory, in accordance with general guidelines laid down by the Principal, to canvass and book cargo, to publicise the services and to maintain contact with Shippers, Consignees, Forwarding Agents, Port and other Authorities and Trade Organisations.

3.12   To provide statistics and information and to report on cargo bookings and use of space allotments. To announce sailing and/or arrivals, and to quote freight rates and announce freight tariffs and amendments.

3.13   To arrange for public relations work (including advertising, press releases, sailing schedules and general promotional material) in accordance with the budget agreed with the Principal and for his account.

3.14   To attend to conference, consortia and /or alliance matters on behalf of the Principal and for the Principal's account.

3.15   To issue on behalf of the Principal Bills of Landing and Manifests, delivery orders, certificates and such other documents.

3.2   Port Agency

3.21   To arrange for berthing of vessels, loading and discharging of the cargo, in accordance with the local custom and conditions.

3.22   To arrange and co-ordinate all activities of the Terminal Operators, Stevedores, Tallymen and all other Contractors, in the interest of obtaining the best possible operation and despatch of the Principal's vessel.

3.23   To arrange for calling forward, reception and loading of outward cargo and discharge and release of inward cargo and to attend to the transhipment of through cargo.

3.24   To arrange for bunkering, repairs, husbandry, crew changes, passengers, ship's stores, spare parts, technical and nautical assistance and medical assistance.

3.25   To carry out the Principal's requirements concerning claims handling, P & I matters, General Average and/or insurance, and the appointment of Surveyors.

3.26   To attend to all necessary documentation and to attend to consular requirements.

3.27   To arrange for and attend to the clearance of the vessel and to arrange for all other services appertaining to the vessel's movements through the port.

3.28   To report to the Principal the vessel's position and to prepare a statement of facts of the call and/or a port log.

3.29   To keep the Principal regularly and timely informed on Port and working conditions likely to affect the despatch of the Principal's vessels.

3.3   Container and Ro/Ro Traffic

Where "equipment" is referred to in the following section it shall comprise container, flat racks, trailers or similar cargo carrying devices, owned, leased or otherwise controlled by the Principal.

3.31   To arrange for the booking of equipment on the vessel.

3.32   To arrange for the stuffing and unstuffing of LCL cargo at the port and to arrange for the provision of inland LCL terminals.

3.33   To provide and administer a proper system, or to comply with the principal's system for the control and registration of equipment. To organise equipment stock within the Territory and make provision for storage, positioning and repositioning of the equipment.

3.34   To comply with Customs requirements and arrange for equipment interchange documents in respect of the movements for which the Agent is responsible and to control the supply and use of locks, seals and labels.

3.35   To make equipment available and to arrange inland haulage.

3.36   To undertake the leasing of equipment into and re-delivery out of the system.

3.37   To operate an adequate equipment damage control system in compliance with the Principal's instructions. To arrange for equipment repairs and maintenance, when and where necessary and to report on the condition of equipment under the Agent's control.

Appendix 16

General Agency

3.41 To supervise, activities and co-ordinate all marketing and sales activities of Port, Inland Agents and/or Sub-agents in the Territory, in accordance with general guidelines laid down by the Principal and to use every effort to obtain business from prospective clients and to consolidate the flow of statistics and information.

3.42 To supervise and co-ordinate all activities of Port, Inland Agents and/or Sub-agents as set forth in the agreement, in order to ensure the proper performance of all customary requirements for the best possible operation of the Principal's vessel in the G.A.'s Territory.

3.43 In consultation with the Principal to recommend and/or appoint on the Principal's behalf and account Port, Inland Agents, and/or Sub-Agents if required.

3.44 To provide Port, Inland Agents and/or Sub-agents with space allocations in accordance with the Principal's requirements.

3.45 To arrange for an efficient rotation of vessels within the Territory, in compliance with the Principal's instructions and to arrange for the most economical despatch in the ports of its area within the scope of the sailing schedule.

3.46 To liaise with Port Agents and/or Sub-agents if and where required, in the Territory in arranging for such matters as bunkering, repairs, crew changes, ship's stores, spare parts, technical, nautical, medical assistance and consular requirements

3.47 To instruct and supervise Port, Inland Agents and/or Sub-Agents regarding the Principal's requirements concerning claims handling. P & I matters and/or insurance, and the appointment of Surveyors. All expenses involved with claims handling other than routine claims are for Principal's account.

3.5 Accounting and Finance

3.51 To provide for appropriate records of the Principal's financial position to be maintained in the Agent's books, which shall be available for inspection and to prepare periodic financial statements.

3.52 To check all vouchers received for services rendered and to prepare a proper disbursement account in respect of each voyage or accounting period.

3.53 To advise the Principal of all amendments to port tariffs and other charges as they become known.

3.54 To calculate freight and other charges according to Tariffs supplied by the Principal and exercise every care and diligence in applying all terms and conditions of such Tariffs or other freight agreements. If the Principal organises or employs an organisation for checking freight calculations and documentation the costs for such checking to be entirely for the Principal's account.

3.55 To collect freight and related accounts and remit to the Principal all freights and other monies belonging to the Principal at such periodic intervals as the Principal may require. All bank charges to be for the Principal's account. The Agent shall advise the Principal of the customary credit terms and arrangements. If the Agent is required to grant credit to customers due to commercial reasons, the risk in respect of outstanding collections is for the Principal's account unless the Agent has granted credit without the knowledge and prior consent of the Principal.

3.56 The Agent shall have authority to retain money from the freight collected to cover all past and current disbursements, subject to providing regular cash position statements to the Principal.

3.57 The Agent in carrying out his duties under this Agreement shall not be responsible to the Principal for loss or damage caused by any Banker, Broker or other person, instructed by the Agent in good faith unless the same happens by or through the wilful neglect or default of the Agent. The burden of proving the wilful neglect of the Agent shall be on the Principal.

Principal's Duties

4.01 To provide all documentation, necessary to fulfil the Agent's task together with any stationery specifically required by the Principal.

4.02 To give full and timely information regarding the vessel's schedules, ports of call and line policy insofar as it affects the port and sales agency activities.

4.03 To provide the Agents immediately upon request with all necessary funds to cover advance disbursements unless the Agent shall have sufficient funds from the freights collected.

4.04 The Principal shall at all times indemnify the Agent against all claims, charges, losses, damages and expenses which the Agent may incur in connection with the fulfilment of his duties under this Agreement. Such indemnity shall extend to all acts, matters and things done, suffered or incurred by the Agent during the duration of this Agreement, notwithstanding any termination thereof, provided always, that this indemnity shall not extend to matters arising by reason of the wilful misconduct or negligence of the Agent.

4.05 Where the Agent provides bonds, guarantees and any other forms of security to Customs or other statutory authorities then the Principal shall indemnify and reimburse the Agent immediately such claims are made, provided they do not arise by reason of the wilful misconduct or the negligence of the Agent.

4.06 If mutually agreed the Principal shall take over the conduct of any dispute which may arise between the Agent and any third party as a result of the performance of the Agent's duties.

5.0 Remuneration

5.01 The Principal agrees to pay the agent and the Agent accepts, as consideration for the services rendered, the commissions and fees set forth on the schedule attached to this Agreement. Any fees specified in monetary units in the attached schedule shall be reviewed every 12 months and if necessary adjusted in accordance with such recognised cost of living index as is published in the country of the Agent.

5.02 Should the Principal require the Agent to undertake full processing and settlement of claims, then the Agent is entitled to a separate remuneration as agreed with the Principal and commensurate with the work involved.

5.03 The remuneration specified in the schedule attached is in respect of the ordinary and anticipated duties of the Agent within the scope of this Agreement. Should the Agent be required to perform duties beyond the scope of this Agreement then the terms on which the Agent may agree to perform such duties will be subject to express agreement between the parties. Without prejudice to the generality of the foregoing such duties may include e.g. participating in conference activities on behalf of the Principal, booking fare-paying passengers, sending out general average notices and making collections under average bonds insofar as these duties are not performed by the average adjuster.

5.04 If the Tariff currency varies in value against the local currency by more than 10% after consideration of any currency adjustment factor existing in the trade the basis for calculation of remuneration shall be adjusted accordingly.

5.05 Any extra expenses occasioned by specific additional requirements of the Principal in the use of computer equipment and systems for the performance of the Agent's duties to the Principal shall be borne by the Principal.

5.06 The Principal is responsible for all additional expenses incurred by the Agent in connecting its computers to any national or local port community system.

6.0 Duration

6.01 This agreement shall remain in force as specified in clause 1.01 of this Agreement. Any notice of termination shall be sent by registered or recorded mail.

6.02 If the Agreement for any reason other than negligence or wilful misconduct of the Agent should by cancelled at an earlier date than on the expiry of the notice given under clause 1.01 hereof, the Principal shall compensate the Agent. The compensation payable by the Principal to the agent shall be determined in accordance with clause 6.04 below.

6.03 If for any reason the Principal withdraws or suspends the service, the Agent may withdraw from this agreement forthwith, without prejudice to its claim for compensation.

6.04 The basis of compensation shall be the monthly average of the commission and fees earned during the previous 12 months or if less than 12 months have passed then a reasonable estimate of the same, multiplied by the number of months from the date of cancellation until the contract would have been terminated in accordance with clause 1.01 above. Furthermore the gross redundancy payments, which the Agent and/or Sub-Agent(s) is compelled to make to employees made redundant by reason of the withdrawal or suspension of the Principal's service, or termination of this Agreement, shall also be taken into account.

6.05 The Agent shall have a general lien on amounts payable to the Principal in respect of any undisputed sums due and owing to the Agent including but not limited to commissions, disbursements and duties.

7.0 Jurisdiction

7.01 a) This Agreement shall be governed by and construed in accordance with the laws of the country in which the Agent has its principle place of business and any dispute arising out of or in connection with this Agreement shall be referred to arbitration in that country subject to the procedures applicable there.

b) This Agreement shall be governed by and construed in accordance with the laws of .... and any dispute arising out of or in connection with this Agreement shall be referred to arbitration at ...., subject to the procedures applicable there.

c) Any dispute arising out of this Agreement shall be referred to arbitration at....................subject to the law and procedures applicable there.

(subclauses [a] [b] & [c] are options. If [b] or [c] are not filled in then [a] shall apply.)

Appendix 16

REMUNERATION SCHEDULE BELONGING TO STANDARD LINER AND GENERAL AGENCY AGREEMENT

Between...and...date............................
       (As Principal)   (As Agent)

The Agent is entitled to the following remuneration based <u>on all total freight</u> earnings (including any surcharges,(eg BAF, CAF) handling charges (eg THC) and freight additionals including inland transport which may be agreed) of the Principal's liner service to and from the Territory to be paid in Agent's local currency. The total remuneration per call shall not in any case be lower than the local fee applicable

I   A.   Where the Agent provides all the services enumerated in this Agreement the Commission shall be:

                Services outward......................%   [Min .... per cont or tonne/cbm]   } MIN

                      inward......................%   [Min .... per cont or tonne/cbm]   } LUMP SUM

      2.   ....% for cargo when only booking is involved. [Min .... per cont] } PER

      3.   ....% for cargo when only handling is involved. [Min........ per cont] } CALL ....

                ("only handling" in the remuneration schedule is so defined that the duties of an Agent are to call forward and otherwise arrange for the cargo to be loaded on board, where the specific booking has been made elsewhere and acknowledged as such by the shipper as nominated for the Principal's service.

      4.   In respect of movements of cargo outside the Agent's Territory......................% of the gross total freight is payable in cases where only collection of freight is involved.

      5.   An additional fee for containers and/or units entering or leaving the inventory control system of the Agent a fee of...................... per unit.

II   A.   ....% for cargo loaded on board in bulk. [Min .... per tonne / cbm]

      2.   ....% for cargo discharged in bulk.   [Min .... per tonne / cbm]

III   Where the Agent provides only the services as non-port agent the remuneration shall be:

    When actually booked/originating from this area:

      1.   Services outward ....%   [Min .... per cont or tonne / cbm]

                      inward ....%   [Min .... per cont or tonne / cbm]

      2.   An additional fee for containers and/or units entering or leaving the inventory control system of the Agent a fee of .... per unit.

IV   Where the Agent provides only the services as non-port agent the remuneration shall be:

      1.   ....% for cargo loaded on board in bulk. [Min .... per tonne / cbm]

      2.   ....% for cargo discharged in bulk.   [Min .... per tonne / cbm]

5.   Clearance and ship's husbandry fee shall be as agreed.

6.   A Commission of .... % shall be paid on all ancillary charges collected by the Agent on behalf of the Principal such as Depot Charges, Container Demurrage, Container Damage etc.

7.   Communications: The Principal will either pay actual communication expenses on a cost plus basis or pay a lumpsum monthly on an average cost plus basis, to be review able.

8.   Travelling expenses: When the Agent is requested by the Principal to undertake journeys of any significant distance and/or duration, all travel expenses including accommodation and other expenses will be for the Principal's account.

9.   Documentary and Administrative Charges: Such charges to be levied as appropriate by the Agent to cargo interests and to remain with the Agent even if related to the trade of the principal.

10.   In case of Transhipment Cargo, a transhipment fee of .... per cont / tonne / cbm is charged by the Agent.

....

    PRINCIPAL   **AGENT**

Appendix 17

Scale of Agency Charges for Dry Cargo Vessels

THE INSTITUTE OF CHARTERED SHIPBROKERS
85, Gracechurch Street, London EC3V 0AA
Tel: (020) 7623 1111; Fax: (020) 7623 8118; E-mail: federation@ics.org.uk
Founded 1911: Incorporated by Royal Charter 21 January 1920,
Supplemental Royal Charter 25 July 1984

SCALE OF AGENCY CHARGES FOR
DRY CARGO VESSELS

Effective 1 January 2005

This scale applies only where agency services are rendered in respect of a vessel registered outside the EU and responsibility for payment rests with a Principal who is outside the EU.

For the purpose of the scale the following definitions apply:

SCALE OF AGENCY CHARGES	**means**	the fees applicable for services rendered to dry cargo vessels as from 1 January 2005.
OVERSEAS	**means**	vessels trading from or to the United Kingdom (including Northern Ireland) and all ports not otherwise specified.
COASTING	**means**	vessels trading between ports within the United Kingdom (including Northern Ireland).
DEADWEIGHT ALL TOLD (DWAT)	**means**	the weight in metric tonnes of cargo, stores and fuel carried by the vessel when loaded to her maximum summer load line as published in Lloyd's Register of Shipping or by vessel's classification society. Where the vessel has dual tonnages, the higher tonnage to apply.
APPROPRIATE FEE	**means**	the fee calculated under Section I modified by Section II, if applicable.

This Edition of the Scale of Agency Charges supersedes all previous editions and amendments thereto.

Appendix 17

DWAT	OVERSEAS 1A	COASTING 1B
	£	£
UP TO 400	306	245
401 - 500	353	283
501 - 600	402	322
601 - 700	457	363
701 - 800	503	402
801 - 900	549	440
901 - 1000	605	483
1001 - 1100	651	520
1101 - 1200	708	567
1201 - 1300	755	604
1301 - 1400	803	643
1401 - 1500	856	684
1501 - 1600	883	707
1601 - 1700	917	733
1701 - 1800	952	761
1801 - 1900	977	783
1901 - 2000	1012	811
2001 - 2200	1072	858
2201 - 2400	1134	907
2401 - 2600	1202	961
2601 - 2800	1263	1010
2801 - 3000	1324	1060
3001 - 3200	1358	1087
3201 - 3400	1398	1119
3401 - 3600	1432	1145
3601 - 3800	1474	1178
3801 - 4000	1508	1206
4001 - 4500	1568	1255
4501 - 5000	1630	1305
5001 - 5500	1696	1357
5501 - 6000	1766	1413
6001 - 6500	1826	1460
6501 - 7000	1887	1510
7001 - 8000	1982	1586
8001 - 9000	2106	1685
9001 - 10000	2273	1819
10001 - 12500	2450	1960
12501 - 15000	2619	2096
15001 - 17500	2796	2237
17501 - 20000	2965	2373
20001 - 22500	3142	2513
22501 - 25000	3319	2655
25001 - 27500	3488	2791
27501 - 30000	3665	2931
30001 - 40000	3828	3062
40001 - 50000	3941	3154
50001 AND OVER	4099	3279

Appendix 17

SECTION II
SUPPLEMENTAL AND MODIFIED FEES

A.   SPECIAL CARGO SUPPLEMENTS

i)	Cargoes wholly or partly bagged, baled, banded, packaged, palletised, containerised or boxed; forest or steel products.		SECTION I plus 12.5%
ii)	Mixed cargo, whether bulk, bagged, baled, banded, packaged, palletised, containerised or boxed; vehicles whether alone or with cased vehicles and/or spare parts.		SECTION I plus 25%
iii)	Perishable vegetables and fruit; Refrigerated cargo.		SECTION I plus 50%
iv)	Hazardous cargo (where extraordinary services are required).		SECTION I plus 100%
v)	Ro-Ro Vehicle carriers.		SECTION I plus 150%

B.   MARITIME STATISTICS

Where expenses are incurred in the collection of Maritime Statistics these will be passed on and a fee may be levied for the production of these statistics.

C.   EXTENDED PORT TIME

i) For ships in port and/or waiting at anchorage over 10 days; for each day or part thereof over 10 days.   5% of SECTION I

ii) Vessels detained in port once cargo operations have completed, for each day or part thereof   10% of SECTION I

D.   SHIP REQUIRED TO BE ENTERED WITH CUSTOMS INWARDS AND/OR CUSTOMS CLEARED OUTWARDS OUTSIDE NORMAL CUSTOMS HOURS, INCLUDING STATUTORY CUSTOMS BOARDING PROCEDURES   15% of SECTION IA (Maximum £372)

E.   CALLING ONLY FOR BUNKERS AND/OR ORDERS AND/OR SHELTERING   50% of SECTION IA

F.   REPAIRING AND/OR DRYDOCKING

i) For each week or part thereof, up to 8 weeks   75% of SECTION IA (Minimum fee £588)

ii) After 8 weeks   Subject to mutual agreement

G.   DELIVERY OR REDELIVERY OF TIME-CHARTERED SHIPS

i) Where an Agent earns also a loading and/or discharging and/or repairing fee from the same Principal.   20% of SECTION IA

ii) If for a different Principal or as an isolated operation.   50% of SECTION IA

H.   ATTENDING DELIVERY OR NEWLY BUILT OR SECOND-HAND SHIPS OR LAID UP SHIPS

i) For each week or part thereof, up to 4 weeks.   25% of SECTION IA

ii) Thereafter for each week or part thereof.   20% of SECTION IA

iii) Attending laid-up ships.   Subject to mutual agreement

I.   INWARD CUSTOMS REPORT OR OUTWARD CLEARANCE IN BALLAST OR CARGO R.O.B. FROM/TO FOREIGN.   15% of SECTION IA

J.   APPOINTMENT AS SUPERVISORY AGENT.   50% of the appropriate fee

K.   OFFSHORE SUPPORT/SUPPLY/STANDBY VESSELS, TUGS, DUMB BARGES OR SIMILAR CRAFT OR ANY LIKE SERVICE VESSELS

i) For first 7 days, per day   £189

ii) Thereafter, for each day   £107

Days spent solely awaiting orders not to count.

L.   GEOPHYSICAL SURVEY VESSELS, SUB-SEA SUPPORT VESSELS OR SIMILAR

i) For the first 7 days, per day   £469

ii) Thereafter, for each day   £234

Appendix 17

M.   CREW ATTENDANCE AND OTHER

     i)   Crew or persons missing/deserting ship or hospitalized
and requiring attention after vessel's departure.
Stowaways, refugees and illegal immigrants.   £95 per person per week

     ii)   Supervising crew or persons arriving/departing rail
stations or air terminals (in addition to (i), if applicable).   £53 per person per week

N.   EXTRA SHIPPERS OR RECEIVERS

     For each one over 3.   £38

O.   ADDITIONAL SERVICES

     Where an Agent is called upon to give a Customs Bond on behalf of his Principal, and/or attends to the distribution and/or collection of Average Bonds and/or Valuations in cases of General Average and/or is involved in processing cargo claims, a charge may be made commensurate with the work involved.

P.   AGENTS ANCILLARY EXPENSES

     (i)   **The Scale Fee does not include agents out of office attendance (except as charged under Section C above); nor does it cover agents out of pocket expenses such as the cost of communications, car expenses, bank charges (including charges levied for cash advanced to Master) and other petties as incurred, together with statutory requirements for cargo and crew attendance, all of which are recoverable in addition to the agency fee.**

     (ii)   The Owners or Disponents are to place the Agent in funds, in advance, to meet the ship's estimated total port disbursements, through freight collected by the Agent and/or by direct remittance if freight collected is insufficient. Where the Owners or Disponents are in default of such immediate advance payment they shall, without prejudice to the Agents' rights to immediate payment in advance, pay in addition a disbursement commission of 5% on any amount not covered by advance funds. One month after presentation of Accounts an additional charge of 2.5% compound interest per month or part of a month is payable.

Q.   CANCELLATION FEE

     Where an agent has spent time and incurred costs in
anticipation of vessel's arrival, subsequently diverted.   25% of SECTION IA

Outline World Map

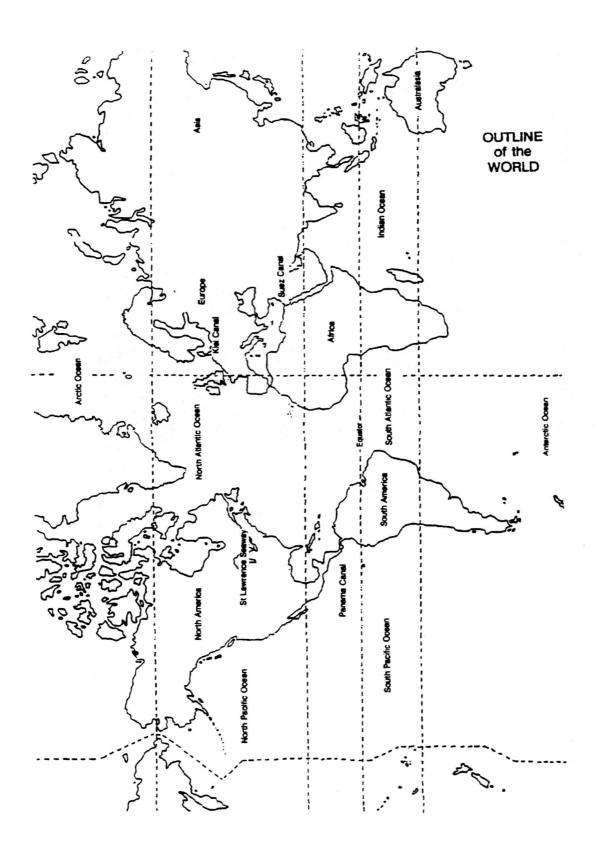

OUTLINE
of the
WORLD

Time Zones

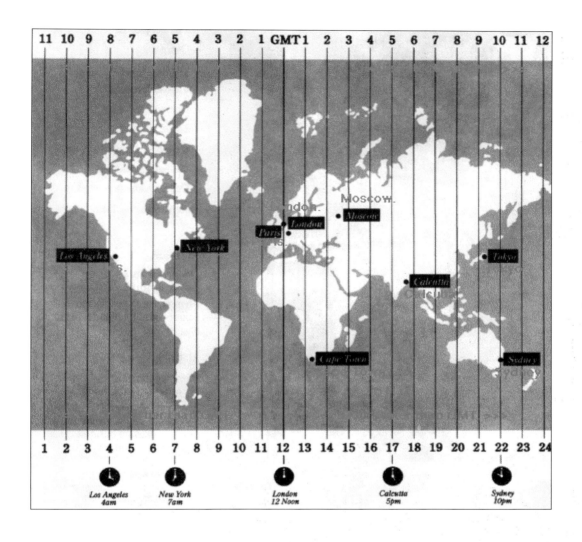

Appendix 20

Beaufort Scale Wind Force Conversions						
Force	Type	Sea Conditions	Knots	Km/Hr	m/sec	mph
0	Calm	Sea like a mirror	Less than 1	Less than 1	Less than 1	Less than 1
1	Very light	Ripples with appearance of scales, no foam crests	1 - 3	1 - 5	1 - 2	1 - 3
2	Light breeze	Wavelets, small but pronounced. Crests with glassy appearance, but do not break.	4 -6	6 - 11	2 -	4 -7
3	Gentle breeze	Large wavelets, crests begin to break. Glassy looking foam, occasional white horses.	7 - 10	12 - 19	3 - 5	8 - 12
4	Moderate breeze	Small waves becoming longer, frequent white horses.	11 - 16	20 - 29	6 - 8	13 - 18
5	Fresh breeze	Moderate waves of pronounced long form. Many white horses, some spray.	17 - 21	30 - 39	9 - 11	19 - 24
6	Strong breeze	Some large waves, extensive white foam crests, some spray.	22 - 27	40 - 50	12 - 14	25 - 31
7	Near gale	Sea heaped up, white foam from breaking waves blowing in streaks with the wind.	28 - 33	51 - 61	14 - 17	32 - 38
8	Gale	Moderately high and long waves. Crests break into spin drift, blowing foam in well marked streaks.	34 - 40	62 - 74	17 - 21	39 - 46
9	Strong gale	High waves, dense foam streaks in wind, wave crests topple, tumble and roll over. Spray reduces visibility.	41 - 47	75 - 87	21 - 24	47 - 54
10	Storm	Very high waves with long overhanging crests. Dense blowing foam, sea surface appears white. Heavy tumbling of sea, shock-like, poor visibility.	48 - 55	88 - 101	24 - 28	55 - 63
11	Violent storm	Exceptionally high waves, sometimes concealing small and medium sized ships. Sea completely covered with long white patches of foam. Edges of wave crests blown into froth. Poor visibility.	56 - 63	102 - 117	28 - 3	64 - 73
12	Hurricane	Air filled with foam and spray, sea white with driving spray, poor visibility.	>64	>119	>33	>74

Ice Clause

BIMCO Special Ice Clause 1947 (Code Name: "Nordice")

I. Should during the time from the fixture of the contract until the Vessel leaves the loading port risk appear of the voyage – including the voyage to the loading port or ports – becoming impossible to perform without damage to the Vessel or substantial delay, or should such risk substantially increase, both the Carrier and the Charterers may cancel the contract without liability in damages.

If the contract is cancelled after the commencement of the loading, the cargo shall be discharged again and be received as fast as the Vessel can deliver. All discharging expenses above usual average discharging expenses for the Carrier's account under this contract, if any, shall be paid by the Charterers.

Should risk of freezing in arise at the loading port the Vessel may leave the port with such cargo as is onboard. The Carrier shall then have the option of completing from and to any port or ports for his own account unless the Charterers choose to pay deadfreight.

II. Should such risk as mentioned in paragraph I exist or arise during the time of the voyage to the discharging port the Charterers shall upon request nominate to the Master an immediately accessible safe port for discharging which does not necessitate a voyage substantially longer than the one agreed upon under this contract.

Provided the Master has not received such nomination within 48 hours after Charterers' receipt of the request he may himself choose a discharging port, in the same country if possible.

III. Should risk arise of the Vessel being frozen in at the discharging port or ports, or of the Vessel being prevented by ice from getting to or out through the only fairway leading to open water, the Vessel may leave the port with such cargo as is onboard. With regard to the choice of discharging port for the cargo left onboard the stipulations in paragraph II shall apply.

IV. The Vessel is entitled to damages at the rate of demurrage entered in the contract of affreightment for any detention by reasons of ice. This shall apply even when the Vessel discharges her cargo at the loading port or if no accessible substitute discharging port is available and when the Vessel is frozen in. In case the Vessel becomes frozen in at the port where the Vessel is discharging but before the discharging is completed the loss of time shall be reckoned from the expiration of the discharging time until the Vessel shall be able to leave the port unhindered by ice.

Any loss of time awaiting the nomination of a substitute discharging port shall not be reckoned until 12 hours after Charterers' receipt of the request.

V. In case of alteration of destination the freight shall be adjusted according to the proportion between the voyage agreed upon and the distance performed. Regard shall also be taken to expenses being increased or saved.

VI. The Carrier shall have a lien on the cargo for all freight, demurrage, damages for detention and expenses due to him under this ice clause.

VII. The Vessel shall not be obliged to force ice or to follow icebreakers.

VIII. Anything done or not done by the Carrier in accordance with this clause shall be deemed to be within this contract.

St. Lawrence Seaway

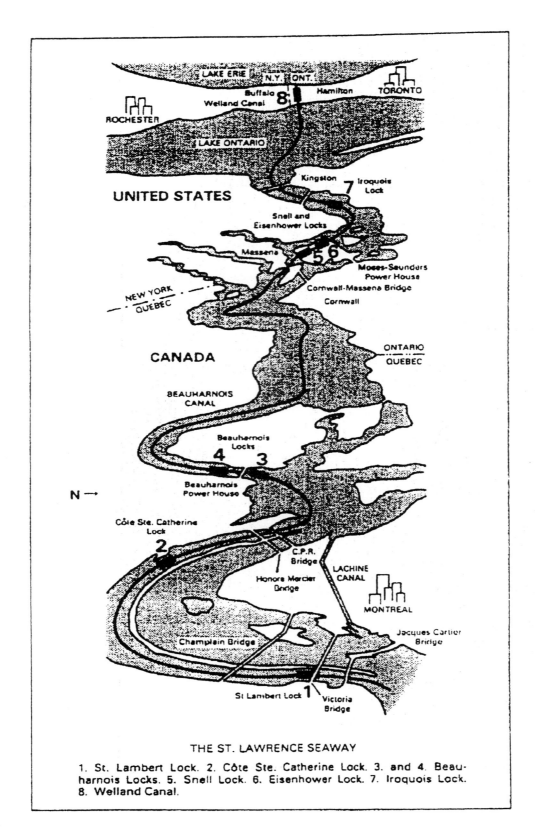

THE ST. LAWRENCE SEAWAY

1. St. Lambert Lock. 2. Côte Ste. Catherine Lock. 3. and 4. Beauharnois Locks. 5. Snell Lock. 6. Eisenhower Lock. 7. Iroquois Lock. 8. Welland Canal.

Kiel Canal

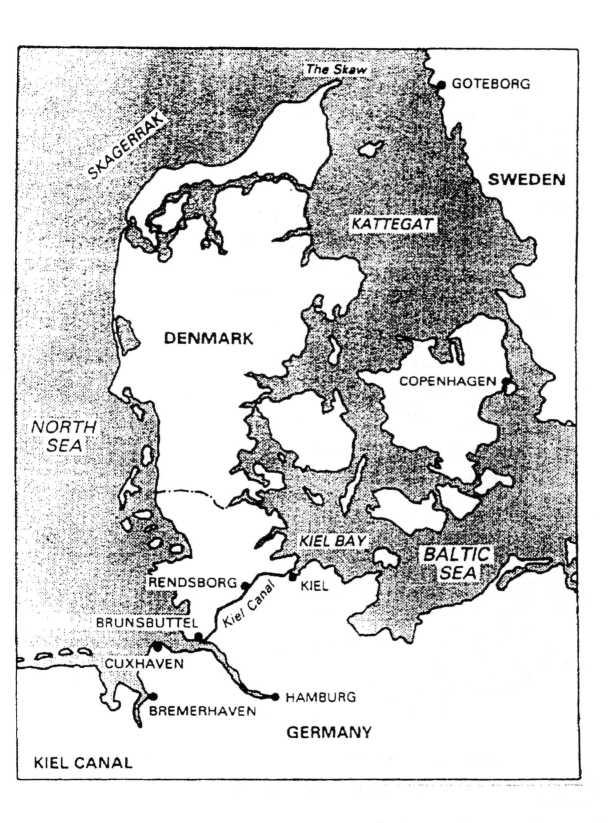

KIEL CANAL

Suez Canal

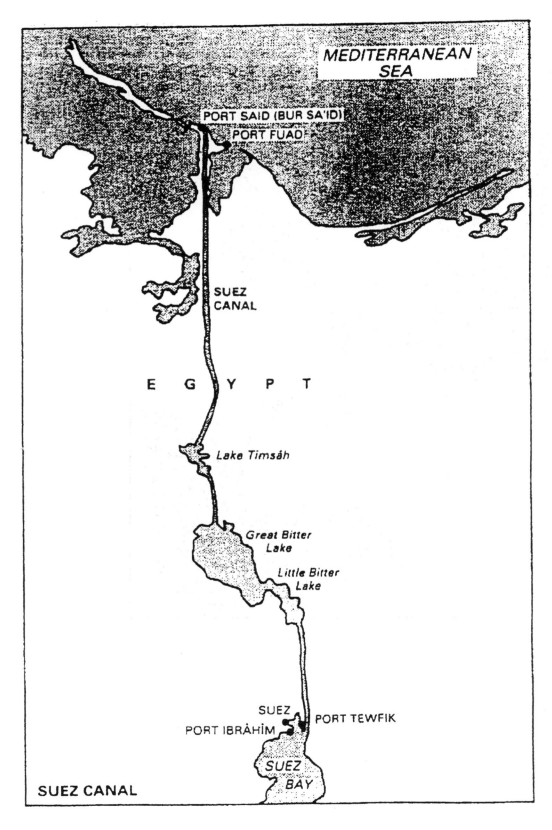

Panama Canal

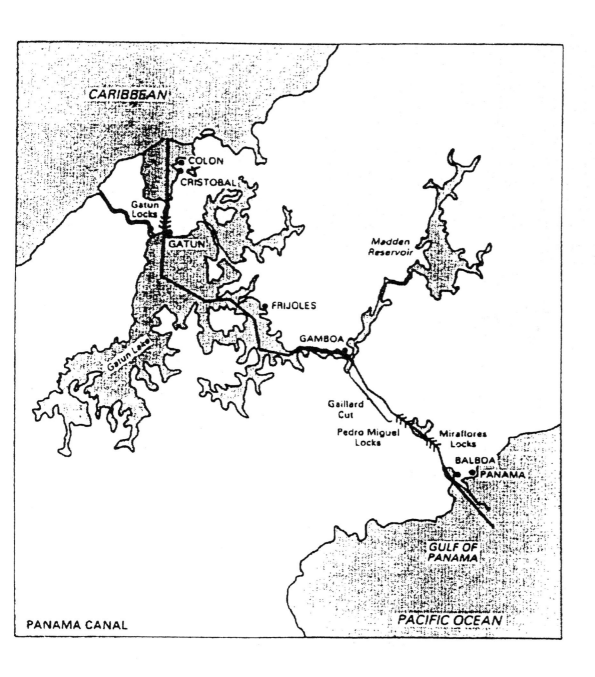

Chartering and Fixture Report

COMPANIES & MARKETS

End in sight for Oz mineral prices?

AUSTRALIA'S major commodity forecaster has dismissed suggestions that China's surging economic growth will continue to underpin high prices for iron ore and coal. The Australian Bureau of Agriculture and Resource Economics (Abare), in its latest commodity outlook, does predict that the Australian commodity export earnings will reach a record A$116Bn ($90.2Bn) for the 2005-6 financial year. But it also predicts that prices will soon start falling.

The report finds that increases in value of minerals and energy exports, to a record $66Bn, are largely caused by higher volumes and prices for metallurgical coal and thermal coal and iron ore. The total value of minerals and energy exports will increase during this year by 23%, it predicts, but prices for most minerals and energy will fall over the next six months. The reason is assumed weaker growth in global industrial activity, reduced Chinese demand for commodities and increases in world supply.

"Part of this forecast slowdown in China's

China Steel Express loads iron ore at Port Hedland, Australia: but will prices soon fall?

demand for raw materials reflects lower growth in the demand for minerals and energy-intensive manufactured products in China's key export mar-

kets," the report says. It dismisses suggestions by some market commentators that commodity prices are in a 'super-cycle', arguing that China's

Dry Fixtures

CARGO	VESSEL	FROM	TO	TONNES	DATE	RATE	CHART.	TERMS
Coal	Cape Kassos, 04	Richards Bay	Rotterdam	150000-10%	Jul 5/20	10.00	Cargill	FIO;ScLd/25000tShinc
Coal	Ocean Cosmos, 00	Richards Bay	Rotterdam	150000-10%	Jun 24/25	10.00	SwissMarin	PtC;FIO;ScLd/25000tShinc
Coal	Ingenious, 99	Richards Bay	Rotterdam	150000-10%	Jul 15/30	10.75	Cargill	FIO;ScLd/25000tShinc
Coal	Steamers, (Cosco)	Richards Bay	Tarragona	150000-10%Ea	2006/2007	11.50	Carboex	FIO;ScLd/24000tShex;7-9Cargoes
Hvy Grain	Mass Glory, 93	US Gulf	Egypt	65000-5%	Jun 25/27	27.00	ACTI	FIO;10000t/6000t
Wheat&Sorghums	Cynthia Fagan, 81	US Gulf	Mombasa & Dar EsSalaam	3960 & 5930	Jul 1/10	210.36	WorldVisio	PtC;BerthTerms
Iron Ore	Eternal Bright, 81	Brazil	China	130000-10%	Jul 20/30	17.60	Cometals	FIO;ScLd/25000t
Iron Ore	Kerkis, 82	Tubarao	Qingdao	170000-10%	Jul 10/20	19.00	Transfield	PtC;FIO;ScLd/25000t
Iron Ore	Steamer	Nouadhibou	Ghent	70000-10%	Jul 10/20	8.25	Sidmar	FIO;4Days
Iron Ore	Steamer, (NYK)	Cape Lambert	Ymuiden	150000-10%	Jul 10/17	11.25	Corus	FIO;6Days
Scrap	Fareast Sunny, 89	ECUS	Marmagoa	35000-5%	Jul 1/5	54.50	Hugo Neu	FIO;10000t/3000t

Timecharter

CONSUMPTION	VESSEL	FROM	TO	TONNES	DATE	RATE	CHART.	TERMS
14kt/30t	Edfu, 97	Del Skaw	Redel Portbury	71752dwt	Jul 5/10	22500 Day	Flame	TripOutviaVentspils
14kt/35t	Samjohn Liberty, 98	Del US Gulf	Redel Egyptian Med	74761dwt	Jul 1/5	24000 Day	Cargill	TripOut+$450000Bonus
14.2kt/28.1t	Konkar Georgios, 97	Del Surabaya	Redel Japan via Indo	46670dwt	Jul 7/15	21500 Day	GlobalBulk	Trip out
13.8kt/31.8t	Wadi Al Arish, 94	Del Kosichang	Redel Japan	64214dwt	Jul 1/3	11000 Day	Norden	PtHedlandRd
14.5kt/35.5t	Iran Kermanshah, 01	Del Hong Kong	Redel Taiwan	75249dwt	Jul 1/5	13000 Day	Daebo	IndonesiaRd
13.7kt/49t	Hebei Angel, 93	Del Rizhao	Redel China	165133dwt	Jul 5/10	23000 Day	BHP-Billit	WAusRd
14.5kt/58t	Alpha Era, 00	Del Beilun	Redel China	170387dwt	Jul 5/10	27500 Day	BHP-Billit	WAusRd
14kt/31.5t	Captain Diamantis, 00	Del Gijon	Redel Fos	74757dwt	Jul 1/3	22500 Day	D'Amico	PrtoBolivarRd
14.3kt/32t	Armia Krajowa, 91	Del So Korea	Redel Singapore/Japan	73505dwt	Jul 2/3	13500 Day	PanOcean	3020000GrnBl;NoPacRd;DC
14.5kt/55t	Sa Fortius, 01	Del Japan	Redel Fos	172509dwt	Jul 15/20	16000 Day	SK Shipp	TripOutviaAus&SoAfrica
14kt/31.5t	Christina Iv, 00	Del Cape Passero	Redel FEviaECSoAm	72493dwt	Jun 24/26	25000 Day	Dreyfus	Trip out
14kt/52t	Bulk Australia, 03	Del Cape Passero	Redel FEviaBrazil	170578dwt	Jul 5/7	45000 Day	PanOcean	Trip out
13.5kt/28t	Clipper Gem, 90	Del Jorf Lasfar	Redel FEviaECSoAm	65619dwt	Jun 21/22	25000 Day	Dreyfus	2897000GrnBl;Trip out
14kt/31.5t	Hanjin New Orleans, 94	Del Pt Kelang	Redel MedviaRichardsBay	70337dwt	Jun 23/24	12500 Day	Daeyang	Trip out
14kt/40t	Stefania, 81	Del Taiwan	Redel Skaw/Passero	61636dwt	Jun 29/30	9000 Day	Bunge	2640000GrnBl;TripOut

Appendix 26

economic growth alone is not sufficient to sustain high prices. Abare points out that it is often overlooked that China's growth is driven by demand from the US for its cheap manufactured goods. Although difficult to quantify, a significant proportion of China's consumption of minerals and energy commodities is exported in the form of manufactured products.

Also, a reduction in export growth for China will impede growth in manufacturing output and infrastructure development, flowing through to reduced demand for minerals and energy commodities.

China's economic growth depends more on exports than on growth in developed countries, with exports accounting for about 30% of China's gross domestic product in 2003. "The current cycle may already qualify as a 'super-cycle', but the sup-

ply and demand outlook for the rest of 2005 and into 2006 suggests that many prices have already peaked," the report says. Abare forecasts that the volume of Australian mine production will rise by nearly eight per cent in 2005-6. A forecast six per cent jump in the output of energy minerals is supported by production rises of oil and natural gas.

Crude oil production will rise 17% because of higher output from Santos's new 100,000 barrels-a-day project in Western Australia's Carnarvon Basin.

Higher output from the North West Shelf's fourth LNG train and the start-up in 2006 of the new Darwin LNG plant will underpin a 17% increase in natural gas production. A 10% increase in Australia's production of minerals and metals is expected to come mainly from higher output of gold, iron ore and alumina. An anticipated 10% increase in iron

ore output is attributed to the commissioning of new production capacity at Rio Tinto and BHP Billiton operations in Western Australia.

China's insatiable demand for minerals has underpinned a 140% price increase in the 54 months to May 2005. Most recent increases in the price index came from significant rises in coal and iron ore prices. The report also predicts that the value of iron ore exports will increase by 60% to $13Bn in 2005-6, after rising 53% in 2004-5. Coking coal exports will rise by 57% to $18.2Bn and thermal coal by 16% to $7.5Bn.

More output from new LNG production facilities and higher prices will cause a 40% rise in the value of Australia's LNG exports to $4.5Bn. Abare predicts that prices for some commodities will cut farm export earnings by 2.5%, to $27.2Bn.

Wet Fixtures

CARGO	VESSEL	FROM	TO	TONNES	DATE	RATE	CHART.	TERMS
Oil Dirty	Angelica Schulte, 05	WC US	Far East	80000	Jul 1	1200000	CNR	PtC;Lump Sum
Oil Dirty	Hellesp Trader. 96	St Lucia	Wilhelmshaven	130000	Jul 2	W75	PDVMarine	
Oil Dirty	SKS Tyne, 96	Trinidad	US Gulf	70000	Jul 1	W161.25	ExxonMobil	Part cargo
Oil Dirty	Elisabeth Maersk, 99	Hound Point	US Gulf	280000	Jul 6	W67	Koch	Part cargo
Oil Dirty	Bravery, 94	Tallinn	US Atlantic US Gulf	80000	Jul 6	W165	Vitol	Part cargo
Oil Dirty	Seatriumph/Racer 02	Novorossiysk	UK/Continent Med	135000	Jul 8	W150	Lukoil	Part cargo
Oil Dirty	Minerva Eleonora, 04	Black Sea	Mediterranean	80000	Jun 29	W130	Alpine	Part cargo
Oil Dirty	Cape Ancona, 98	Libya	Wilhelmshaven	80000	Jun 29	W145	Dreyfus	Part cargo
Oil Dirty	Erviken, 04	Arzew	Philadelphia	130000	Jul 14	W110	Sun	
Oil Dirty	Titan Glory, 00	Arzew	US Gulf	265000	Jul 20	W65	Valero	
Oil Dirty	African Ruby, 94	W Africa	US Atlantic	130000	Jul 13	W132	Sun	
Oil Dirty	Bourgogne, 96	W Africa	Indonesia	260000	Jul 20	W65	Vitol	
Oil Dirty	Arlene, 03	ME Gulf	US Gulf	130000	Jul 20	W100	Chevron	
Oil Dirty	Loul'wat Qatar, 90	Ras Tanura	Chittagong	80000	Jul 10	W89	BSC	
Oil Dirty	Titan Neptune, 88	ME Gulf	Japan op Singapore	257500	Jul 18	W52 op W55	ExxonMobil	
Oil Dirty	Front Lillo, 91	Bushire	Far East	130000	Jul 11	W95	Arcadia	
Oil Dirty	Hebei Ambition, 90	Kharg Island	China	260000	Jul 13	W50	Zhenrong	
Oil Dirty	Poseidon M, 95	Dumai	Taiwan	80000	Jul 4	465000	CPC	Lump Sum
Oil Clean	Hans Scholl, C4	US Gulf	EC Mexico	30000	Jun 28	270000	PMI	Lump Sum
Oil Clean	Alam Bitara, 99	US Gulf	UK/Continent	38000	Jun 29	W150	BP	
Oil Clean	Lion, 85	Caribbeans	Continent	38000	Jun 29	W150	CNR	
Oil Clean	Rosetta, 03	UK/Continent	US Atlantic	37000	Jul 5	W265	CSSA	Part cargo
Oil Clean	Smooth Hound, 89	Ant Rott Amsterdam	Mediterranean	70000	Jun 25	W125	Shell	
Oil Clean	Seaexplorer, 76	Black Sea	Mediterranean	30000	Jul 1	W290	Petraco	Part cargo
Oil Clean	Elka Hercules, 02	Mediterranean	US Atlantic	37000	Jul 5	W270	Shell	
Oil Clean	Morning Glory Vii, 99	ME Gulf	Japan	55000	Jul 12	W179	SK Shipp	Part cargo
Oil Clean	Dynamic Express, 93	Singapore	Japan	30000	Jul 14	W190	CNR	Part cargo
Oil Clean	Da Qing 453, 02	Ning Bo	Ulsan	30000	Jul 7	300000	SK Shipp	PtC;Lump Sum

Source: Maritime Research Inc

Group Profit and Loss Account

For the year ended 31st March XXXX

	This Yr £M	Last Yr £M
Turnover	2920.2	1981.7
Net Operating Costs	(2620.9)	(1791.1)
	299.3	190.6
Share of pre-tax profits of Associated Companies	28.3	21.1
Operating Profit	327.6	211.7
Interest Payable less interest receivable	(45.6)	(33.2)
Profit on ordinary activities before Profit-share and taxation	282.0	178.5
Employee Profit-share	(7.3)	(4.4)
Profit on ordinary activities before taxation	274.7	174.1
Taxation on profit on ordinary activities	(79.5)	(49.4)
Profit on ordinary activities after taxation	195.2	124.7
Minority interests	(8.8)	(2.5)
Extraordinary and Capital Items	25.3	29.8
Profit for the financial year attributable to shareholders	211.7	152.0
Dividends	(91.8)	(70.3)
Profit transferred to other reserves	(41.1)	(30.2)
Profit for the year retained in this account	78.8	51.5
Dividends per £ of deferred stock	22.0p	19.0p
Earnings per £ of deferred stock	47.1p	41.7p

Appendix 28

Balance Sheet

As at 31st March XXXX

	This Yr £M	Last Yr £M
ASSETS EMPLOYED		
Fixed Assets		
Tangible Assets		
Ships	645.2	435.7
Properties	1068.7	855.9
Other fixed assets	252.4	118.8
Interest in leased assets	33.9	34.7
Investments	168.5	139.6
	2168.7	1584.7
Current Assets		
Stocks	309.9	226.6
Debtors	573.9	437.3
Investments	8.5	11.9
Cash at bank and in hand	57.0	54.8
	949.3	730.6
	3,118.0	2,315.3
Financed by		
CAPITAL AND RESERVES		
Called up share capital	545.0	376.7
Share premium	30.9	10.4
Revaluation reserve	232.7	142.7
Other reserves	373.1	357.6
Profit and Loss Account	284.7	225.3
Stockholders' Funds	1,446.4	1,112.7
Minority interests	32.4	34.5
Provsions for liabilities and charges	77.4	55.6
Loans	610.0	363.4
Creditors	931.8	749.1
	1,651.6	1,202.6
	3,118.0	2,513.3

The Hague Rules as Amended by the Brussels Protocol 1968

Commonly referred to as

The Hague-Visby Rules

Article I

In these Rules the following words are employed, with the meanings set out below:

(a) 'Carrier' includes the owner or the charterer who enters into a contract of carriage with a shipper.

(b) 'Contract of carriage' applies only to contracts of carriage covered by a bill of lading or any similar document of title, in so far as such document relates to the carriage of goods by sea, including any bill of lading or any similar document as aforesaid issued under or pursuant to a charter party from the moment at which such bill of lading or similar document of title regulates the relations between a carrier and a holder of the same.

(c) 'Goods' includes goods, wares, merchandise, and articles of every kind whatsoever except live animals and cargo which by the contract of carriage is stated as being carried on deck and is so carried.

(d) 'Ship' means any vessel used for the carriage of goods by sea.

(e) 'Carriage of goods' covers the period from the time when the goods are loaded on to the time they are discharged from the ship.

Article II

Subject to the provisions of Article VI, under every contract of carriage of goods by sea the carrier, in relation to the loading, handling, stowage, carriage, custody, care and discharge of such goods, shall be subject to the responsibilities and liabilities and entitled to the rights and immunities hereinafter set forth.

Article III

1. The carrier shall be bound before and at the beginning of the voyage to exercise due diligence to:

   (a) Make the ship seaworthy;

   (b) Properly man, equip and supply the ship;

   (c) Make the holds, refrigerating and cool chambers, and all other parts of the ship in which goods are carried, fit and safe for their reception, carriage and preservation.

2. Subject to the provisions of Article IV, the carrier shall properly and carefully load, handle, stow, carry, keep, care for, and discharge the goods carried.

3. After receiving the goods into his charge the carrier or the master or agent of the carrier shall, on demand of the shipper, issue to the shipper a bill of lading showing among other things:

   (a) The leading marks necessary for identification of the goods as the same are furnished in writing by the shipper before the loading of such goods starts, provided such marks are stamped or otherwise shown clearly upon the goods if uncovered, or on the cases or coverings in which such goods are contained, in such a manner as should ordinarily remain legible until the end of the voyage.

(b) Either the number of packages or pieces, or the quantity, or weight, as the case may be, as furnished in writing by the shipper.

(c) The apparent order and condition of the goods.

Provided that no carrier, master or agent of the carrier shall be bound to state or show in the bill of lading any marks, number, quantity or weight which he has reasonable ground for suspecting not accurately to represent the goods actually received, or which he has had no reasonable means of checking.

4. Such a bill of lading shall be *prima facie* evidence of the receipt by the carrier of the goods as therein described in accordance with paragraph 3 (a), (b) and (c). However, proof to the contrary shall not be admissible when the bill of lading has been transferred to a third party acting in good faith.

5. The shipped shall be deemed to have guaranteed to the carrier the accuracy at the time of shipment of the marks, number, quantity and weight, as furnished by him, and the shipper shall indemnify the carrier against all loss, damages and expenses arising or resulting from inaccuracies in such particulars. The right of the carrier to such indemnity shall on no way limit his responsibility and liability under the contract of carriage to any person other than the shipper.

6. Unless notice of loss or damage and the general nature of such loss or damage be given in writing to the carrier or his agent at the port of discharge before or at the time of the removal of the goods into the custody of the person entitled to delivery thereof under the contract of carriage, or, if the loss or damage be not apparent, within three days, such removal shall be *prima facie* evidence of the delivery by the carrier of the goods as described in the bill of lading.

The notice in writing need not be given if the state of the goods has, at the time of their receipt, been the subject of joint survey or inspection.

Subject to paragraph 6 bis the carrier and the ship shall in any event be discharged from all liability whatsoever in respect of the goods, unless suit is brought within one year of their delivery or of the date when they should have been delivered. This period, may however, be extended if the parties so agree after the cause of action has arisen.

In the case of any actual or apprehended loss or damage the carrier and the receiver shall give all reasonable facilities to each other for inspecting and tallying the goods.

6bis. An action for indemnity against a third person may be brought even after the expiration of the year provided for in the preceding paragraph if brought within the time allowed by the law of the Court seized of the case. However, the time allowed shall be not less than three months, commencing from the day when the person bringing such action for indemnity has settled the claim or has been served with process in the action against himself.

7. After the goods are loaded the bill of lading to be issued by the carrier, master, or agent of the carrier, to the shipper shall, if the shipper so demands be a 'shipped' bill of lading provided that if the shipper shall have previously taken up any document of title to such goods, he shall surrender the same as against the issue of the 'shipped' bill of lading, but at the option of the carrier such document of title may be noted at the port of shipment by the carrier, master, or agent with the name or names of the ship or ships upon which the goods have been shipped and the date or dates of shipment, and when so noted, if it shows the particulars mentioned in paragraph 3 of Article III. shall for the purpose of this article be deemed to constitute a 'shipped' bill of lading.

8. Any clause, covenant, or agreement in a contract of carriage relieving the carrier or the ship from liability for loss or damage to, or in connection with goods arising from negligence, fault, or failure in the duties and obligations provided in this article or lessening such liability otherwise than as provided in these Rules, shall be null and void and of no effect. A benefit of insurance in favour of the carrier or similar clause shall be deemed to be a clause relieving the carrier from liability.

Article IV

1. Neither the carrier nor the ship shall be liable for loss or damage arising or resulting from unseaworthiness unless caused by want of due diligence on the part of the carrier to make the ship seaworthy, and to secure that the ship is properly manned, equipped and supplied, and to make the holds, refrigerating and cool chambers and all other parts of the ships in which goods are carried fit and safe for their reception, carriage and preservation in accordance with the provisions of paragraph 1 of Article III. Whenever loss or damage has resulted from unseaworthiness the burden of proving the exercise of due diligence shall be on the carrier or other person claiming exemption under this article.

2. Neither the carrier nor she ship shall be responsible for loss or damage arising or resulting from:

(a) Act, neglect, or default of the master, mariner pilot, or the servants of the carrier in the navigation or in the management of the ship.

(b) Fire, unless caused by the actual fault or privity of the carrier.

(c) Perils, dangers and accidents of the sea or other navigable waters.

(d) Act of God.

(e) Act of war.

(f) Act of public enemies.

(g) Arrest or restraint of princes, rulers or people, or seizure under legal process.

(h) Quarantine restrictions.

(i) Act or omission of he shipper or owner of the goods, his agent or representative.

(j) Strikes or lockouts or stoppage or restraint of labour from whatever cause, whether partial or general.

(k) Riots and civil commotions.

(l) Saving of attempting to save life or property at sea.

(m) Wastage in bulk of weight or any other loss or damage arising from inherent defect, quality or vice of the goods.

(n) Insufficiency of packing.

(o) Insufficiency of inadequacy of marks.

(p) Latent defects not discoverable by due diligence.

(q) Any other cause arising without the actual fault or privity of the carrier, or without the fault or neglect of the agents or servants of the carrier, but the burden of proof shall be on the person claiming the benefit of this exception to show that neither the actual fault or privity of the carrier nor the fault of neglect of the agents or servants of the carrier contributed to the loss or damage.

3. The shipped shall not be responsible for loss or damage sustained by the carrier or the ship arising or resulting from any cause without the act, fault or neglect of the shipper, his agents or his servants.

4. Any deviation in saving or attempting to save life or property at sea or any reasonable deviation shall not be deemed to be an infringement or breach of these Rules or of the contract of carriage, and the carrier shall not be liable for any loss or damage resulting therefrom.

5. **(a)** Unless the nature and value of such goods have been declared by the shipper before shipment and inserted in the bill of lading, neither the carriage nor the ship shall in any event be or become liable for any loss or damage to or in connection with the goods in an amount exceeding the equivalent of 666.67 units of account per package or unit or units of account per kilo of gross weight of the goods lost or damaged, whichever is the higher.

(b) The total amount recoverable shall be calculated by reference to the value of such goods at the place and time at which the goods are discharged from the ship in accordance with the contract or should have been so discharged.

The value of the goods shall be fixed accordingly to the commodity exchange price, or, if there be no such price, according to the current market price, or, if there be no commodity price or current market price, by reference to the normal value of goods of the same kind and quality.

(c) Where a container, pallet or similar article of transport is used to consolidate goods, the number of packages or units enumerated in the bill of lading as packed in such article of transport shall be deemed the number of packages or units for the purpose of this paragraph as far as these packages or units are concerned. Except as aforesaid such article of transport shall be considered the package or unit.

(d) The unit of account mentioned in this Article is the special drawing right as defined by the International Monetary Fund. The amounts mentioned in h_visby/art/art/04_5a sub-paragraph (a) of this paragraph shall be converted into national currency on the basis of the value of that currency on a date to be determined by the law of the Court sized of the case.

(e) Neither the carrier nor the ship shall be entitled to the benefit of the limitation of liability provided for in this paragraph if it is proved that the damage resulted from an act or omission of the carrier done with intent to cause damage, or recklessly and with knowledge that damage would probably result.

(f) The declaration mentioned in sub-paragraph (a) of this paragraph, if embodied in the bill of lading, shall be *prima facie* evidence, but shall not be binding or conclusive on the carrier.

(g) By agreement between the carrier, master or agent of the carrier and the shipper other maximum amounts than those mentioned in sub-paragraph (a) of this paragraph may be fixed, provided that no maximum amount so fixed shall be less than the appropriate maximum mentioned in that sub-paragraph.

(h) Neither the carrier nor the ship shall be responsible in any event for loss or damage to, or in connection with, goods if the nature or value thereof has been knowingly mis-stated by the shipper in the bill of lading.

6. Goods of an inflammable, explosive or dangerous nature to the shipment whereof the carrier, master or agent of the carrier has not consented with knowledge of their nature and character, may at any time before discharge be landed at any place, or destroyed or rendered innocuous by the carrier without compensation and the shipper of such goods shall be liable for all damages and expenses directly of indirectly arising out of or resulting from such shipment. If any such goods shipped with such knowledge and consent shall become a danger to the ship or cargo, they may in like manner be landed at any place, or destroyed or rendered innocuous by the carrier without the liability on the part of the carrier except to general average, if any.

Article IV bis

1. The defences and limits of liability provided for in these Rules shall apply in any action against the carrier in respect of loss or damage to goods covered by a contract of carriage whether the action be founded in contract or in tort.

2. If such an action is brought against a servant or agent of the carrier (such servant or agent not being an independent contractor), such servant or agent shall be entitled to avail himself of the defences and limits of liability which the carrier is entitled to invoke under these Rules.

3. The aggregate of the amounts recoverable from the carrier, and such servants and agents, shall in no case excel the limit provided for in these Rules.

4. Nevertheless, a servant or agent of the carrier shall not be entitled to avail himself of the provisions of this article, if it is proved that the damage resulted from an act or omission of the servant or agent done with intent to cause damage or recklessly and with knowledge that damage would probably result.

Article V

A carrier shall be at liberty to surrender in whole or in part all or any of his rights and immunities or to increase any of his responsibilities and obligations under these Rules, provided such surrender or increase shall be embodied in the bill of lading issued to the shipper. The provisions of these Rules shall not be applicable to charter parties, but if bills of lading are issued in the case of a ship under a charter party they shall comply with the terms of these Rules. Nothing in these Rules shall be held to prevent the insertion in a bill of lading of any lawful provision regarding general average.

Article VI

Notwithstanding the provisions of the preceding articles, a carrier, master or agent of the carrier and a shipper shall in regard to any particular goods be at liberty to enter into any agreement in any terms as to the responsibility and liability of the carrier for such goods, and as to the rights and immunities of the carrier in respect of such goods, or his obligation as to seaworthiness, so far as this stipulation is not contrary to public policy, or the care or diligence of his servants or agents in regard to the loading, handling, stowage, carriage, custody, care and discharge of the gods carried by sea, provided that in this case no bill of lading has been or shall be issued and that the terms agreed shall be embodied in a receipt which shall be a non-negotiable document and shall marked as such.

An agreement so entered into shall have full legal effect.

Provided that this article shall not apply to ordinary commercial shipments made in the ordinary course of trade, but only to other shipments where the character or condition of the property to be carried or the circumstances, terms and conditions under which the carriage is to be performed are such as reasonably to justify a special agreement.

Article VII

Nothing herein contained shall prevent a carrier or a shipper from entering into any agreement, stipulation, condition, reservation or exemption as to the responsibility and reliability of the carrier or the ship for the loss or damage to, or in connection with, the custody and care and handling of goods prior to the loading on, and subsequent to the discharge from, the ship on which the goods are carried by sea.

Article VIII

The provisions of these Rules shall not affect the rights and obligations of the carrier under any statute for the time being in force relating to the limitation of the liability of owners of sea-going vessels.

Article IX

These Rules shall not affect the provisions of any international Convention or national law governing liability for nuclear damage.

Article X

The provisions of these Rules shall apply to every bill of lading relating to the carriage of goods between ports in two different States if:

(a) the bill of lading is issued in a contracting State, or

(b) the carriage is from a port in a contracting State, or

(c) the contract contained in or evidenced by the bill of lading provides that these Rules or legislation of any State giving effect to them are to govern the contract;

whatever may be the nationality of the ship, the carrier, the shipper, the consignee, or any other interested person.

(The last two paragraphs of this Article are not reproduced. They require contracting States to apply the Rules to bills of lading mentioned in the Article and authorise them to apply the Rules to other bills of lading).

(Article 11 to 16 of the International Convention for the unification of certain rules of law relating to bills of lading signed at Brussels on August 25, 1974 are not reproduced. They deal with the coming into force of the Convention, procedure for ratification, accession and denunciation and the right to call for a fresh conference to consider amendments to the Rules contained in the Convention).

General Clause Paramount

The International Convention for the Unification of Certain Rules of Law relating to Bills of Lading signed at Brussels on 25 August 1925 ("the Hague Rules") as amended by the Protocol signed at Brussels on 23 February 1968 ("the Hague-Visby Rules") and as enacted in the country of shipment shall apply to this contract. When the Hague-Visby are not enacted in the country of shipment, the corresponding legislation of the country of destination shall apply, irrespective of whether such legislation may only regulate outbound shipments.

When there is no enactment of the Hague-Visby Rules in either the country of shipment or in the country of destination, the Hague-Visby Rules shall apply to this contract save where the Hague Rules as enacted in the country of shipment or if no such enactment is in place, the Hague Rules as enacted in the country of destination apply compulsorily to this Contract.

The Protocol signed in Brussels on 21 December 1979 ("the SDR Protocol 1979") shall apply where the Hague-Visby Rules apply, whether mandatorily or by the Contract.

The Carrier shall in no case be responsible for loss or damage to cargo arising prior to loading, after discharging, or while the cargo is in the charge of another carrier, or with respect to deck cargo and live animals.

New Jason Clause

In the event of accident, danger, damage or disaster before or after commencement of the voyage, resulting from any cause whatsoever, whether due to negligence or not, for which, or for the consequences of which, the carrier is not responsible. By statute, contract or otherwise, the goods, shippers, consignees or owners of the goods shall contribute with the carrier in general average to the payment of any sacrifice, losses or expenses of a general average nature that may be made or incurred, and shall pay salvage and special charges incurred in respect of the goods.

If a salving ship is owned or operated by the carriers, the salvage shall be paid for as fully as if such salving ship or ships belonged to strangers. Such deposit as the carrier or his agents may deem sufficient to cover the estimated contribution of the goods, and any salvage and special charges thereon shall, if required, be made by the goods, shippers, consignees or owners of the goods to the carrier before delivery.

Both to Blame Collision Clause

If the ship comes into collision with another ship as a result of the negligence of the other ship and any act, neglect or default of the master mariner, pilot or the servants of the carrier in the navigation or in the management of the ship, the owners of the goods carried hereunder will indemnify the carrier against all loss or liability to the other non-carrying ship or her owners in so far as such loss or liability represents loss of, or damage to, or any claim whatsoever of the owners of the said goods, paid or payable by the other non-carrying ship or her owners as part of their claim against the carrying ship or carrier.

The foregoing provisions shall also apply where the owners, operators or those in charge of any ship or ships or objects other than, or in addition to, the colliding ships or objects are the fault in respect to a collision or contract.Appendix 10:6.

Appendix 33

War Risks Clauses

BIMCO Standard War Risks Clause for Voyage Chartering, 1993 Code Name: "Voywar 1993"

(1) For the purpose of this Clause, the words:

(a) "Owner" shall include the shipowners, bareboat charterers, disponent owners, managers or other operators who are charged with the management of the Vessel, and the Master; and

(b) "War Risks" shall include any war (whether actual or threatened), act of war, civil war, hostilities, revolution, rebellion, civil commotion, warlike operations, the laying of mines (whether actual or reported), acts of piracy, acts of terrorists, acts of hostility or malicious damage, blockades (whether imposed against all vessels or imposed selectively against vessels of certain flags or ownership, or against certain cargoes or crews or otherwise howsoever), by any person, body, terrorist or political group, or the Government of any state whatsoever, which, in the reasonable judgement of the Master and/or the Owners, may be dangerous or are likely to be or to become dangerous to the Vessel, her cargo, crew or other persons on board the Vessel.

(2) If at any time before the Vessel commences loading, it appears that, in the reasonable judgement of the Master and/or the Owners, performance of the Contract of Carriage, or any part of it, may expose, or is likely to expose, the Vessel, her cargo, crew or other persons on board the Vessel to War Risks, the Owners may give notice to the Charterers cancelling this Contract of Carriage, or may refuse to form such part of it as may expose, or may be likely to expose, the Vessel, her cargo, crew or other persons on board the Vessel to War Risks; provided always that if this Contract of Carriage provides that loading or discharging is to take place within a range of ports, and at the port or ports nominated by the Charterers the Vessel, her cargo,, crew, or other persons onboard the Vessel may be exposed, or may be likely to be exposed, to War Risks, the Owners shall first require the Charterers to nominate any other safe port which lies within the range for loading or discharging, and may only cancel this Contract of Carriage if the Charterers shall not have nominated such safe port or ports within 48 hours of receipt of notice of such requirement.

(3) The Owners shall not be required to continue to load cargo for any voyage, or to sign Bills of Lading for any port or place, or to proceed or continue on any voyage, or on any part thereof, or to proceed through any canal or waterway, or to proceed to or remain at any port or place whatsoever, where it appears, either after the loading of the cargo commences, or any any stage of the voyage thereafter before the discharge of the cargo is completed, that, in the reasonable judgement of the Master and/or the Owners, the Vessl, her cargo (or any part thereof), crfew or other persons on board the Vessel (or any one or ore of them) may be, or are likely to be, exposed to War Risks. If it should so appear, the Owners may by notice request the Charters to nominate a safe port for the discharge of the cargo or any part thereof, and if within 48 hours of the receipt of such notice, the Charterers shall not have nominated such a port, the Owners may discharge the cargo at any safe port of their choice (including the port of loading) in complete fulfillment of the Contract of Carriage. The Owners shall be entitled to recover from the Charterers the extra expenses of such discharge and, if the discharge takes place at any port other than the loading port, to receive the full freight as though the cargo had been carried to the discharging port and if the extra distance exceeds 100 miles, to additional freight which shall be the same percentage of the freight contracted for as the percentage which the extra distance represents to the distance of the normal and customary route, the Owners having a lien on the cargo for such expenses and freight.

(4) If at any stage of the voyage after the loading of the cargo commences it appears that, in the reasonable judgement of the Master and/or the Owners, the Vessel, her cargo, crew or other persons on board the Vessel may be, or are likely to be, exposed to War Risks on any part of the route (including any canal or waterway) which is normally and customarily used in a voyage of the nature contracted for, and there is another longer route to the discharging port, the Owners shall give notice to the Charterers that this route will be taken. In this event the Owners shal lbe entitled, if the total extra distance exceeds 100 miles to additional freight which shall be the same percentage of the freight contracted for as the percentage which the extra distance represents to the distance of the normal and customary route.

(5) The Vessel shall have liberty:

(a) to comply with all orders, directions, recommendations or advice as to departure, arrival, routes, sailing in convoy, ports of call, stoppages, destinations, discharge of cargo, delivery or in any way whatsoever which are given by the Government of the Nation under whose flag the Vessel sails, or other Government to whose laws the Owners are subject, or any other Government which so requires, or any body or group acting with the power to compel compliance with their orders or directions;

(b) to comply with the orders, directions or recommendations of any war risks underwriters who have the authority to give the same under the terms of the war risks insurance;

(c) to comply with the terms of any resolution of the Security Council of the United Nations, and directives of the European Community, the effective orders of any other Supranational body which has the right to issue and give the same, and with national laws aimed at enforcing the same to which the Owners are subject, and to obey the orders and directions of those who are charged with their enforcement;

(d) to discharge at any other port any cargo or part thereof which may render the Vessel liable to confiscation as a contraband carrier;

(e) to call at any other port to change the crew or any part thereof or other persons on board the Vessel when there is reason to believe that they may be subject to internment, imprisonment or other sanctions;

(f) where cargo has been loaded or has been discharged by the Owners under any provisions of this Clause, to load other cargo for the Owners' own behalf and carry it to any other port or ports whatsoever, whether backwards or forwards or in a contrary direction to the ordinary or customary route.

(6) If in compliance with any of the provisions of sub-clauses (2) to (5) of this Clause anything is done or not done, such shall not be deemed to be a deviation, but shall be considered as due fulfilment of the Contract of Carriage.

United Nations Convention on the Carriage of Goods by Sea (1978)

Hamburg Rules

PREAMBLE

THE STATES PARTIES TO THIS CONVENTION,

HAVING RECOGNIZED the desirability of determining by agreement certain rules relating to the carriage of goods by sea,

HAVING DECIDED to conclude a convention for this purpose and have thereto agreed as follows:

PART I. GENERAL PROVISIONS

Article 1. Definitions

In this Convention:

1. "Carrier" means any person by whom or in whose name a contract of carriage of goods by sea has been concluded with a shipper.

2. "Actual carrier" means any person to whom the performance of the carriage of the goods, or of part of the carriage, has been entrusted by the carrier, and includes any other person to whom such performance has been entrusted.

3. "Shipper" means any person by whom or in whose name or on whose behalf a contract of carriage of goods by sea has been concluded with a carrier, or any person by whom or in whose name or on whose behalf the goods are actually delivered to the carrier in relation to the contract of carriage by sea.

4. "Consignee" means the person entitled to take delivery of the goods.

5. "Goods" includes live animals; where the goods are consolidated in a container, pallet or similar article of transport or where they are packed, goods includes such article of transport or packaging if supplied by the shipper.

6. "Contract of carriage by sea" means any contract whereby the carrier undertakes against payment of freight to carry goods by sea from one port to another; however, a contract which involves carriage by sea and also carriage by some other means is deemed to be a contract of carriage by sea for the purposes of this Convention only in so far as it relates to the carriage by sea.

7. "Bill of lading" means a document which evidences a contract of carriage by sea and the taking over or loading of the goods by the carrier, and by which the carrier undertakes to deliver the goods against surrender of the document. A provision in the document that the goods are to be delivered to the order of a named person, or to order, or to bearer, constitutes such an undertaking.

8. "Writing" includes, *inter alia*, telegram and telex.

Article 2. Scope of application

1. The provisions of this Convention are applicable to all contracts of carriage by sea between two different States, if:

    (a) the port of loading as provided for in the contract of carriage by sea is located in a Contracting State, or

    (b) the port of discharge as provided for in the contract of carriage by sea is located in a Contracting State, or

    (c) one of the optional ports of discharge provided for in the contract of carriage by sea is the actual port of discharge and such port is located in a Contracting State, or

    (d) the bill of lading or other document evidencing the contract of carriage by sea is issued in a Contracting State, or

    (e) the bill of lading or other document evidencing the contract of carriage by sea provides that the provisions of this Convention or the legislation of any State giving effect to them are to govern the contract.

2. The provisions of this Convention are applicable without regard to the nationality of the ship, the carrier, the actual carrier, the shipper, the consignee or any other interested person.

3. The provisions of this Convention are not applicable to charter-parties. However, where a bill of lading is issued pursuant to a charter-party, the provisions of the Convention apply to such a bill of lading if it governs the relation between the carrier and the holder of the bill of lading, not being the charterer.

4. If a contract provides for future carriage of goods in a series of shipments during an agreed period, the provisions of this Convention apply to each shipment. However, where a shipment is made under a charter-party, the provisions of paragraph 3 of this article apply.

Article 3. Interpretation of the Convention

In the interpretation and application of the provisions of this Convention regard shall be had to its international character and to the need to promote uniformity.

PART II. LIABILITY OF THE CARRIER

Article 4. Period of responsibility

1. The responsibility of the carrier for the goods under this Convention covers the period during which the carrier is in charge of the goods at the port of loading, during the carriage and at the port of discharge.

2. For the purpose of paragraph 1 of this article, the carrier is deemed to be in charge of the goods

    (a) from the time he has taken over the goods from:

    (i)   the shipper, or a person acting on his behalf; or

    (ii)   an authority or other third party to whom, pursuant to law or regulations applicable at the port of loading, the goods must be handed over for shipment;

    (b) until the time he has delivered the goods:

    (i)   by handing over the goods to the consignee; or

    (ii)   in cases where the consignee does not receive the goods from the carrier, by placing them at the disposal of the consignee in accordance with the contract or with the law or with the usage of the particular trade, applicable at the port of discharge; or

    (iii) by handing over the goods to an authority or other third party to whom, pursuant to law or regulations applicable at the port of discharge, the goods must be handed over.

3. In paragraphs 1 and 2 of this article, reference to the carrier or to the consignee means, in addition to the carrier or the consignee, the servants or agents, respectively of the carrier or the consignee.

Article 5. Basis of liability

1. The carrier is liable for loss resulting from loss of or damage to the goods, as well as from delay in delivery, if the occurrence which caused the loss, damage or delay took place while the goods were in his charge as defined in article 4, unless the carrier proves that he, his servants or agents took all measures that could reasonably be required to avoid the occurrence and its consequences.

2. Delay in delivery occurs when the goods have not been delivered at the port of discharge provided for in the contract of carriage by sea within the time expressly agreed upon or, in the absence of such agreement, within the time which it would be reasonable to require of a diligent carrier, having regard to the circumstances of the case.

3. The person entitled to make a claim for the loss of goods may treat the goods as lost if they have not been delivered as required by article 4 within 60 consecutive days following the expiry of the time for delivery according to paragraph 2 of this article.

4. *(a)* The carrier is liable

    (i) for loss of or damage to the goods or delay in delivery caused by fire, if the claimant proves that the fire arose from fault or neglect on the part of the carrier, his servants or agents;

    (ii) for such loss, damage or delay in delivery which is proved by the claimant to have resulted from the fault or neglect of the carrier, his servants or agents in taking all measures that could reasonably be required to put out the fire and avoid or mitigate its consequences.

    (b) In case of fire on board the ship affecting the goods, if the claimant or the carrier so desires, a survey in accordance with shipping practices must be held into the cause and circumstances of the fire, and a copy of the surveyors report shall be made available on demand to the carrier and the claimant.

5. With respect to live animals, the carrier is not liable for loss, damage or delay in delivery resulting from any special risks inherent in that kind of carriage. If the carrier proves that he has complied with any special instructions given to him by the shipper respecting the animals and that, in the circumstances of the case, the loss, damage or delay in delivery could be attributed to such risks, it is presumed that the loss, damage or delay in delivery was so caused, unless there is proof that all or a part of the loss, damage or delay in delivery resulted from fault or neglect on the part of the carrier, his servants or agents.

6. The carrier is not liable, except in general average, where loss, damage or delay in delivery resulted from measures to save life or from reasonable measures to save property at sea.

7. Where fault or neglect on the part of the carrier, his servants or agents combines with another cause to produce loss, damage or delay in delivery, the carrier is liable only to the extent that the loss, damage or delay in delivery is attributable to such fault or neglect, provided that the carrier proves the amount of the loss, damage or delay in delivery not attributable thereto.

Article 6. Limits of liability

1. *(a)* The liability of the carrier for loss resulting from loss of or damage to goods according to the provisions of article 5 is limited to an amount equivalent to 835 units of account per package or other shipping unit or 2.5 units of account per kilogram of gross weight of the goods lost or damaged, whichever is the higher.

(b) The liability of the carrier for delay in delivery according to the provisions of article 5 is limited to an amount equivalent to two and a half times the freight payable for the goods delayed, but not exceeding the total freight payable under the contract of carriage of goods by sea.

(c) In no case shall the aggregate liability of the carrier, under both subparagraphs *(a)* and *(b)* of this paragraph, exceed the limitation which would be established under subparagraph *(a)* of this paragraph for total loss of the goods with respect to which such liability was incurred.

2. For the purpose of calculating which amount is the higher in accordance with paragraph 1 *(a)* of this article, the following rules apply:

(a) Where a container, pallet or similar article of transport is used to consolidate goods, the package or other shipping units enumerated in the bill of lading, if issued, or otherwise in any other document evidencing the contract of carriage by sea, as packed in such article of transport are deemed packages or shipping units. Except as aforesaid the goods in such article of transport are deemed one shipping unit.

(b) In cases where the article of transport itself has been lost or damaged, that article of transport, if not owned or otherwise supplied by the carrier, is considered one separate shipping unit.

3. Unit of account means the unit of account mentioned in article 26.

4. By agreement between the carrier and the shipper, limits of liability exceeding those provided for in paragraph 1 may be fixed.

Article 7. Application to non-contractual claims

1. The defences and limits of liability provided for in this Convention apply in any action against the carrier in respect of loss of or damage to the goods covered by the contract of carriage by sea, as well as of delay in delivery whether the action is founded in contract, in tort or otherwise.

2. If such an action is brought against a servant or agent of the carrier, such servant or agent, if he proves that he acted within the scope of his employment, is entitled to avail himself of the defences and limits of liability which the carrier is entitled to invoke under this Convention.

3. Except as provided in article 8, the aggregate of the amounts recoverable from the carrier and from any persons referred to in paragraph 2 of this article shall not exceed the limits of liability provided for in this Convention.

Article 8. Loss of right to limit responsibility

1. The carrier is not entitled to the benefit of the limitation of liability provided for in article 6 if it is proved that the loss, damage or delay in delivery resulted from an act or omission of the carrier done with the intent to cause such loss, damage or delay, or recklessly and with knowledge that such loss, damage or delay would probably result.

2. Notwithstanding the provisions of paragraph 2 of article 7, a servant or agent of the carrier is not entitled to the benefit of the limitation of liability provided for in article 6 if it is proved that the loss, damage or delay in delivery resulted from an act or omission of such servant or agent, done with the intent to cause such loss, damage or delay, or recklessly and with knowledge that such loss, damage or delay would probably result.

Article 9. Deck cargo

1. The carrier is entitled to carry the goods on deck only if such carriage is in accordance with an agreement with the shipper or with the usage of the particular trade or is required by statutory rules or regulations.

2. If the carrier and the shipper have agreed that the goods shall or may be carried on deck, the carrier must insert in the bill of lading or other document evidencing the contract of carriage by sea a statement to that effect. In the absence of such a statement the carrier has the burden of proving that an agreement for carriage on deck has been entered into; however, the carrier is not entitled to invoke such an agreement against a third party, including a consignee, who has acquired the bill of lading in good faith.

3. Where the goods have been carried on deck contrary to the provisions of paragraph 1 of this article or where the carrier may not under paragraph 2 of this article invoke an agreement for carriage on deck, the carrier, notwithstanding the provisions of paragraph 1 of article 5, is liable for loss of or damage to the goods, as well as for delay in delivery, resulting solely from the carriage on deck, and the extent of his liability is to be determined in accordance with the provisions of article 6 or article 8 of this Convention, as the case may be.

4. Carriage of goods on deck contrary to express agreement for carriage under deck is deemed to be an act or omission of the carrier within the meaning of article 8.

Article 10. Liability of the carrier and actual carrier

1. Where the performance of the carriage or part thereof has been entrusted to an actual carrier, whether or not in pursuance of a liberty under the contract of carriage by sea to do so, the carrier nevertheless remains responsible for the entire carriage according to the provisions of this Convention. The carrier is responsible, in relation to the carriage performed by the actual carrier, for the acts and omissions of the actual carrier and of his servants and agents acting within the scope of their employment.

2. All the provisions of this Convention governing the responsibility of the carrier also apply to the responsibility of the actual carrier for the carriage performed by him. The provisions of paragraphs 2 and 3 of article 7 and of paragraph 2 of article 8 apply if an action is brought against a servant or agent of the actual carrier.

3. Any special agreement under which the carrier assumes obligations not imposed by this Convention or waives rights conferred by this Convention affects the actual carrier only if agreed to by him expressly and in writing. Whether or not the actual carrier has so agreed, the carrier nevertheless remains bound by the obligations or waivers resulting from such special agreement.

4. Where and to the extent that both the carrier and the actual carrier are liable, their liability is joint and several.

5. The aggregate of the amounts recoverable from the carrier, the actual carrier and their servants and agents shall not exceed the limits of liability provided for in this Convention.

6. Nothing in this article shall prejudice any right of recourse as between the carrier and the actual carrier.

Article 11. Through carriage

1. Notwithstanding the provisions of paragraph 1 of article 10, where a contract of carriage by sea provides explicitly that a specified part of the carriage covered by the said contract is to be performed by a named person other than the carrier, the contract may also provide that the carrier is not liable for loss, damage or delay in delivery caused by an occurrence which takes place while the goods are in the charge of the actual carrier during such part of the carriage. Nevertheless, any stipulation limiting or excluding such liability is without effect if no judicial proceedings can be instituted against the actual carrier in a court competent under paragraph 1 or 2 of article 21. The burden of proving that any loss, damage or delay in delivery has been caused by such an occurrence rests upon the carrier.

2. The actual carrier is responsible in accordance with the provisions of paragraph 2 of article 10 for loss, damage or delay in delivery caused by an occurrence which takes place while the goods are in his charge.

PART III. LIABILITY OF THE SHIPPERS

Article 12. General rule

The shipper is not liable for loss sustained by the carrier or the actual carrier, or for damage sustained by the ship, unless such loss or damage was caused by the fault or neglect of the shipper, his servants or agents. Nor is any servant or agent of the shipper liable for such loss or damage unless the loss or damage was caused by fault or neglect on his part.

Article 13. Special rules on dangerous goods

1. The shipper must mark or label in a suitable manner dangerous goods as dangerous.

2. Where the shipper hands over dangerous goods to the carrier or an actual carrier, as the case may be, the shipper must inform him of the dangerous character of the goods and, if necessary, of the precautions to be taken. If the shipper fails to do so and such carrier or actual carrier does not otherwise have knowledge of their dangerous character:

    (a) the shipper is liable to the carrier and any actual carrier for the loss resulting from the shipment of such goods, and

    (b) the goods may at any time be unloaded, destroyed or rendered innocuous, as the circumstances may require, without payment of compensation.

3. The provisions of paragraph 2 of this article may not be invoked by any person if during the carriage he has taken the goods in his charge with knowledge of their dangerous character.

4. If, in cases where the provisions of paragraph 2, subparagraph (b), of this article do not apply or may not be invoked, dangerous goods become an actual danger to life or property, they may be unloaded, destroyed or rendered innocuous, as the circumstances may require, without payment of compensation except where there is an obligation to contribute in general average or where the carrier is liable in accordance with the provisions of article 5.

PART IV. TRANSPORT DOCUMENTS

Article 14. Issue of bill of lading

1. When the carrier or the actual carrier takes the goods in his charge, the carrier must, on demand of the shipper, issue to the shipper a bill of lading.

2. The bill of lading may be signed by a person having authority from the carrier. A bill of lading signed by the master of the ship carrying the goods is deemed to have been signed on behalf of the carrier.

3. The signature on the bill of lading may be in handwriting, printed in facsimile, perforated, stamped, in symbols, or made by any other mechanical or electronic means, if not inconsistent with the law of the country where the bill of lading is issued.

Article 15. Contents of bill of lading

1. The bill of lading must include, *inter alia*, the following particulars:

    (a) the general nature of the goods, the leading marks necessary for identification of the goods, an express statement, if applicable, as to the dangerous character of the goods, the number of packages or pieces, and the weight of the goods or their quantity otherwise expressed, all such particulars as furnished by the shipper;

    (b) the apparent condition of the goods;

(c)   the name and principal place of business of the carrier;

(d)   the name of the shipper;

(e)   the consignee if named by the shipper;

(f)   the port of loading under the contract of carriage by sea and the date on which the goods were taken over by the carrier at the port of loading;

(g)   the port of discharge under the contract of carriage by sea;

(h)   the number of originals of the bill of lading, if more than one;

(i)   the place of issuance of the bill of lading;

(j)   the signature of the carrier or a person acting on his behalf;

(k)   the freight to the extent payable by the consignee or other indication that freight is payable by him;

(l)   the statement referred to in paragraph 3 of article 23;

(m)   the statement, if applicable, that the goods shall or may be carried on deck;

(n)   the date or the period of delivery of the goods at the port of discharge if expressly agreed upon between the parties; and

(o)   any increased limit or limits of liability where agreed in accordance with paragraph 4 of article 6.

2.   After the goods have been loaded on board, if the shipper so demands, the carrier must issue to the shipper a "shipped" bill of lading which, in addition to the particulars required under paragraph 1 of this article, must state that the goods are on board a named ship or ships, and the date or dates of loading. If the carrier has previously issued to the shipper a bill of lading or other document of title with respect to any of such goods, on request of the carrier the shipper must surrender such document in exchange for a "shipped" bill of lading. The carrier may amend any previously issued document in order to meet the shippers demand for a "shipped" bill of lading if, as amended, such document includes all the information required to be contained in a "shipped" bill of lading.

3.   The absence in the bill of lading of one or more particulars referred to in this article does not affect the legal character of the document as a bill of lading provided that it nevertheless meets the requirements set out in paragraph 7 of article 1.

Article 16. Bills of lading: reservations and evidentiary effect

1.   If the bill of lading contains particulars concerning the general nature, leading marks, number of packages of pieces, weight or quantity of the goods which the carrier or other person issuing the bill of lading on his behalf knows or has reasonable grounds to suspect do not accurately represent the goods actually taken over or, where a "shipped" bill of lading is issued, loaded, or if he had no reasonable means of checking such particulars, the carrier or such other person must insert in the bill of lading a reservation specifying these inaccuracies, grounds of suspicion or the absence of reasonable means of checking.

2.   If the carrier or other person issuing the bill of lading on his behalf fails to note on the bill of lading the apparent condition of the goods, he is deemed to have noted on the bill of lading that the goods were in apparent good condition.

3.   Except for particulars in respect of which and to the extent to which a reservation permitted under paragraph 1 of this article has been entered:

(a)   the bill of lading is prima facie evidence of the taking over or, where a "shipped" bill of lading is issued, loading, by the carrier of the goods as described in the bill of lading; and

(b)   proof to the contrary by the carrier is not admissible if the bill of lading has been transferred to a third party, including a consignee, who in good faith has acted in reliance on the description of the goods therein.

4.   A bill of lading which does not, as provided in paragraph 1, subparagraph (k), of article 15, set forth the freight or otherwise indicate that freight is payable by the consignee or does not set forth demurrage incurred at the port of loading payable by the consignee, is prima facie evidence that no freight or such demurrage is payable by him. However, proof to the contrary by the carrier is not admissible when the bill of lading has been transferred to a third party, including a consignee, who in good faith has acted in reliance on the absence in the bill of lading of any such indication.

Article 17. Guarantees by the shipper

1.   The shipper is deemed to have guaranteed to the carrier the accuracy of particulars relating to the general nature of the goods, their marks, number, weight and quantity as furnished by him for insertion in the bill of lading. The shipper must indemnify the carrier against the loss resulting from inaccuracies in such particulars. The shipper remains liable even if the bill of lading has been transferred by him. The right of the carrier to such indemnity in no way limits his liability under the contract of carriage by sea to any person other than the shipper.

2.   Any letter of guarantee or agreement by which the shipper undertakes to indemnify the carrier against loss resulting from the issuance of the bill of lading by the carrier, or by a person acting on his behalf, without entering a reservation relating to particulars furnished by the shipper for insertion in the bill of lading, or to the apparent condition of the goods, is void and of no effect as against any third party, including a consignee, to whom the bill of lading has been transferred.

3.   Such a letter of guarantee or agreement is valid as against the shipper unless the carrier or the person acting on his behalf, by omitting the reservation referred to in paragraph 2 of this article, intends to defraud a third party, including a consignee, who acts in reliance on the description of the goods in the bill of lading. In the latter case, if the reservation omitted relates to particulars furnished by the shipper for insertion in the bill of lading, the carrier has no right of indemnity from the shipper pursuant to paragraph 1 of this article.

4.   In the case of intended fraud referred to in paragraph 3 of this article, the carrier is liable, without the benefit of the limitation of liability provided for in this Convention, for the loss incurred by a third party, including a consignee, because he has acted in reliance on the description of the goods in the bill of lading.

Article 18. Documents other than bills of lading

Where a carrier issues a document other than a bill of lading to evidence the receipt of the goods to be carried, such a document is prima facie evidence of the conclusion of the contract of carriage by sea and the taking over by the carrier of the goods as therein described.

PART V. CLAIMS AND ACTIONS

Article 19. Notice of loss, damage or delay

1.   Unless notice of loss or damage, specifying the general nature of such loss or damage, is given in writing by the consignee to the carrier not later than the working day after the day when the goods were handed over to the consignee, such handing over is prima facie evidence of the delivery by the carrier of the goods as described in the document of transport or, if no such document has been issued, in good condition.

2.   Where the loss or damage is not apparent, the provisions of paragraph 1 of this article apply correspondingly if notice in writing is not given within 15 consecutive days after the day when the goods were handed over to the consignee.

3.   If the state of the goods at the time they were handed over to the consignee has been the subject of a joint survey or inspection by the parties, notice in writing need not be given of loss or damage ascertained during such survey or inspection.

4.   In the case of any actual or apprehended loss or damage, the carrier and the consignee must give all reasonable facilities to each other for inspecting and tallying the goods.

5.   No compensation shall be payable for loss resulting from delay in delivery unless a notice has been given in writing to the carrier within 60 consecutive days after the day when the goods were handed over to the consignee.

6.   If the goods have been delivered by an actual carrier, any notice given under this article to him shall have the same effect as if it had been given to the carrier; and any notice given to the carrier shall have effect as if given to such actual carrier.

7.   Unless notice of loss or damage, specifying the general nature of the loss or damage, is given in writing by the carrier or actual carrier to the shipper not later than 90 consecutive days after the occurrence of such loss or damage or after the delivery of the goods in accordance with paragraph 2 of article 4, whichever is later, the failure to give such notice is *prima facie* evidence that the carrier or the actual carrier has sustained no loss or damage due to the fault or neglect of the shipper, his servants or agents.

8.   For the purpose of this article, notice given to a person acting on the carriers or the actual carriers behalf, including the master or the officer in charge of the ship, or to a person acting on the shippers behalf is deemed to have been given to the carrier, to the actual carrier or to the shipper, respectively.

Article 20. Limitation of actions

1.   Any action relating to carriage of goods under this Convention is time-barred if judicial or arbitral proceedings have not been instituted within a period of two years.

2.   The limitation period commences on the day on which the carrier has delivered the goods or part thereof or, in cases where no goods have been delivered, on the last day on which the goods should have been delivered.

3.   The day on which the limitation period commences is not included in the period.

4.   The person against whom a claim is made may at any time during the running of the limitation period extend that period by a declaration in writing to the claimant. This period may be further extended by another declaration or declarations.

5.   An action for indemnity by a person held liable may be instituted even after the expiration of the limitation period provided for in the preceding paragraphs if instituted within the time allowed by the law of the State where proceedings are instituted. However, the time allowed shall not be less than 90 days commencing from the day when the person instituting such action for indemnity has settled the claim or has been served with process in the action against himself.

Article 21. Jurisdiction

1.   In judicial proceedings relating to carriage of goods under this Convention the plaintiff, at his option, may institute an action in a court which according to the law of the State where the court is situated, is competent and within the jurisdiction of which is situated one of the following places:

    (a)   the principal place of business or, in the absence thereof, the habitual residence of the defendant; or

    (b)   the place where the contract was made, provided that the defendant has there a place of business, branch or agency through which the contract was made; or

(c)   the port of loading or the port of discharge; or

(d)   any additional place designated for that purpose in the contract of carriage by sea.

2.   *(a)*   Notwithstanding the preceding provisions of this article, an action may be instituted in the courts of any port or place in a Contracting State at which the carrying vessel or any other vessel of the same ownership may have been arrested in accordance with applicable rules of the law of that State and of international law. However, in such a case, at the petition of the defendant, the claimant must remove the action, at his choice, to one of the jurisdictions referred to in paragraph 1 of this article for the determination of the claim, but before such removal the defendant must furnish security sufficient to ensure payment of any judgement that may subsequently be awarded to the claimant in the action.

     (b)   All questions relating to the sufficiency or otherwise of the security shall be determined by the court of the port or place of the arrest.

3.   No judicial proceedings relating to carriage of goods under this Convention may be instituted in a place not specified in paragraph 1 or 2 of this article. The provisions of this paragraph do not constitute an obstacle to the jurisdiction of the Contracting States for provisional or protective measures.

4.   *(a)*   Where an action has been instituted in a court competent under paragraphs 1 or 2 of this article or where judgement has been delivered by such a court, no new action may be started between the same parties on the same grounds unless the judgement of the court before which the first action was instituted is not enforceable in the country in which the new proceedings are instituted;

     (b)   For the purpose of this article, the institution of measures with a view to obtaining enforcement of a judgement is not to be considered as the starting of a new action;

     (c)   For the purpose of this article, the removal of an action to a different court within the same country, or to a court in another country, in accordance with paragraph 2 (a) of this article, is not to be considered as the starting of a new action.

5.   Notwithstanding the provisions of the preceding paragraphs, an agreement made by the parties, after a claim under the contract of carriage by sea has arisen, which designates the place where the claimant may institute an actions, is effective.

Article 22. Arbitration

1.   Subject to the provisions of this article, parties may provide by agreement evidenced in writing that any dispute that may arise relating to carriage of goods under this Convention shall be referred to arbitration.

2.   Where a charter-party contains a provision that disputes arising thereunder shall be referred to arbitration and a bill of lading issued pursuant to the charter-party does not contain special annotation providing that such provision shall be binding upon the holder of the bill of lading, the carrier may not invoke such provision as against a holder having acquired the bill of lading in good faith.

3.   The arbitration proceedings shall, at the option of the claimant, be instituted at one of the following places:

     (a)   a place in a State within whose territory is situated:

         (i)   the principal place of business of the defendant or, in the absence thereof, the habitual residence of the defendant; or

         (ii)   the place where the contract was made, provided that the defendant has there a place of business, branch or agency through which the contract was made; or

  (iii) the port of loading or the port of discharge; or

 (b) any place designated for that purpose in the arbitration clause or agreement.

4. The arbitrator or arbitration tribunal shall apply the rules of this Convention.

5. The provisions of paragraphs 2 and 4 of this article are deemed to be part of every arbitration clause or agreement, and any term of such clause or agreement which is inconsistent therewith is null and void.

6. Nothing in this article affects the validity of an agreement relating to arbitration made by the parties after the claim under the contract of carriage by sea has arisen.

PART VI. SUPPLEMENTARY PROVISIONS

Article 23. Contractual stipulations

1. Any stipulation in a contract of carriage by sea, in a bill of lading, or in any other document evidencing the contract of carriage by sea is null and void to the extent that it derogates, directly or indirectly, from the provisions of this Convention. The nullity of such a stipulation does not affect the validity of the other provisions of the contract or document of which it forms a part. A clause assigning benefit of insurance of goods in favour of the carrier, or any similar clause, is null and void.

2. Notwithstanding the provisions of paragraph 1 of this article, a carrier may increase his responsibilities and obligations under this Convention.

3. Where a bill of lading or any other document evidencing the contract of carriage by sea is issued, it must contain a statement that the carriage is subject to the provisions of this Convention which nullify any stipulation derogating therefrom to the detriment of the shipper or the consignee.

4. Where the claimant in respect of the goods has incurred loss as a result of a stipulation which is null and void by virtue of the present article, or as a result of the omission of the statement referred to in paragraph 3 of this article, the carrier must pay compensation to the extent required in order to give the claimant compensation in accordance with the provisions of this Convention for any loss of or damage to the goods as well as for delay in delivery. The carrier must, in addition, pay compensation for costs incurred by the claimant for the purpose of exercising his right, provided that costs incurred in the action where the foregoing provision is invoked are to be determined in accordance with the law of the State where proceedings are instituted.

Article 24. General average

1. Nothing in this Convention shall prevent the application of provisions in the contract of carriage by sea or national law regarding the adjustment of general average.

2. With the exception of article 20, the provisions of this Convention relating to the liability of the carrier for loss of or damage to the goods also determine whether the consignee may refuse contribution in general average and the liability of the carrier to indemnify the consignee in respect of any such contribution made or any salvage paid.

Article 25. Other conventions

1. This Convention does not modify the rights or duties of the carrier, the actual carrier and their servants and agents provided for in international conventions or national law relating to the limitation of liability of owners of seagoing ships.

2. The provisions of articles 21 and 22 of this Convention do not prevent the application of the mandatory provisions of any other multilateral convention already in force at the date of this Convention relating to matters dealt with in the said articles, provided that the dispute arises

exclusively between parties having their principal place of business in States members of such other convention. However, this paragraph does not affect the application of paragraph 4 of article 22 of this Convention.

3. No liability shall arise under the provisions of this Convention for damage caused by a nuclear incident if the operator of a nuclear installation is liable for such damage:

    (a) under either the Paris Convention of 29 July 1960 on Third Party Liability in the Field of Nuclear Energy as amended by the Additional Protocol of 28 January 1964, or the Vienna Convention of 21 May 1963 on Civil Liability for Nuclear Damage, or

    (b) by virtue of national law governing the liability for such damage, provided that such law is in all respects as favourable to persons who may suffer damage as is either the Paris Convention or the Vienna Convention.

4. No liability shall arise under the provisions of this Convention for any loss of or damage to or delay in delivery of luggage for which the carrier is responsible under any international convention or national law relating to the carriage of passengers and their luggage by sea.

5. Nothing contained in this Convention prevents a Contracting State from applying any other international convention which is already in force at the date of this Convention and which applies mandatorily to contracts of carriage of goods primarily by a mode of transport other than transport by sea. This provision also applies to any subsequent revision or amendment of such international convention.

Article 26. Unit of account

1. The unit of account referred to in article 6 of this Convention is the special drawing right as defined by the International Monetary Fund. The amounts mentioned in article 6 are to be converted into the national currency of a State according to the value of such currency at the date of judgement or the date agreed upon by the parties. The value of a national currency, in terms of the special drawing right, of a Contracting State which is a member of the International Monetary Fund is to be calculated in accordance with the method of valuation applied by the International Monetary Fund in effect at the date in question for its operations and transactions. The value of a national currency, in terms of the special drawing right, of a Contracting State which is not a member of the International Monetary Fund is to be calculated in a manner determined by that State.

2. Nevertheless, those States which are not members of the International Monetary Fund and whose law does not permit the application of the provisions of paragraph 1 of this article may, at the time of signature, or at the time of ratification, acceptance, approval or accession or at any time thereafter, declare that the limits of liability provided for in this Convention to be applied in their territories shall be fixed as 12,500 monetary units per package or other shipping unit or 37.5 monetary units per kilogram of gross weight of the goods.

3. The monetary unit referred to in paragraph 2 of this article corresponds to sixty-five and a half milligrams of gold of millesimal fineness nine hundred. The conversion of the amounts referred to in paragraph 2 into the national currency is to be made according to the law of the State concerned.

4. The calculation mentioned in the last sentence of paragraph 1 and the conversion mentioned in paragraph 3 of this article is to be made in such a manner as to express in the national currency of the Contracting State as far as possible the same real value for the amounts in article 6 as is expressed there in units of account. Contracting States must communicate to the depositary the manner of calculation pursuant to paragraph 1 of this article, or the result of the conversion mentioned in paragraph 3 of this article, as the case may be, at the time of signature or when depositing their instruments of ratification, acceptance, approval or accession, or when availing themselves of the option provided for in paragraph 2 of this article and whenever there is a change in the manner of such calculation or in the result of such conversion.

PART VII. FINAL CLAUSES

Article 27. Depositary

The Secretary-General of the United Nations is hereby designated as the depositary of this Convention.

Article 28. Signature, Ratification, Acceptance, Approval, Accession

1. This Convention is open for signature by all States until 30 April 1979 at the Headquarters of the United Nations, New York.

2. This Convention is subject to ratification, acceptance or approval by the signatory States.

3. After 30 April 1979, this Convention will be open for accession by all States which are not signatory States.

4. Instruments of ratification, acceptance, approval and accession are to be deposited with the Secretary-General of the United Nations.

Article 29. Reservations

No reservations may be made to this Convention.

Article 30. Entry into force

1. This Convention enters into force on the first day of the month following the expiration of one year from the date of deposit of the twentieth instrument of ratification, acceptance, approval or accession.

2. For each State which becomes a Contracting State to this Convention after the date of the deposit of the twentieth instrument of ratification, acceptance, approval or accession, this Convention enters into force on the first day of the month following the expiration of one year after the deposit of the appropriate instrument on behalf of that State.

3. Each Contracting State shall apply the provisions of this Convention to contracts of carriage by sea concluded on or after the date of the entry into force of this Convention in respect of that State.

Article 31. Denunciation of other conventions

1. Upon becoming a Contracting State to this Convention, any State Party to the International Convention for the Unification of certain Rules relating to Bills of Lading signed at Brussels on 25 August 1924 (1924 Convention) must notify the Government of Belgium as the depositary of the 1924 Convention of its denunciation of the said Convention with a declaration that the denunciation is to take effect as from the date when this Convention enters into force in respect of that State.

2. Upon the entry into force of this Convention under paragraph 1 of article 30, the depositary of this Convention must notify the Government of Belgium as the depositary of the 1924 Convention of the date of such entry into force, and of the names of the Contracting States in respect of which the Convention has entered into force.

3. The provisions of paragraphs 1 and 2 of this article apply correspondingly in respect of States Parties to the Protocol signed on 23 February 1968 to amend the International Convention for the Unification of certain Rules relating to Bills of Lading signed at Brussels on 25 August 1924.

4. Notwithstanding article 2 of this Convention, for the purposes of paragraph 1 of this article, a Contracting State may, if it deems it desirable, defer the denunciation of the 1924 Convention and of the 1924 Convention as modified by the 1968 Protocol for a maximum period of five years from the entry into force of this Convention. It will then notify the Government of Belgium of its intention. During this transitory period, it must apply to the Contracting States this Convention to the exclusion of any other one.

Article 32. Revision and amendment

1. At the request of not less than one third of the Contracting States to this Convention, the depositary shall convene a conference of the Contracting States for revising or amending it.

2. Any instrument of ratification, acceptance, approval or accession deposited after the entry into force of an amendment to this Convention is deemed to apply to the Convention as amended.

Article 33. Revision of the limitation amounts and unit of account or monetary unit

1. Notwithstanding the provisions of article 32, a conference only for the purpose of altering the amount specified in article 6 and paragraph 2 of article 26, or of substituting either or both of the units defined in paragraphs 1 and 3 of article 26 by other units is to be convened by the depositary in accordance with paragraph 2 of this article. An alteration of the amounts shall be made only because of a significant change in their real value.

2. A revision conference is to be convened by the depositary when not less than one fourth of the Contracting States so request.

3. Any decision by the conference must be taken by a two-thirds majority of the participating States. The amendment is communicated by the depositary to all the Contracting States for acceptance and to all the States signatories of the Convention for information.

4. Any amendment adopted enters into force on the first day of the month following one year after its acceptance by two thirds of the Contracting States. Acceptance is to be effected by the deposit of a formal instrument to that effect with the depositary.

5. After entry into force of an amendment a Contracting State which has accepted the amendment is entitled to apply the Convention as amended in its relations with Contracting States which have not within six months after the adoption of the amendment notified the depositary that they are not bound by the amendment.

6. Any instrument of ratification, acceptance, approval or accession deposited after the entry into force of an amendment to this Convention is deemed to apply to the Convention as amended.

Article 34. Denunciation

1. A Contracting State may denounce this Convention at any time by means of a notification in writing addressed to the depositary.

2. The denunciation takes effect on the first day of the month following the expiration of one year after the notification is received by the depositary. Where a longer period is specified in the notification, the denunciation takes effect upon the expiration of such longer period after the notification is received by the depositary.

Done at Hamburg, this thirty-first day of March, one thousand nine hundred and seventy-eight, in a single original, of which the Arabic, Chinese, English, French, Russian and Spanish texts are equally authentic.

In witness whereof the undersigned plenipotentiaries, being duly authorized by their respective Governments, have signed the present Convention.

Common understanding adopted by the
United Nations Conference on the Carriage of Goods by Sea.

It is the common understanding that the liability of the carrier under this Convention is based on the principle of presumed fault or neglect. This means that, as a rule, the burden of proof rests on the carrier but, with respect to certain cases, the provisions of the Convention modify this rule

MOCK EXAMINATION

Do not turn to the next page until you have followed the suggestions below.

Overleaf is a sample examination paper. In your own interest do not look at it yet but instead, do the same revision of the course as you would do for any examination.

On completing your revision, put away your notes, have pen and paper ready and set aside three hours when you will not be interrupted. In other words create as near as possible examination room conditions.

It is recommended that you hand write this mock examination. You will have to write the actual examination and many students find that it is difficult to write legibly for three hours without practice. If your writing is illegible you will lose marks. Examiners cannot mark what they cannot read.

Carry out the instructions on the question paper and send your answers to your course tutor for marking (Note your start and finish times on the front of your answer paper).

THE INSTITUTE OF CHARTERED SHIPBROKERS

MOCK EXAM

INTRODUCTION TO SHIPPING

Time allowed – Three hours

Answer any FIVE questions – All questions carry equal marks

1. Discuss the principle factors which would create an increase in international trade.

2. A triangle drawn between the world's three principle **canals** contain some of the busiest transit trade routes. Draw this triangle.

    For each canal discuss one cargo; ship type and likely countries of origin and destination.

3. Explain the meaning of 'intermodalism' with particular reference to the importer who buys a small parcel of goods from an inland Canadian source for delivery to an Indian Ocean island destination.

4. Explain the role and function of Port State Control.

5. Analyse the manner in which a divisional manager can monitor the performance of his branch offices.

6. A fixture is usually confirmed in the form of a charter party, of which there are two basic types. Discuss the essential differences.

7. Trace the reasons why the greater proportion of world crude oil is refined closer to the consuming area, than at source.

8. Describe in detail the properties of a traditional first original Bill of Lading.

    In today's world of electronic transmission, is there any significant difference between the bill of lading and the seawaybill?

THE PURPOSE AND SCOPE OF THIS BOOK AND COURSE GUIDE

COMMERCIAL GEOGRAPHY

Continents: Geographical regions for example Far East, Mediterranean, S.E. Asia. Location of major countries and ports. All the continents, the major centres of which they are comprised and the manner in which they are grouped in geographical regions.

The location of major ports, canals and waterways.

Oceans of the world and the seas of which they are comprised. The effects of tides, currents, climate and weather.

An awareness of different map projections; latitude and longitude.

INTERNATIONAL TRADE

Understand the role of different markets that comprise the global market. Be aware of the difference between absolute and comparative advantage. Understand the role of shipping arising from derived demand.

CARGOES AND TRADE ROUTES

Thoroughly understand the different roles of liners and tramps. In liners understand the main unitised systems and break bulk operations. Be aware of major liner routes.

Understand the major dry bulk trades and the origins and distribution of principle cargoes.

The oil and other liquid trades.

Understand the origin and distribution of principle cargoes distinguishing between crude oil and products.

Be aware of the categorisation of cargoes into clean, dirty, chemicals, gas, vegetable oils and juices.

SHIP TYPES

Thoroughly understand the basic characteristics of bulk carriers etc and the types of trades in which they are used.

Understand the main sizes of vessel in each class.

Expect to illustrate any answers with simple sketches.

CONTRACTS OF CARRIAGE

Thoroughly understand the basic contracts:

Charter Parties for tramp and tankers.

Bills of Lading for liners.

Be aware of the role of the Bill of Lading under a Charter Party.

Understand the difference between Voyage and Time Charter Parties and the basic elements of each.

Understand the three functions of the Bill of Lading and its role in international trade.

Understand the main specialist abbreviations, terms and expressions used in Charter Parties and Bills of Lading.

LAW OF CARRIAGE

Understand the duty of care and the nature of tortious acts outside of contracts.

Be aware of the way in which international conventions are established and the major conventions relative to shipping.

Understand the basic application of Hague/Hague-Visby/Hamburg rules, their requirement for seaworthiness and the limitation of carrier liability. Be aware of the differences between these rules.

Understand the legal effect of the Bill of Lading as a document of title and the implication of its role in the delivery of goods.

Be aware of the role of marine insurance and P & I Associations.

SHIP REGISTRATION AND CLASSIFICATION

Thoroughly understand the concept of ship registration and its flag state.

Understand the differences between registering in the country of beneficial ownership, offshore registry and flag of convenience.

Be aware of Port State Control.

Understand the need for classification and the role of classification societies.

THE PRACTIONERS IN SHIPPING BUSINESS

Thoroughly understand the difference between principals and intermediaries.

Understand the role and function of:

Principals –	shipowners, charterers, shippers and NVOCs (non vessel operating carriers)
Intermediaries –	Brokers in dry cargo chartering, tanker chartering, ship sale and purchase
	Port agents and liner agents and the differences between them
	Ship managers and freight forwarders.

Be aware that all classes of intermediaries may be independent businesses or in-house departments of the principal.

BASIC ACCOUNTING

Understand the fundamentals of bookkeeping & corporate accounts.

Thoroughly understand the definitions and functions of Revenue, Cost, Profit, Capital, Cash-flow, Interest.

Thoroughly understand the importance of maintaining positive cash flow.

Be aware of the structure of various different types of business entity and understand the concept of limited liability.

Order Form – TutorShip

Shipping guides LTD
The Port Information Specialists

This voucher entitles the student to a £10 discount off the price of *The Ships Atlas*. **This offer is only available through Shipping Guides Ltd. Please contact us at the address below to find out the current price or visit our website www.portinfo.co.uk.**

Company:

Address:

Post/Zip Code: Country:

VAT No.   (EC only)

Contact: Title:

Tel No: Fax:

Email:

SHIPPING GUIDES LIMITED
75 Bell Street, Reigate, Surrey,
RH2 7AN, United Kingdom

Tel: +44 1737 242255
Fax: +44 1737 222449

Email: sales@portinfo.co.uk
Telex: 917070 Shipg G

VAT Registration Number
GB 243 9546 43

Nature of business

○ Ship master   ○ Ship owner/operator/manager   ○ Ship broker/agent

○ Ship charterer   ○ Legal services   ○ Financial services   ○ Other

If other, please specify:

Required Products

Product Name	Quantity	Price
The Ships Atlas		
	Subtotal	
	Postage	
	VAT	
	Total	

Please note that prices may be subject to VAT

Order Details

○ Please send a (proforma) invoice   ○ We have arranged direct payment to your bank   ○ We wish to pay by cheque/bank draft/credit card
(Delete as applicable)

The amount of £   Customers within the EU should quote their VAT numbers where appropriate

Please note that prices may be subject to VAT

Amex ○   Mastercard ○   Visa ○   Delta ○   Switch ○

Cardholder's Name:

Card Number:

Expiry Date: /

Signature: Date: /   /

Method of payment

1. Sterling bank draft drawn on a bank in the UK made payable to Shipping Guides Ltd.
2. Credit card (complete section left).
3. Direct payment in Pounds Sterling to our bank (details below). Payment to be made in full
   - All charges to your account
   - All direct payments to state company name and complete address

Our Bank Details
Barclays Bank plc,
90 - 92 High Street, Crawley,
West Sussex, RH10 1BP, UK.

Account Number: 30079332
Sort Code: 20-23-97
IBAN No: GB32 BARC 202397 30079332
Swiftcode: BARCGB22